Love & Family

Love & Family

*Raising a Traditional Family
in a Secular World*

by

Mercedes Arzú Wilson

Ignatius Press   San Francisco

The Family of the Americas Foundation
Post Office Box 1170
Dunkirk, Maryland 20754–1170
U.S.A.
(301) 627–3346

Cover by Riz Boncan Marsella

First edition 1996
Ignatius Press, San Francisco
ISBN 0–89870–607–6
Library of Congress catalogue card number 96–75715
Printed in the United States of America

This work is dedicated to His Holiness Pope John Paul II, Mother Teresa of Calcutta and to the memory of Professor Jérôme Lejeune. Their leadership, courage and example have been my inspiration for many years and have encouraged and supported our work.

This work is further dedicated to my parents, who gave me life and taught me by their unselfish example how to live and be compassionate toward others. Finally, it is dedicated to my own family, whose love and support have enabled me to continue this work.

Contents

PART ONE
The Family: Center of Life

PART TWO

Raising Responsible Adults

PART THREE
Educational Warfare

PART FOUR

Natural versus Unnatural Family Planning

Foreword

Jérôme Lejeune, M.D., Ph.D.
(June 13, 1926–April 3, 1994)

Chairman, Department of Fundamental Genetics
Pediatric Hospital, Paris, France
Recipient, Kennedy Prize, 1962

Love and family; these two words should never be separated. The family is where we discover the meaning of love, and the greatest achievement of which lovers can dream is founding a new family.

In her excellent book, Mercedes Arzú Wilson explores masterfully, but with rare clarity of language, this center of Love and Life, the family. But this citadel of hope is being severely attacked. Youngsters are brainwashed by the so-called sex education which desecrates the dignity of the body, and the elderly are cursed by the camouflaged elimination, unduly called "good death" (euthanasia). It must always be remembered that this abomination has been written, in history, in bloody letters: EUTHANAZI.

Covering all the ages one after the other, this book teaches parents how to teach their own children. Expressed in a vivid manner—precise, matter of fact, but also very poetic—the four parts of the book cover all situations. Mercedes Arzú Wilson knows and explores equally well the psyche of the baby and the teenager, the young adult. Not only is her teaching extremely competent, it is really convincing. From the self-worth of the young to healthy education in sexuality, up to natural family planning, all the answers to the psychological, physiological and sociological problems are given.

This book is a kind of visitation.

A charming educator is revealing to an attentive future mother all the secrets of life and love she has verified in her own family.

Happy are the children whose parents read this book and put into action these counsels. The children will be preserved from venereal disease, including AIDS, for they will be told the truth: There is no such thing as safe sex in promiscuity. But a much greater secret will be revealed to them: Safe love really does exist; it even has a name—happiness in fidelity.

Endorsements

Your work with the families is so important. If there is no peace in the world today, it is because there is no peace in the family. Help your families to make their homes centres of compassion and forgive constantly and so bring peace. Your first duty is to be a family—to be the presence of Christ to one another—to reveal to one another something of His Love, compassion and tenderness. If we bring prayer back into our families, we can bring love also back, for prayer gives a pure heart and a pure heart can see and serve Jesus in another. I pray for you that you make your home another Nazareth where prayer and sacrifice, work and love bound the Holy Family and helped them to grow together in holiness. Pray for me as I do for you.

God bless you.

Mother Teresa of Calcutta, M.C.

Those who have followed your dedicated work in the field of Natural Family Planning will welcome your publication, with extensive references to research, and with its special emphasis on abstinence and on teaching children about sexuality in the one place and the one way in which it deserves to be taught: at home, in the context of family and morality.

+ John Cardinal O'Connor
Archbishop of New York

At once inspirational and full of practical wisdom, Mercedes Arzú Wilson's *Love & Family* is a sure guide for parents facing the vital task of introducing sexuality to their children. While modern cultural and economic pressures seek to strip the family of its central functions, this book is a tool that strengthens the family, helping parents to recover their God-given role as moral teachers.

Allan Carlson, Ph.D.
President, The Rockford Institute

Mercedes Arzú Wilson's *Love & Family* offers specific guidelines that will prove helpful to parents who desire that their children develop constructive, healthy sexual attitudes. The book makes unmistakably clear that an individual's sexual life may be one of the most fulfilling of human experiences but also—paradoxically—one of the most painful. The information and wisdom provided here will help families guide their children toward health and away from the misinformation and confusion toward sexuality that characterize this last decade of the twentieth century.

Armand M. Nicholi, Jr., M.D.
Professor of Psychiatry
Harvard Medical School,
Massachusetts General Hospital
Boston, Massachusetts

You and your work have addressed a vital sector of human behavior, that very place where modern man so often comes to grief—and where modern science, spectacular though it might be in the physical and biological sciences, has itself stumbled so badly. This is of course human sexuality, not its pleasures but its pathologies: teenage promiscuity and unwanted pregnancies, the millions of abortions, the vast array of contraceptive devices and drugs with their very real danger to the health, physical and psychological, of the women who use them. You and your Family of the Americas Foundation have achieved that rarest of goals, the combining of scientific technique with our Western value system of family, love and respect for God and man, for body and spirit. One all too often gets divorced from the other.

As for values, there is a unique value in your technique of family planning by which a woman, using a natural yet scientifically impeccable method, can determine for herself the precise time when she can conceive human life, God's greatest gift to us, and plan her family accordingly.

It's really a remarkable achievement—a wonderful piece of work—pulling all this information together. You've done a tremendous piece of work and I'm proud of you.

Walker Percy, M.D.
(May 28, 1916–May 10, 1990)
Fellow of the American Academy of Arts and Sciences
Member of the National Institute of Arts and Sciences
Recipient of the National Book Award 1962

Mercedes Arzú Wilson has written a book that's filled with valuable information and bristling with challenging ideas. You don't have to agree with every point she makes to recognize the significance of her contribution. It will help provide a sense of empowerment for parents, helping them overcome feelings of reticence and helplessness in teaching their children about some of life's most sensitive issues.

Michael Medved
co-host of "Sneak Previews," PBS
chief film critic for *The New York Post*
author of *Hollywood vs. America*

Mercedes Arzú Wilson recognizes that a mother and father need insightful, honest counsel in dealing with their child's sexual development. *Love & Family* answers the questions all parents committed to raising a healthy, happy child need to explore. This book is also an excellent resource for anyone who wants to know more about the natural family planning method Wilson has taught with success all over the world. She gives not only the facts about why the family is involved in our current cultural crisis, but what steps can be taken to instill value and meaning into a child's life.

Beverly LaHaye
President, Concerned Women for America

Acknowledgments

I am deeply grateful to each of the men and women who have assisted in the preparation of this book and in the continuing implementation of the Love & Family program. Heartfelt thanks to my distinguished colleagues who provided essays and other materials for the text; to the pro-family leaders who generously agreed to review the final manuscript; to Daniel J. Engler and Teresa A. Donovan for their editorial assistance; and to my dedicated staff in Maryland and Louisiana, especially Brenda Williams, Jim Landi, Sharon Cook, Faith Torsani, Amy Walton, Jennifer Siegmund and Laura Pennefather, who worked many long days and late nights while providing patient assistance to both the author and editor.

Special thanks to Patricia Peacock for her untiring editorial assistance, John Preble and Mariano Garzaro for the beautiful charts and graphs, and Delaine Johnson and the rest of my staff and volunteers for their steadfast support. Thanks also goes to Dr. William Gibbons, Professor Denis St. Marie, Dr. Francesca Kearns, and especially William Carrigan, a board member whose wisdom and advice I greatly cherish. I equally extend my gratitude for the encouragement and support of my Board of Directors and spouses: José and Celia Carredano, Bud and Eileen Hansen, Paul and Barbara Henkels, Frank and Patricia Lynch, John and Carol Saeman, and Alberto and Christine Vollmer.

Why Read This Book?

Human beings cannot live without love. If it is not given unconditionally, young people are going to look for it elsewhere. It is with this essential fact in mind that we have designed and tested this uplifting, family-centered program so you can give your children the priceless gift of appreciating their sexuality as a joyful and sacred part of their humanity. You will be able to show them why sexual intimacy is meant only for the lifelong commitment of marriage.

Using this program will enable you to fulfill—and enjoy to the fullest —your roles as the most important teachers of your children in these vital matters. Since the Love & Family program explains how premarital chastity fosters real adulthood, self-respect, true friendship and lasting love, it will help you teach your youngsters to resist such strong currents as peer pressure and popular culture, which seek to rob them of these benefits. At the same time, the program promotes their lifelong health and happiness. Since we present expert views on family life and the latest information about human fertility, sexually transmitted diseases, contraception, sterilization and abortion, the program can also help your children to "unlearn" harmful *mis*information about marriage, sex and family. That is vital, of course; all of us need as much help as possible in confronting the problems which threaten the many rewards of raising a family in these times.

Today's families are facing challenges that were virtually unknown to earlier generations. Economic trends have forced many parents to juggle additional work demands along with family responsibilities, and demographic changes have often led to the dispersion of the extended family— grandparents, aunts, uncles and cousins—whose constant presence might otherwise greatly enrich a child's development. Most troubling, however, is the proliferation of anti-family forces in contemporary society: in films, music, videos and magazines, parental authority and traditional moral values are undermined or ridiculed. Unlike past eras, public agencies and edu-

23

cational institutions no longer reinforce parents' efforts to teach their children chastity, obedience, honesty and virtue. Instead, they force upon us school-based clinics that encourage premarital sex, as well as homosexual and other unnatural behaviors.

At the international level, powerful government agencies and private organizations that profit from the distribution of contraceptives continue to exert incredible pressure on couples and families—especially in the developing world—in the name of "population control." Today we hear innumerable protests against the use of chemicals in natural environments like the wetlands. Similarly, the use of artificial hormones like steroids by athletes is denounced as an intolerable evil. Why, then, do so many of the same people who oppose these harmful practices advocate the use of such artificial poisons by women?

Together, all of these forces are helping to foment a destructive spirit of materialism, self-gratification and contempt for the poor. It is a spirit that threatens individuals, families and society as a whole. (If you turn to chapters nine and ten, you will learn about the personal and political damage caused by contraception and abortion, which these forces promote.) It is not surprising, therefore, that many parents feel isolated and unsure of their role as the most important teachers of their children. Increasingly discouraged and confused, some parents have begun to question their ability (and even their right and obligation) to impart to their children clear, unequivocal lessons about modesty, self-control, personal responsibility and love of God.

Most sexuality programs promote promiscuous behavior by ignoring and/or undermining the role of parents and by encouraging youngsters to experiment with sex. Few programs affirm the importance of the family and the positive influence of loving parents on their children's development. In contrast, the Love & Family program presents not only pertinent scientific information but also expert opinions on a range of subjects such as marriage, communication, responsible decision-making and fertility appreciation, to name but a few. In so doing, the program alerts parents to current dangers and helps them orient their children against misinformation and temptation. *The instruction and example of loving parents is the greatest deterrent to promiscuous behavior among teens.* By striving to live by the high ideals set forth in this program, you will help your children recognize that sex is truly meant for the lifelong commitment of marriage.

The Love & Family program works. That is clear from the impressively low rate of teen pregnancy achieved during the first three-year demonstration phase of the program. Begun as a demonstration project called Fertility Appreciation for Families, the program was initially funded by the United States Department of Health and Human Services (HHS) under the Adolescent Family Life Act. With the HHS grant, teacher training and curricula were developed and pilot programs were established at four testing sites: Corpus Christi, Texas; Wichita, Kansas; Charleston, South Carolina; and New Orleans, Louisiana. Nearly sixty-two hundred parents and adolescents were exposed to the program during the demonstration period. Studies show that Fertility Appreciation for Families adolescent participants had a pregnancy rate of only five per thousand as compared to the average of ninety-six per thousand for one program and 111 per thousand for another. This record underscores the program's immense potential for helping young people avoid sex until marriage, while also fostering increased communication and friendship between parents and teenagers.

While you, as parents, have the best understanding of your child's particular needs (regardless of what others may want you to believe), you will want to become familiar with all of the important topics discussed in this book. Doing so will not only equip you for one of your most challenging and rewarding tasks as parents, but it will also give you a deeper appreciation of your own sexuality within marriage. What better way is there to discover the full joys and wonder of love and family life?

PART ONE

The Family: Center of Life

CHAPTER ONE

Understanding the Family as a Center of Love and Life

The family is the natural and fundamental group unit of society and is entitled to protection by society and the State.

United Nations General Assembly,
Universal Declaration of Human Rights, 1948,
Article 16, Section 3

Throughout history and in cultures around the world, the ideas, attitudes and values of the family shape each child and help determine his development into a happy, responsible and productive adult. In spite of the strain of constant change in the world, the family remains the best means of educating and nurturing children and conveying cherished values and traditions from one generation to the next. The family is also the best forum in which to foster the love, decency and morality that are at the heart of life.

The family, historians tell us, is "the nucleus of civilization." It is our oldest and most enduring institution. The family is the building block of society; its strength and stability determine the strength and stability of communities and nations. There has never been an enduring society without the family serving to educate and foster children, to shape their morals and to pass on essential values.

Discussions with your children about sexuality and marriage, love and parenthood, will be much more effective if you can give your children a true understanding of the family's critical importance, which was so eloquently described by Dr. Allan Carlson, president of the Rockford Institute and consultant to the Love & Family program:

> The creation of a family is the central act of human existence, a task beside which all others are secondary. It is within the family that sexuality finds its proper place, a setting where love creates a new human life to be cared for and nourished by its parents. Sex outside the family bond is often personally and socially destructive. Within the family, though, it gains deep meaning and constructive purpose. . . .
>
> The family also serves as the vital heart of a healthy society. . . . It gives protection and nurture to infants, children, and youth during their formative years. . . . It teaches young people, mainly by example, how to live, co-exist, and cooperate in the broader society. It is the arena where social responsibility is learned as a child and exercised when grown. It offers adults a haven from the world, a place of unconditional affection into which they can retreat in times of stress. And, most importantly, it provides individuals with their historical being, binding them to a past through their parents and grandparents and to the future through their children and grandchildren.[1]

Parents and Sexuality Education

The family is the fundamental social unit. As its heads, parents are the most important educators of their children in all matters—including, of course, human sexuality.

Some parents may be uncomfortable discussing family, love and sexuality with their children. Some might provide a mistaken view of these matters or find that family problems are a barrier to speaking about them. Nevertheless, parents are the true experts when it comes to education in human sexuality. This is so for a number of reasons:

---

[1] Allan C. Carlson, "On the Importance and History of the Family," unpublished paper submitted to Family of the Americas Foundation, Inc., February 24, 1984.

1. Parents love their children and have their best interests at heart.

2. Parents know their children and their needs better than anyone.

3. Parents convey attitudes and values about life and sexuality as they interact with one another and with their children each day. In fact, children learn primarily from this "modeling" by the parents.

4. Parents are the real guardians of their vulnerable children and need to protect them from sexually explicit information that breaks down the natural innocence and modesty of children.

5. Parents are available to their children for support, questions and direction.

6. Parents have much wisdom to share that comes from the faithful living out of their commitment as husband and wife and as parents.

In providing an education in sexuality to their children, parents must begin by refuting the propaganda that outside "experts" can do the job better than they can. When anyone else is permitted to serve as the primary educator, parental authority is undermined and both the right and obligation of parents to educate and protect their children are violated. Parents must become much more active if they wish to overcome today's many threats to their control over the education of their children.

Parents need to teach their children how to recognize and reject the profanation of sexuality on television and in movies, videos, music, books and magazines. Human sexuality is spiritual and psychological, as well as physical—much more than mere lust. *It is a deep feeling of desire that should ripen into love and find fulfillment within the lifelong commitment of marriage.* Therein, love is transformed into the creation of children who will carry family, community and nation into the future.

As you discuss these topics with your children, remember that there are two primary ways that teaching and learning take place in the home. One sort occurs when parents intentionally instruct their children about something they want them to learn. The other, the parents' own example, is the way children most frequently learn. This happens spontaneously as children observe their parents throughout the day. Parents' values about life are expressed through their day-to-day activities—including interaction with family members and friends. Children unconsciously absorb these attitudes. Therefore, parents must be constantly aware of their own conduct. *Parents are indeed the first and most influential teachers of their children, whether they choose to be or not.*

It is clear, for example, that if a child observes the parents retreating from problems into alcohol or drugs or by simply a hostile silence, the child may do the same as an escape from similar difficulties. Children observe and copy parental attitudes and habits and often carry them into adult life. Simply put, the manner in which you handle life's challenges may well determine how your children will do so. A positive influence can significantly benefit their overall quality of life.

In the same way, a child's sexual identity and role are learned from the parents whether anything is said or not. Just as young boys and girls imitate the dress, hairstyles, gestures and problem-solving behavior of their parents, they also look to their parents for examples of being a man or woman.

Human sexuality is the characteristic that makes a person uniquely masculine or feminine throughout life. It develops as an integral part of one's spiritual, emotional, intellectual and physical growth; it is not something that springs into being merely as a result of puberty; it develops in stages. Each of us is conceived as a sexual being—the result of the union of the father with the mother. Our gender (our biological maleness or femaleness) is determined at the moment of conception, and every cell in the body carries the mark of that first union.

Conception as male or female is only the first step in a lifelong process. Sexuality is not limited to gender but includes spiritual and psychological aspects as well; being biologically male or female is but one of the many qualities that define a man or a woman. Human sexuality is a hallmark of the human personality that manifests itself in all the dimensions of living: social roles, relationships with others, the sharing of affection, love, intimacy, and so on. We cannot think of or describe ourselves without including the characteristic of our sexuality. It is possible to isolate this part of our personality in order to discuss it, but as it is such an integral part of who we are, we cannot separate its influence from our larger thoughts, feelings and behavior.

Due to its pervasiveness in our natures, sexuality has moral relevance for each of us. Dr. Josef Seifert, director of the International Academy of Philosophy, explains the source of our moral obligations regarding sex:

> [W]e can comprehend the moral relevance of human procreation only when we transcend the purely biological conception of human sexuality and grasp the fact that in the case of man sexuality serves the coming into existence of a *human* being.[2]

Our reverence for the dignity of every human person leads us to appreciate the wonder of our ability to bring new persons into the world and the magnificence of the family—the institution that makes possible this miraculous transmitting of human life.

Early Family Life

Moral considerations play an important role in education about sexuality and family life, especially since early family experience molds, to a great extent, a person's future in society. However, parents never stop teaching or serving as role models to their children. This continues until the parents' age and health impair their abilities and they become dependent on the care and kindness of their children.

Since the primary function of the family has remained unchanged throughout history, the profound effect of family on the development of mature, healthy children remains unchanged. This experience determines, in large part:

---

[2] Josef Seifert, Ph.D., "The Moral Difference between Natural Regulation of Conception and Contraception," unpublished paper submitted to Family of the Americas Foundation, Inc., 1984, p. 6.

- our adult character; our sense of ideals, responsibility and morality.

- whether we respect ourselves and have confidence in our abilities.

- how we see others and feel about them; when we respect others as we do ourselves, we will not want to do or say things that could harm them.

- our ability to establish warm, close, friendly relationships; when we experience warm, caring relationships within our families, we are better able to love others.

- the way that we try to make and find meaning in our existence; parents must communicate to their young children that life does have true meaning and that everyone has a unique purpose and mission.

Early family life, and how it is interpreted by children, contributes a great deal to the formation of attitudes, values and behavior that are likely to persist into and throughout adult life. It is true that the family is not the only molding force in a child's life; schools, friends and institutions of higher learning also influence lifelong attitudes and values. *Yet nothing has greater impact on a child's life than his family experience—in particular, parental love and discipline—but this can only have the greatest impact on the life of a child when the parents realize this fact and make proper use of it.* When children receive proper training at home, they will develop the ability to recognize the truth when they hear it and to reject falsehood and propaganda when they encounter it. If children's identification with their family is well developed, they will not have great difficulty in relating to things beyond and greater than themselves: church, country, relatives, friends, community groups, and so forth. Having a healthy bond with a family allows children to experience loving relationships as well as the demands of cooperation, responsibility, contribution and compromise. It will also help them understand that their behavior and decisions affect others. Children will carry this early training with them, and it will continue to shape them whether they realize it or not.

Changes within society have resulted in many variations of the traditional family structure, but the basic needs of children have not changed: the need for unconditional love and affection and the knowledge that they are unique and irreplaceable.

The traditional family can be defined as a married man and woman and their biological and/or adopted children. Today, though, there are many one-parent families resulting from the loss of a parent through death, separation or divorce, or because one parent never assumed responsibility. Single-parent families are the only category of growing poverty in some wealthy countries. In the United States, for example, the poverty rate among families headed by married couples is 5.7 percent. Among families where fathers are absent, the poverty rate is 33.4 percent—more than five times higher.[3] Trends are equally alarming in less-developed nations.

Former U.S. Secretary of Education William Bennett has noted disturbing trends for the family in his "Index of Leading Cultural Indicators." Since 1960, Bennett writes, "the U.S. population has increased 41%. . . . But during the same 30-year period [1960–1990] there has been a . . . 419% increase in illegitimate births; a quadrupling in divorce rates, a tripling of the percentage of children living in single-parent homes; more than a 200% increase in the teenage suicide rate; and a drop of almost 80 points in SAT [Scholastic Aptitude Test] scores."[4]

Whether headed by women or men, whether residing in rural or urban areas or in wealthy or less-developed nations, single-parent families face additional hardships in providing for the emotional, physical and spiritual needs of their children. It is important to continue promoting and striving for the ideal family structure in which children are cared for by both a mother and a father in an unbroken marriage bond. An adequate response to the needs of family members is often more difficult for those who have lost a parent to death, separation or divorce, but it is both possible and necessary to compensate for such losses to the child and the family.

---

[3] United States Census Bureau statistics, as cited by President George Bush in proclamation of National Children's Day, 1992.

[4] William J. Bennett, "Quantifying America's Decline," *Wall Street Journal*, March 15, 1993.

Circle of Love and Life

Teaching your children about the family becomes easier when you help them to picture love and life as a circle of personal bonds—the continuation of love and life through family members caring for each other. The circle begins with parents lovingly bringing children into the world. A husband and wife's first child often creates a dramatic, positive change in the couple's life. Before the baby is born, the parents often wonder how they will have enough love to share with this new little person because they already love each other so very much. Yet, what then happens shows that love is truly without limits. For this child, the parents become willing to sacrifice their sleep, their independence and, if necessary, their lives. When subsequent children arrive, this love continues to grow and expand.

If a child is born with congenital abnormalities or is later disabled by some accident or illness, the parents will understandably be distressed at first, but with courage and acceptance they usually begin to overcome this challenge. Parents who have faced such a challenge eventually see that this special child becomes, in the words of one mother to Mother Teresa, "the professor of love" in the family.

Today we often hear parents talk about how very much they look forward to the time when their children will be out of the house or college so their burden will be lifted. Yet parents' responsibilities toward their children never come to an end. Moreover, children are extremely sensitive and must never be made to think they are burdens. Instead, children should be told that no matter what moral, psychological or physical crisis might arise, their parents will always stand by them. When children have this kind of assurance they are more likely to trust their parents and seek them first for advice about their problems.

Consider what might happen in the case of a teenage boy whose best friend, distraught over the separation of his parents, has resorted to using drugs and is pressuring him to try them as well. The teenager needs the confidence and support of his parents to deal with this problem and to help his troubled friend. If his parents have communicated their unconditional love and acceptance over the years, the teenager will be able to approach them with confidence. They will understand his concern and help him determine how best to help the friend and to rebuff peer pressure to take drugs. The teenager and his parents may even agree to invite the friend to spend some time at their home so he can have the warmth and support of another family during this difficult time in his life.

In this example we see how the circle of love established within a family continues to expand and to enrich the larger human community—much like the concentric waves that are set in motion when a stone is cast into a pond—the love that parents show toward each other and toward their son inspires and enables him to reach out, in the spirit of love, to a friend in need. That is the beauty and wonder of love—it has its own special kind of ripple effect.

The more we learn in this book about the miracle of life and the precious gifts of love and fertility, the more deeply we appreciate the intricate pattern of our earthly existence. Just as nature repeats its seasons year after year, and just as a woman's fertility is renewed cycle after cycle, so does all life seem to follow a steady circular pattern as each generation is born, ages, marries and rears the next.

People who were prized by their parents in childhood are, of course, most likely to love and care for their parents in later years, as one generation succeeds another. For example, Noreen Rackow, a fifty-eight-year-old housewife from the midwestern United States, has been taking care of her eighty-eight-year-old mother for more than five years. (Mrs. Rackow's father died in 1991. Her mother has Alzheimer's disease, a debilitating illness that gradually leaves patients totally dependent on the care of others.) "My mother and dad always had love for me and helped me out," says Mrs. Rackow, "so I decided that is the way it should be for them now." Mrs. Rackow adds a wise observation about society in general:

Children should take care of their parents if they are able to. I think most of us are able to, but we don't want to. We're just too selfish. People think it's a burden, but it's really the thought that's the burden. If they once tried taking care of their folks, it isn't so bad. Lots of things in life are hard. You have to work at it. You have to try it. . . . I really would like [Mother] to stay with me until the end. I would never consider ending her life by euthanasia.[5]

Speaking at the National Prayer Breakfast in Washington, D.C., in February 1994, Mother Teresa of Calcutta related the following:

I can never forget the experience I had in visiting a home where they kept all these old parents of sons and daughters who had just put them into an institution and forgotten them—maybe. I saw that in that home these old people had everything—good food, comfortable place, television, everything, but everyone was looking toward the door. And I did not see a single one with a smile on the face. I turned to Sister and I asked: "Why do these people who have every comfort here, why are they all looking toward the door? Why are they not smiling?"

I am so used to seeing the smiles on our people, even the dying ones smile. And Sister said: "This is the way it is nearly every day. They are expecting, they are hoping that a son or daughter will come to visit them. They are hurt because they are forgotten."

And see, this neglect to love brings spiritual poverty. Maybe in our own family we have somebody who is feeling lonely, who is feeling sick, who is feeling worried. Are we there? Are we willing to give until it hurts in order to be with our families, or do we put our own interests first? These are the questions we must ask ourselves, especially as we begin this year of the family. We must remember that love begins at home and we must also remember that "the future of humanity passes through the family."

We are not social workers. We may be doing social work in the eyes of some people, but we must be contemplatives in the heart of the world. For we must bring that presence of God into your family, for the family that prays together, stays together. There is so much hatred, so much misery, and we with our prayer, with our sacrifice, are beginning at home. Love begins at home, and it is not how much we do, but how much love we put into what we do.

---

[5] Noreen Rackow, as told to Mark Torinus, "The Faces of Euthanasia: Alzheimer's: A Caregiver Speaks Out," *Life Cycle*, no. 114 (April 1992): 7.

If we are contemplatives in the heart of the world with all its problems, these problems can never discourage us. We must always remember what God tells us in Scripture: "Even if a mother could forget the child in her womb—something impossible, but even if she could forget—I will never forget you."

And so here I am talking with you. I want you to find the poor here, right in your own home first. And begin love there. Bring that good news to your own people first. And find out about your next-door neighbors. Do you know who they are?

I had the most extraordinary experience of love of neighbor with a Hindu family. A gentleman came to our house and said: "Mother Teresa, there is a family who have not eaten for so long. Do something." So I took some rice and went there immediately. And I saw the children—their eyes shining with hunger. I don't know if you have ever seen hunger. But I have seen it very often. And the mother of the family took the rice I gave her and went out. When she came back, I asked her: "Where did you go? What did you do?" And she gave me a very simple answer: "They are hungry also." What struck me was that she knew—and who are they? A Muslim family—and she knew. I didn't bring any more rice that evening because I wanted them, Hindus and Muslims, to enjoy the joy of sharing.

But there were those children, radiating joy, sharing the joy and peace with their mother because she had the love to give until it hurts. And you see this is where love begins—at home in the family.

So as the example of this family shows, God will never forget us and there is something you and I can always do. We can keep the joy of loving Jesus in our hearts, and share that joy with all we come in contact with. Let us make that one point—that no child will be unwanted, unloved, uncared-for, or killed and thrown away. And give until it hurts—with a smile.[6]

---

[6] Mother Teresa of Calcutta, "Whatever You Did unto One of the Least, You Did unto Me," speech at the National Prayer Breakfast, Washington, D.C., February 3, 1994.

Sadly euthanasia (or "mercy killing," as its proponents would have us view it) has become routine in some countries of the world. In the Netherlands, 65 percent of family physicians offer the choice of euthanasia *without* first receiving a request from the patient.[7] Many physicians admit that they kill patients on their own initiative.

In the United States, advocates of the so-called "right to die" began to promote "living wills" during the 1970s as an acceptable first step toward euthanasia. It is not surprising that by 1985, more "mercy killings" occurred during that one twelve-month period than in the preceding twenty-three years combined. In fact, more than 75 percent of those cases occurred in states with living-will legislation.[8]

In 1991, Derek Humphrey, founder of the pro-death Hemlock Society, published a "how-to" manual on suicide titled *Final Exit*. It has been sold at popular bookstores nationwide and appeared on *The New York Times* best-seller list for several weeks (even reaching the number one spot). Today, led to believe they must not become a "burden" to anyone, many ill older Americans suffer from severe depression. Some even opt to kill themselves, as demonstrated by the gruesome work of Jack Kevorkian, an ex-pathologist who has collaborated in the early deaths of several dozen people across the United States.

In Europe, by the year 2010, the pension and health care systems will be so "overburdened" by the increase in the number of pensioners compared to workers contributing to these systems[9] that euthanasia is likely to receive even greater support from those who advocate material welfare over human compassion. This lack of respect for the elderly and handicapped emanates from the time abortion was legalized and the mother and

---

[7] Barbara L. Lyons, "The Case against Euthanasia and Assisted Suicide," *Life Cycle*, no. 114 (April 1992): 8–9. Cites "Medische Beslissingen Rond het Levenseinde, II: Het Onderzoek voor de Commissie Onderzoek Medische Praktijk inzake Euthanasie" (Medical Decisions about the End of Life, II: The Study Ordered by the Committee to Investigate Medical Practice concerning Euthanasia), *The Hague* 2 (1991): 83.

[8] Edward R. Grant, J.D. et al., "Repackaging the Euthanasia Debate: 25 Years of Change in Public Policy and Language," *AUL Insights* 3, no. 1 (February 1992): 9.

[9] William Drozdiak, "Europe's 'Birth Dearth' Spawns Reappraisal of Immigration," *The Washington Post*, January 20, 1994, p. A19.

her doctor were given a license to kill the unborn child. If human life is not respected from the moment of conception, who would expect that it be respected until its natural death?

Supporters of assisted suicide and other forms of euthanasia refuse to recognize the intrinsic value of human life in all its stages. They fail to see the wisdom and love that elderly grandparents bring to a family; the profile in faith and courage that a terminally ill relative shares with others as he bravely endures suffering and prepares for a peaceful, holy death is lost.

Experience shows that caring for ill or elderly family members in the home brings great benefits to the family. Children learn to be loving, caring and considerate as a result of doing things for grandparents and other elderly relatives in the home, which adds to each child's sense of self-worth. That is how the circle of love and life continues through the centuries. Parents bring children into the world with love, and these same children see the aging parents out of this world with love.

Dangers for the Family

The beneficial process of caring for others and forgetting self is currently under attack as unrealistic and "unnatural." Many family experts maintain that this assault on the family, the basic unit of society, is completely unprecedented.

The family has always had to contend with threats to its survival. In ancient times, the threats were tangible and easily identified: wild animals, lack of food and shelter, storms, tribal wars and disease. The dangers confronting families today are more subtle and, in many ways, more sinister. The following discussion is meant to bring into sharper focus a few of the forces that currently undermine family stability.

Perhaps the foremost of the forces that threaten the family today is the failure to recognize a higher meaning and purpose in life. This causes many people to pursue material gratification and pleasure as life's chief goals, and so they engage in drug and alcohol abuse, promiscuity and other ruinous vices. Dr. Viktor E. Frankl, the famed psychotherapist and author known for his profound sense of human dignity and worth, describes the syndrome of meaninglessness:

> [I]t is the very problem of our time that people are caught by a pervasive feeling of meaninglessness . . . accompanied by a feeling of emptiness. . . . Our industrial society is out to satisfy all needs, and our consumer society is even out to *create* needs in order to satisfy them; but the most human of all needs—the need to see a meaning in one's life—remains unsatisfied. People may have enough to live by; but more often than not they do not have anything to live for.[10]

Young people suffer greatly from this absence of meaning, and the results show in a tragic toll of suicides, illicit drug use, deaths and injuries from drunk driving, venereal disease and AIDS. Despite being born in a nation blessed with tremendous material prosperity and technological development, more than two thousand American adolescents between the ages of fifteen and nineteen committed suicide in 1989. (Suicide is the second leading cause of death in this age group.)[11] Planned Parenthood's research arm, the Alan Guttmacher Institute, estimates that twelve million new sexually transmitted diseases occur every year. Two-thirds of these cases impact the lives of men and women under the age of twenty-five.[12] Some three million teenagers contract sexually transmitted diseases annually.[13] Among the more than 289,000 reported cases of AIDS in America, 1,167 impacted young people between the ages of thirteen and nineteen. A total of 10,949 were between the ages of twenty and twenty-four.[14] Shockingly, in 1989,

---

[10] Viktor Frankl, M.D., Ph.D., "The Meaning of Love," Ninth International Congress for the Family, World Organization for the Family, September 1986, as printed in *Ninth International Congress for the Family: The Fertility of Love* (Paris: Fayard, 1987), p. 39.

[11] National Institute of Mental Health, Office of Scientific Information, "Suicide Facts", March 1992.

[12] "Facts in Brief: Sexually Transmitted Diseases (STDs) in the United States," The Alan Guttmacher Institute, September 1993.

[13] Ibid.

[14] United States Department of Health and Human Services, HIV/AIDS Surveillance Report, first quarter (through March 1993), vol. 5, no. 1 (May 1993): 10.

"HIV infection and AIDS became the sixth leading cause of death among 15- to 24-year-olds in the United States."[15]

This sense of meaninglessness is not incurable. Teens who have been taught to love and respect themselves and others, who have received loving discipline at home and who have observed and been inspired by the generosity and gentleness of their parents, will have a realistic sense of optimism about the future. Efforts to supply these things where they have been lacking in a family can be successful.

Without the love properly provided in generous amounts by parents, children will usually seek it in the first person who gives them any kind of attention. This can and does lead to serious problems, such as sexual promiscuity. Many teens lack a positive attitude toward the future because they have not experienced unconditional love from their parents. This is often aggravated by fragmentation of their families and, in some cases, poor economic status. They see little opportunity for employment for themselves and lack the skills to deal with the challenges of a high-pressure, success-oriented society. Under these circumstances, it is easy to understand how young people can become discouraged and eventually resort to such false escapes as premature sexual intimacy (fornication) in trying to dispel feelings of hopelessness and despair. Such attempts, however, fail. As Harvard professor Dr. Armand Nicholi, Jr., explains:

> Many who have worked closely with adolescents over the past decade have realized that the new sexual freedom has by no means led to greater pleasure, freedom, and openness, more meaningful relationships between the sexes, or exhilarating relief from stifling inhibitions. Clinical experience has shown that the new permissiveness has often led to empty relationships, feelings of self-contempt and worthlessness, an epidemic of venereal disease, and a rapid increase in unwanted pregnancies. . . . They have noted that students caught up in this new sexual freedom found it "unsatisfying and meaningless". . . . [A]lthough their sexual behavior by and large appeared to be a desperate attempt to overcome a profound sense of loneliness, they described their sexual relationships as less than

---

[15] Centers for Disease Control and Prevention, "HIV/AIDS Prevention: Facts about Adolescents and HIV/AIDS," February 1993, p. 1.

satisfactory and as providing little of the emotional closeness they desired. They described pervasive feelings of guilt and haunting concerns
that they were using others and being used as "sexual objects."[16]

Values and Meaning

Even within intact families, a frequent absence of values and goals to guide
family decisions and activities can cause members to lose sight of what is
truly worthwhile in their lives, such as acts of mercy and kindness toward
the less fortunate. Material possessions and fleeting liaisons cannot satisfy
our deeply rooted desire for meaning and fulfillment; there is a hunger inside the human heart that cannot be satisfied by the relentless pursuit of
temporal appetites. Sharing with others brings rich meaning to life, produces emotional and spiritual growth, and becomes a family's greatest contribution to its own future, as well as that of community and nation. Many
families that are financially, spiritually and emotionally well-off could share
their blessings with children who do not have these benefits. Community
organizations are always looking for families that are willing to share their
love and lives with youngsters who desperately need the experience of stable family living.

Dr. Viktor E. Frankl tells us that young people initially learn to find
meaning in their lives through the influence and example of other people—
primarily their parents—who have found it in their own. One of the more
important tasks of the family is to lead the child to the discovery that happiness is a natural consequence of forgetting oneself and reaching out to
others. That is a priceless lesson you can give your children. Children begin
learning and practicing the virtues of discipline and generosity within the
family through the example and loving guidance of their parents.

---

[16] Armand M. Nicholi, Jr., M.D., "The Adolescent," unpublished paper submitted to Family of
the Americas Foundation, Inc., 1984, pp. 4–5. See also *The Harvard Guide to Modern Psychiatry*
(Cambridge: Bel-Knap Press, 1980), p. 530.

Mother Teresa reminds us of what Scripture teaches: "On the last day He [Jesus] will say to those on His right, 'whatever you did to the least of these, you did to Me,' and He will also say to those on His left, 'whatever you neglected to do for the least of these, you neglected to do it for Me.'"[17]

---

[17] Mother Teresa of Calcutta, "Whatever You Did."

CHAPTER TWO

Building a Stronger Family: Challenges and Solutions

So long as parents are willing to place their careers and goals ahead of the very lives of their children, the world will become an increasingly hostile and sad place in which to live.

Douglas R. Scott
President, Life Decisions International

As we have seen, problems for the family include outside influences that encroach on the parents' role as the most important teachers of their children and attack their beliefs. British family life educator Valerie Riches notes the erosion of family values and parental authority:

> When a nation is threatened by enemies from outside or confronted with economic policies which may damage future national stability, there is public controversy, advocacy of solutions and the emergence of alternative strategies and policies. Where matters of family policy and social morals are concerned, however, political and public debate seems to become stricken with paralysis, closed to scrutiny, fearful of the word "morality". Yet the issue at stake concerns the very fabric of society, the very future of the human race. The threat posed should command immediate response, energetic debate and the formation of counter-policies.
>
> It is imperative that people of good will investigate and unravel the strands which have been cleverly woven round the policies, laws and institutions in their own countries. The investigators need to be iden-

tified and exposed, because they function with impunity, in secrecy or behind a screen of pseudo-respectability given when governments fund their activities and policies.

It is an awesome situation to contemplate and act upon. It is one which requires coordinated effort by those who believe in and support the family and the sanctity of life. It is a battle to be fought *now* by those who cherish the true meaning of freedom.[1]

Dr. James Hitchcock of St. Louis University expresses the same concern in more specific terms:

The "profession" of sex education now largely adheres to the idea that no kind of sexual behavior is wrong if it does not "hurt anyone," and that traditional ideas of chastity are actually damaging to children. One of the purposes of sex education programs is to make students tolerant of all forms of sexual behavior. It is one of the ways in which the very idea of the family is undermined, since students are taught in effect that the traditional, stable family structure is in no way superior to any other form of living together, including cohabitation among homosexuals.[2]

Dr. Paul Vitz, professor of psychology at New York University, identifies this approach to sexuality as similar to that of the "values clarification" system taught to our schoolchildren since the 1960s. That approach calls the direct teaching of morality "outdated" and leads children to base their actions on relativism—the notion that what is good or bad is only so for a given person. This contradictory system and others like it, such as secular humanism, which rejects God and promotes a man-centered view of life, create real dangers for youngsters who learn from them to justify immoral and illegal behavior.[3]

---

[1] Valerie Riches, "Sex & Social Engineering" (Wicken, U.K.: Family and Youth Concern, 1986), pp. 24–25.

[2] James Hitchcock, Ph.D., "Forces Working against the Family," unpublished paper submitted to Family of the Americas Foundation, Inc., 1984, p. 13.

[3] Paul C. Vitz, Ph.D., "Defending Traditional Values: Comments for Parents," unpublished paper submitted to Family of the Americas Foundation, Inc., 1984.

In addition to these challenges, parents are having an increasingly difficult time offsetting the influence of the media and the massive obstacles they create for the family. Many movies and television programs, for instance, seduce teenagers into approving of sexual promiscuity/fornication. The combination of violence and sex, which is frequently heard in rock music and seen in music videos, is especially dangerous. Dr. Hitchcock says this about the influence of some rock music:

> Commercial entertainment is in many instances overtly hostile to family values. Rock music, the most extreme case, celebrates drug-taking and promiscuous sex and creates heroes who at least play the role of being depraved personalities. The whole world of popular music thrives on artificially induced excitement and sensation. It is a world from which parents often feel shut out—a world which, if they do penetrate it, they find inimical to the values that they have tried to inculcate in their children.[4]

Lest it appear that anyone who criticizes the popular culture today is merely a middle-aged, graying prude or similar stereotype, consider this sage observation by Jeff Jacoby, a young, single journalist with the editorially liberal *Boston Globe*:

> I've become jaded. And if a decade and a half of being exposed to this stuff (explicit/violent films, etc.) can leave me jaded—with my background, my religious schooling, my disciplined origins—what impact does it have on . . . a generation growing up amid dysfunctional families, broken-down schools, and a culture of values-free secularism? . . . And what happens to an unblushing society? Why, everything. Central Park joggers get raped and beaten into comas. Sixth graders sleep around. Los Angeles rioters burn down their neighborhood. . . . To suggest that Snoop Doggy Dogg's barbaric gang-rape fantasies somehow follow in the tradition of Sophocles' tragic drama, Chaucer's romantic poetry or Solzhenitsyn's moral testimony is to suggest that there is no difference between meaning and meaninglessness.[5]

---

[4] Hitchcock, "Forces Working against the Family," p. 15.

[5] Jeff Jacoby, "A Desensitized Society Drenched in Sleaze," *Boston Globe*, June 7, 1995.

Values Have Consequences

While current dangers to the family are often subtle, far more obvious are the results of the breakdown in traditional home life. A recent study by the United States Census Bureau comparing the U.S. and other developed countries found that the U.S. has the highest:

- divorce rate

- number of children affected by divorce

- teenage pregnancy rate

- abortion rate

- percentage of teen abortions in the world

- percentage of children living in single-parent households

- percentage of violent deaths among youth[6]

If this were not enough, the United States also has 5 percent of the world's population but consumes 50 percent of the world's illegal drugs.[7] In brief, despite its general economic prosperity and abundant resources, the United States suffers from a cultural crisis—in many ways, a crisis of values—that is damaging both children and their families. Patrick F. Fagan, a longtime observer of public policy and trends that affect the family, writes, "This is a crisis not of children, not caused by children . . . but

---

[6] List derived from Center for International Research, "Children's Well-Being: An International Comparison," U.S. Department of Commerce, Bureau of the Census, International Population Reports Series, P-95, no. 80, November 1989, as summarized by Patrick F. Fagan, "The Social Teaching of John Paul II on the Family: Towards a More Generous Gift of Self in the Family," unpublished and undated paper (circa 1990), p. 3. See also *U.S. Children and Their Families: Current Conditions and Recent Trends*, Report of the Select Committee on Children, Youth and Families, United States Congress, 1989.

[7] Tim Russert, "Meet the Press" interview of Barry McCaffrey, director, Drug Control Policy, broadcast on April 28, 1996.

a crisis in marriage, in its stability, its standing, and in societal support for it."[8]

Fagan cites a number of developments that compound marital and family weakness, including several previously mentioned: the fact that increasingly both parents work outside the home and delegate the care of their children to outsiders; television's ever-growing hold, which not only replaces the time that families have together but also promotes "self-gratification" and "junk food for the mind." He adds that, for many children, these dangers combine to form an "emotional vacuum."[9] According to Fagan, "The major social problem arising from dysfunction in families is not just familial breakdown, divorce, separation and children born out of wedlock, but even more fundamentally *the breakdown of the ability to form close relationships within the family.*"[10]

What You Can Do

Parents must be aware that, regardless of Hollywood "ratings" or media reviews, many television programs, movies, videos, books and magazines are poisonous for children—and for grownups as well. Parents have to protect their children from what is harmful. They also need to understand how much peer pressure causes teenagers to act against conscience and instinct.

Promiscuity often results from peer pressure. Indeed, even a Planned Parenthood survey found that peer pressure is the number one reason adolescents initiate sexual activity, followed by reasons of curiosity and thinking that "everyone is doing it."[11] As Dr. Hitchcock notes, parents can neu-

---

[8] Patrick F. Fagan, "The Social Teaching of John Paul II on the Family: Towards a More Generous Gift of Self in the Family," p. 3.

[9] Ibid., p. 4.

[10] Ibid., p. 6. Cites the National Institute of Drug Abuse (NIDA) summary of the process leading to addictions, *The Psychodynamics of Drug Dependence*, NIDA/ADAMHA, 1977.

[11] "American Teens Speak: Sex, Myths, TV, and Birth Control—The Planned Parenthood Poll," public opinion survey commissioned by Planned Parenthood Federation of America and conducted by Louis Harris and Associates Inc., 1986.

tralize peer pressure by pointing out to their children that their peers may be demanding strict control over their entertainment, friendships and even their behavior and basic attitudes toward life.[12] No one—especially children —wants to feel controlled or used. The respected family commentator and scholar Michael Keating says parents can also remind children that the notion that people should form all of their ideas about life exclusively from persons of their own age makes no sense. Keating's other recommendations for countering peer pressure include: teaching children independence from their peers; limiting children's time among their peers and averting them from potentially hazardous situations; encouraging children toward healthy relationships with both older and younger individuals; and seeking to affect the entire peer group in a positive manner by contact with outstanding teachers, youth leaders and other good role models.[13]

What else can you do to warn your children about negative peer pressure and other dangers outlined here? Dr. Vitz makes some excellent suggestions. To start with, parents must have some kind of alternative in mind:

> First, be willing to criticize—gently but clearly—the permissive and relativistic "new" morality.

> Second, be willing to defend traditional values and to show them in your own life. What are these traditional values? Well here is a list of traditional values as they can be found in amost [sic] everyone's heritage: honesty, hard work, respect for others, also courage, persistence, justice, leadership. . . .

> Third, don't overlook the traditional American values of hard work and achievement combined with compassion and generosity toward others. As for sexual morality, all the major cultural and religious heritages have great respect for chastity and self-control; all are critical of people who are sexually permissive and lacking in self-control. It is hard to respect a young man who can't control his body, who is, so weak that he is, "pushed around by his hormones."[14]

---

[12] Hitchcock, "Forces Working against the Family."

[13] Michael Keating, "The Stolen Generation," *Eleventh International Congress on the Family* (Brussels: Les Editions Européennes, 1988), pp. 61–69.

[14] Vitz, "Defending Traditional Values," pp. 10–11.

Parents may be afraid of being called "old-fashioned" or too straight or square or whatever. Don't worry! Deep down inside, most kids know that, when you insist on high standards, it is because you care for them. Even while they rebel, many children know in their hearts that Mom and Dad are right. *Stand for what you know is good and pray for the best.* (Remember that by setting limits of acceptable behavior, you not only show your children that you care about them, you also provide a way of "saving face" should they encounter a situation where peer pressure is especially strong. Teens are often thankful to be able to say, "No way, I can't! My old man would probably ground me for weeks if we got caught.")

Marriage and Divorce

Another gift that you can offer your children is the message that a strong, lasting marital relationship is superior to any other arrangement. Society no longer conveys to people that a stable marriage is necessary to healthy families. This may well be the single most important reason why divorce has become so common since 1960 and why divorce rates continue to rise.

Marital breakdown has not only become acceptable, it is even condoned. In contrast to this trend, though, many people continue to suggest the need for a permanent bond in marriage. Reverend Edward O'Connor of the University of Notre Dame is one of them:

Even apart from the needs of the children, spousal love itself strongly recommends such a union. The completeness and intimacy of the gift of self signified by the marital union calls for a bond that will remain unbroken. Casual sex is an intrinsic contradiction: the deep hurts, frustration, and disgust for which it is notorious are simply signs of this. Marital love is different from friendship, which can be more or less superficial, more or less transitory. There is no doubt a place for casual friendships in human life; but the human heart has need also for another kind of bond, stable and all-embracing: for a love given in such a way that it may never be retracted. Thus marital love has by its very nature the character of a complete and hence inviolable union. In this imperfect world of ours, spouses do of course fail in their fidelity, and a realistic social order has to have ways of dealing with these failures. But it also needs to acknowledge them as failures, not options.[15]

Children and the rest of us need to discover that many modern marriages could be made to work in the same way that marriages have always been made to work—by the partners being willing to sacrifice a certain measure of self in the interests of other members of the family. As Dr. Nicholi of Harvard states:

The answer to a successful marriage lies not in the number or intensity of the conflicts, but in the willingness and emotional and spiritual resources of the parents to work through the conflicts. Any close relationship requires continuous effort, time and work to maintain it. We need to invest this time and effort because adults, as well as our children, need the close, warm, sustained relationships that only a healthy family environment can provide. I have found in my own life as a busy physician that the time necessary to maintain and nurture these relationships seldom becomes available unless I schedule it into my day—and give it no less priority than a medical emergency.[16]

On the other side of the coin, Professor Nicholi has discussed how the absence of one or both parents affects children:

If one factor influences the character development and emotional stability of a person, it is the quality of the relationship he experiences as a child with both of his parents. . . . [A] parent's accessibility, either physically, emotionally or both, can exert a profound influence on the child's emotional health.[17]

Nicholi adds:

Vast research over the past three decades shows that many forms of psychoneuroses and character disorders can be laid to a child's separation

---

[15] Edward D. O'Connor, C.S.C., *The Catholic Vision* (Huntington, Ind.: Our Sunday Visitor, 1992), pp. 208–9.

[16] Armand M. Nicholi, Jr., M.D., "The Impact of Separation and Divorce on Children," unpublished paper submitted to Family of the Americas Foundation, Inc., undated (circa 1984).

[17] Ibid.

from mother or father. . . . [W]hat has been shown over and over again to contribute most to the emotional development of the child is a close, warm, sustained and continuous relationship with both parents.[18]

Despite this fact, the divorce rate remains high, and an increasing number of children have missing parents. In addition, it is one of the chief reasons child-rearing has shifted from the home and parents to outside agencies and individuals. Nicholi suggests that continued high divorce rates will mean additional deterioration in family life and a higher incidence of mental illness and social problems. He calls family disintegration "the most painful and most frightening of human experiences." He is convinced that "because of divorce and family disintegration, millions struggle with loneliness at some level throughout their lives." Entire nations, as well as individuals, bear the consequences of divorce and the resulting ruined families. For example, a study by sociologists at Princeton University (in the United States) found that high school students whose parents are divorced or separated are three times more likely than their peers to abandon their studies. In addition, researchers at Cambridge University in Great Britain found that children of divorced parents are three times more likely to leave home after a dispute, and four-and-a-half times more likely to cohabit at a younger age. As noted in the British financial journal *The Economist*, the breakdown in family life and values also has large-scale economic consequences:

> When children are badly educated, when a chunk of national income must be set aside to house, care for, or cure those who cannot provide for themselves, when a not much smaller chunk has to be spent on policing and security to ward off crime; then a country will find it hard to grow rich.[19]

Fortunately, there are steps many one-parent families take to strengthen themselves, including counseling as appropriate, but also efforts to reinforce love, respect, sharing, prayer together, forgiveness and hope for the future. Persistence is a key element in this process.

---

[18] Ibid.

[19] "Children of Divorce, An Economic Burden on Society," *Europe Today*, no. 16 (March 29, 1993): 2. Cites *The Economist* (no date or page number cited).

CHAPTER THREE

The Family: A Reservoir of Hope

[L]ove is not understood as a mere side effect of sex but sex as a way of expressing the experience of that ultimate togetherness that is called love.

Viktor E. Frankl
Man's Search for Meaning

Despite higher divorce rates and other problems, many people not only remain family-conscious, they also see the home as a haven of love and life in our troubled world. Such folk understand the need to revitalize their own families and those in their communities and countries.

Dr. James Hitchcock's suggestions for doing this are echoed by many other family specialists: take action to plan and work for family life, learn about anti-family forces and warn children against them, join with like-minded families and groups to defend yourself and your ideals, pray together and help the many other people who would love to recapture healthy and loving family life if they had the knowledge and encouragement to do so.

Parents as Leaders and Teachers

Time must be set aside to discuss love, life and family matters with your children. You can gain a great deal of confidence by considering your capacities as your children's leaders, teachers, protectors and guides. These are roles you have been performing since the birth of your children. Reverend Edward D. O'Connor talks about parents' responsibilities for the care of their children:

> The rationale for marriage comes principally from the needs of the offspring. It is not sufficient for humans to be engendered, like turtles or tadpoles. They need also to be fed, clothed, protected and educated. . . . They have to be taught innumerable things, from the basics of personal hygiene to the subtle demands of interpersonal relationships. Their conscience has to be formed. They must learn how to earn a living and how to develop their intellectual and social potential. Finally, they need a loving environment in order to learn to love others. All this calls for devoted care—care that none but the parents are likely to provide. It requires the combined strength and tenderness of a father and mother. In order that all this might be assured, the procreation of children needs to take place in the framework of a stable, personal union, which is what we call marriage.[1]

Parents must respond to the needs of the child in such a way that the child will eventually achieve independence while maintaining a healthy connection with the family. Parents will play many roles as they help the child to grow into a responsible adult; primary will be those of leader and teacher.

A healthy family has the qualities of strong leadership, ideally shared by the mother and father. Parents will be effective leaders and teachers if they first have a strong, loving relationship with each other. This will show their children what it means to share affection, feelings, ideas and dreams; what it means to be sensitive to each other's needs and accepting of each other's faults.

On the other hand, problems in the parents' relationship can be a major stumbling block in the rearing of children. Ill will between parents often causes one parent deliberately to oppose the other, especially on issues related to discipline. One parent may attempt to compensate for unfairness

---

[1] Edward D. O'Connor, C.S.C., *The Catholic Vision* (Huntington, Ind.: Our Sunday Visitor Publishing, 1992), p. 10.

or harshness toward the child on the part of the other parent. The compensating parent may put up with misbehavior, shower the child with gifts or permit the child to do something that he was previously not allowed to do. When parents get into this kind of "power struggle," the child can use it as an opportunity to manipulate both parents to get what he wants. The child learns which parent is willing to be the "pushover" and will consistently go to this parent with requests. Deep down the parents know this "contest of wills" is damaging to the child and the marriage. However, it can become a way to get the attention of the other spouse.

Children who experience strong and loving parental leadership within the family feel secure. Children respect and trust parents who are not afraid to be strong leaders. When this strong leadership is present, the children have no confusion about "who's in charge" and "what's the rule."

There are families in which children attempt to assume primary leadership roles because the parents neglect to assume this important responsibility. Such situations are always tragic, because while the children sense the family's need for leadership, they are not equipped for the task and are overwhelmed by it.

This responsibility of primary leadership does not exclude creative approaches to lesser responsibilities and tasks in the home. Mom may manage household finances better; Dad may be the best disciplinarian; older children may assume leadership in upkeep of the house, car repairs, grocery shopping, and so forth. Many families display outstanding creativity in this area, which merits recognition. However, this is quite a different issue and should not be confused with the primary leadership and responsibility for the family.

The role of parents as leaders and teachers stems from the very purpose of parenthood, which is to develop capable young people who will become loving, responsible adults. This is of the utmost importance, because this goal will determine how the parents guide children as they develop and mature. Parenting, by far, is the most important thing you will ever do.

Parents always hope their children will thrive in the society in which they live. Worldly honor and success may not always be possible or even desirable because as honorable people they may have to act contrary to the popular mores of the day and be at odds with society and its attitudes. When this happens—and nowadays it is inevitable if parenthood has been effective—we trust that our children will courageously do what they know to be right and good for themselves and for society, just as their parents have tried to do.

The Healthy Family

As you guide your children in learning about sexuality and marriage, you will want to help them understand the traits of a healthy family. When these traits are studied closely, it becomes clear just how complex and demanding it is to keep a family system working in a healthy way. Yet when a family works as a team, it is a wonderful experience and a real asset in solving problems.

The popular columnist Dolores Curran has compiled a list of characteristics of a healthy family. All of us can profit by referring to this list, which describes a healthy family as one that:

1. communicates and listens

2. affirms and supports one another

3. teaches respect for others

4. develops a sense of trust

5. has a sense of play and humor

6. exhibits a sense of shared responsibility

7. teaches a sense of right and wrong

8. has a strong sense of family in which rituals and tradition abound

9. has a balance of interaction among members

10. has a shared religious core

11. respects the privacy of one another

12. values service to others

13. fosters family table time and conversation

14. shares leisure time

15. admits and seeks help with problems

Values and Family

Healthy families are impossible without sound family values. Almost everywhere, people have always believed in honesty, courage, chastity, respect for parents, fidelity in marriage and self-control. Both history and current statistics on divorce prove that when these core values are not central to a culture or an individual family, that culture or family cannot endure.

Every family, whatever its ethnic or religious background, has a core set of values in its heritage that exemplifies and inspires its members. These values are remarkably similar all over the world. The core notion that one should live a life of self-control is common to these values because when self-control is lost to anger, addiction, abuses of sexuality, and so forth, life goes downhill in a hurry.

As will later be addressed in detail, there is a strong push today to break down the moral restraints of young people. Not the least among those pushing are the money-making entities that stand to gain from the increased spending that such a breakdown ensures: pharmaceutical companies that sell contraceptive pills and devices, birth control clinics that dispense such items and demand taxpayer dollars for their support, and filmmakers and pornographers who exploit the natural curiosity of the young and appeal to the lusts of those who should be old enough to know better.

While the harmful side effects of contraceptive pills and devices will be discussed in detail in Part Four, it is appropriate to note here the deliberate attempts by many pharmaceutical companies and other special-interest groups to downplay and even conceal scientific research that shows such pills and devices are unsafe, while emphasizing more "favorable" studies. For example, following a 1988 newspaper report that vital research studies on triphasic contraceptive pills were fabricated, government drug-licensing agencies in the United States, Canada, Australia and the United Kingdom said they would reexamine the submitted data. British journalist Brian Deer provides one example:

> A computer analysis of Wyeth's 1986 promotions to doctors discloses that claims made in support of the new generation triphasic oral contraceptive were based substantially on material in second rank publications or those paid for by drug companies.
>
> The analysis prepared for *The Sunday Times* by the Institute for Scientific Information in Philadelphia reveals that only seven references in a 73-item "worldwide bibliography" issued by Wyeth were from any of the 1,000 top biomedical science journals.
>
> Of the rest, 27 were in transcripts of special symposia or journal supplements financed by drug companies. . . . Eight of the references were to work published by senior staff of Schering AG or Wyeth.[2]

To take a stand against such forces, parents must be able to offer a viable alternative to their children. Solid, loving family values are such an alternative. They can and do work, as millions know.

Values are not just proscriptions *against* certain behaviors, they are ideals to live *for*, standards to live *by*. They serve as the basis for actions and judgments and are crucial to making decisions. Such values are concrete ways of describing what is important. In essence, decision-making is acting on them. When people are able to define their values clearly, decision-making becomes more effective. Values are shaped by many sources, including parents, churches or religious groups, teachers and friends. They help us decide which paths to choose and ultimately determine our character.

Values are taught by word and example. Who we are makes more of an impression than what we say. In a healthy family unit, parents are com-

---

[2] Brian Deer, "Inquiry Ordered on Professor's Bogus Pill Tests," *Child and Family* 20, no. 2 (1988): 116–17. Reprinted from *The Sunday Times* (London), October 5, 1986.

mitted to a clear set of values and have the integrity to abide by them. Likewise, family members express and share values.

Children need to see in their parents the strength and conviction of a firm moral code, especially during the early formative years. Parents who are good models must not only verbally communicate their code to their children but also live it out from day to day so the children witness their parents' integrity and the efficacy of their standards. For example, parents who duly reprimand or punish their child for calling another by a derisive name such as "fatso" or "stupid" should be careful to ensure that their *own* vocabulary does not include hateful words. If their child later overhears them referring to a neighbor as a "jerk" or a fellow driver as a "[expletive] moron," the child would be rightly confused or, perhaps, angered by his parents' hypocrisy. There is tragic irony in the story of a boy who is sent home from school for stealing pencils from the class supply room. His father, a government employee, asks him sternly, "Why on earth would you do a thing like that? If I had known you wanted some pencils, I would have brought a box home from the office!" Is it really any wonder why the boy saw no wrong in taking what did not belong to him?

Douglas R. Scott, president of Life Decisions International, a world-leading organization concentrating on challenging the agenda of Planned Parenthood, has written of the importance of parents practicing what they preach:

> It is important to remember that children often mimic the actions of the adults in their lives. It is no secret that children will often make the same mistakes as their parents. Therefore, if parents are involved in behavior they are telling their children not to practice, how can they expect their children to take them seriously? Children want to look up to their parents so it is important for parents to do everything possible to enhance this respect. This is particularly true for single parents.[3]

---

[3] Douglas R. Scott, *Bad Choices: A Look Inside Planned Parenthood* (Franklin, Tenn., Legacy Communications, 1992), p. 93.

Love and Family

Love, the greatest power of all, must be transmitted from person to person. It is not something that can be transmitted by words alone. One cannot read a dictionary definition of love to know what it means. Wonderful living examples of love exist for each of us and for our children—in persons who have been lovers in the truest sense of the word and whose love has transcended borders, cultures and traditions. One of them is Mother Teresa of Calcutta, who is readily identified by people of every faith as an embodiment and living presence of love. Among her many works of love is a home for the dying in Calcutta. There she and her fellow Missionaries of Charity have brought tens of thousands of dying people from the streets so that they would not die alone, but in true dignity, love and peace. Mother Teresa and her Sisters and Brothers help those who can be healed as well. She tells of one such man:

> We took him to our home. He was so drunk, but the Sisters gave him much love, such care, such everything. After a couple of days, he told a Sister: "My heart is open. I have realized God loves me. I now understand His tender love for me. I want to go home." And we helped him go home. A month later he came back to the home and gave the Sisters his first salary and said to them: "Do to the others what you have done to me." He left; he was a different human being. Love had brought him back to his family, back to the love and tenderness of his children.[4]

Mother Teresa, in her writings and her public speeches around the world, has offered many suggestions about building strong families. She says that if parents have love and concern for each other, their children will learn from that and then know what to do when the time comes for them to start their own family. She notes that parents are often "the only ones left to help their children today" and tells us to teach our children to love and respect each other, to talk and recreate together, and to learn to

---

[4] Mother Teresa of Calcutta, "Children—Wealth of Nations," *Ninth International Congress for the Family* (Paris: Fayard Publications, 1987), p. 456.

share, sacrifice and give to those in need. She recently related the following during a speech in Washington, D.C.:

> Because I talk so much of giving with a smile, once a professor from the United States asked me: "Are you married?" And I said: "Yes, and I find it sometimes very difficult to smile at my spouse, Jesus, because He can be very demanding—sometimes." This is really something true. And there is where love comes in—when it is demanding, and yet we can give it with joy.[5]

Mother Teresa urges families to pray together and thus discover "the joy of loving." She says that to live together, it is necessary to pray together. Finally, she reminds us that "what counts is not how much we give but how much we love." These are values that we, our children and our world truly need.

The fruit of silence is prayer
The fruit of prayer is faith
The fruit of faith is love
The fruit of love is service
The fruit of service is peace.

— Mother Teresa

Values and Children

In the same way that Mother Teresa and her Sisters reach out to others, parents can teach their children about love and its value in their lives. Parents show by example what it means to love one's spouse and what it means to love one's children. They are the best model of this because they have "lived love" through times of pain and sorrow as well as joy.

Throughout life, children observe their parents, and parents gradually begin to see the results of their upbringing in the home. What parents pro-

---

[5] Mother Teresa of Calcutta, "Whatever You Did unto One of the Least, You Did unto Me," speech at the National Prayer Breakfast, Washington, D.C., February 3, 1994.

vide for their children during their formative years will ultimately determine the course of their children's lives and what they will become.

In early childhood, education in sexuality is not so much a matter of instruction regarding the physical aspects of sex and reproduction as it is the development of an attitude about self that is acquired primarily from interaction with the mother, father and other members of the family. Children unconsciously learn to value their own sexuality based on the way they perceive parents feel about themselves and each other. If the child perceives that the mother enjoys being a woman and the father a man, the child is likely to want to be like one of them some day. A little girl will want to grow up to be like her mother if she sees her as a basically happy person, satisfied with herself and loved by her husband. Likewise, a little boy who experiences his father as a strong and loving man will want to grow up to be like him and be loved and cherished by someone like his mother.

Values affect how people treat themselves and others; they have a direct bearing on a person's attitudes and decisions. People who value themselves and others, for example, are more likely to treat others as persons instead of as mere entertainment objects. Children who have learned moral values like respect, chastity, honesty and integrity within their own families stand a better chance of enjoying meaningful and productive adult lives.

Adolescence is the time to plan one's life and to set goals which reflect proper values. This is a difficult process because all adolescents are going through many changes of opinion, emotions and interests. Friends must be chosen who have similar morals; otherwise, the adolescent will face strong pressure to conform to values other than his own. Most teens respect people who have the courage to say "No" and to stand on their own beliefs and values.

Every great person in history conformed to many rules but also had the ability and courage in crucial moments to stand up for principle—even against great pressure. A child does not become a leader or even his own person by following the crowd. Joining the herd may feel good for a time, but it keeps the person from becoming a real individual. Being an individual and leader means holding to traditional values and convictions. It says to the world, "I respect you and value others as I do myself."

What Have You Been Teaching?

You can enhance the education of your children about love and life by first becoming more aware of what you have actually been teaching your children and by determining if this is consistent with the values and philosophy of life that you want to pass on to them. The following is an exercise that will help you to do this.

Parents' Priorities

The degree to which parents care about certain rules and issues is one key to healthy, loving and fruitful family life. Some parents establish too many rules. Others institute far too few. The purpose of this exercise is to help you think about what is most important for you to insist upon in your family. It will also help you to recognize if these priorities are reflected in practice.

First, make a list of the rules that you spend the most energy in enforcing. What are the issues that take up your time with your children? Some sample rules or issues:

1. appropriate television programs, movies, videos and music

2. no alcohol or other drugs

3. choice of friends

4. responsibilities at school, home and place of worship

5. manners/politeness

6. guidelines for dating

Now take some time to reflect on your teaching as a parent. What are the things your children will need to learn from you in order to live their lives well? What lessons, beliefs or values do you wish them to remember from their living with you? Make a list of six essential learning goals that you wish your children to remember and possess. Here are some samples:

1. Honor your parents.

2. Take time to think of others and to perform acts of kindness.

3. Share what you have with others, at home and elsewhere.

4. Be faithful to your values.

5. Remember that everyone has a unique purpose and mission in life.

6. Remember that every human being has innate dignity and worth.

7. You are in this world for a purpose and you were chosen to perform it.

A family's strength and character are very much affected by what parents insist on. The rules and organization of a family in many ways are a curriculum that parents teach. The question for parents: Are you teaching what you want and what your children need?

Reflect on the two lists that you have made. Is there a difference between where you are devoting your time and energy and what you think is most important? Are your most important learning goals reflected in the rules and issues that you most frequently enforce? If not, compile a list of possible ways of teaching those that you neglect. Make a list of concrete steps you can take to achieve a different balance in your teaching as a parent.

Action steps:

1. Help your child to become involved in some service to others.

2. Meet the parents of your child's friends.

3. Plan family time together (dinner, recreation, discussions, and so on).

4. Make this time more attractive and inviting than watching television. Make sure that your children realize that such entertainment is usually meaningless, that it has been responsible for much of the increase in crime, as well as in sexual promiscuity and other terrible things. Likewise, help your kids to recognize that the vulgar language and violence in today's films and television programs have been spreading a lack of respect for oneself and one's fellow man. Of course, children should also know that the television you do choose to watch is that which is educational in nature or pure entertainment.

5. Worship together regularly, as this will help your children not only in their everyday lives but also in times of crisis and grief, which all of us encounter at some point. In addition, it establishes a good habit and emphasizes the importance of the child's spiritual well-being.

The Family and Hope

In this chapter, we have examined the family as a center of love and life, dangers to the family and young people today, and ways to defend our children and families. We have also learned of the family's resilience and durability through the centuries. This promise of the family for the future has been described well by Jean Vanier, friend of persons with physical and mental disabilities and founder of the L'Arche Communities and Faith and Light movement:

I am so convinced that the family is the bearer of hope today that there are so many things I'm afraid of. I see immense destructive forces that attack the family, raising a barrier between man and woman, barriers of lack of confidence in each other and barriers relative to fertility and to family hope, barriers against the family, which is called upon to become an oasis, a place of life and peace for a suffering and anguished world. . . .

We are in front of a world where war and division are great. But we know—we, the disciples of Jesus—that we aren't doomed to war and death. . . . The family . . . can be the bearer of peace, be an oasis of compassion for a world where people feel lonely, isolated and guilty. These communities can be sources of hope and we then discover that our world is not doomed to anguish, to death, and each of us to isolation, but that we are destined for life, the covenant, love, and to give our world hope.[6]

---

[6] Jean Vanier, "Family = Hope = The Fertility of Love," *Ninth International Congress for the Family* (Paris: Fayard Publications, 1987), p. 106.

PART TWO

Raising Responsible Adults

CHAPTER FOUR

Discovering Self-Worth and Establishing Communication

When families are strong and united, children can see God's special love in the love of their father and mother and can grow to make their country a loving and prayerful place. The child is God's best gift to the family and needs both mother and father because each one shows God's love in a special way. The family that prays together stays together, and if they stay together they will love one another as God has loved each one of them. And works of love are always works of peace.

Mother Teresa of Calcutta
Message to delegates at the United Nations
Fourth International Conference on Women
Beijing, Communist China

Child and adult alike, we all need to understand the roles of self-worth and communication in developing healthy sexual attitudes and behavior. You can help your children, now and for years to come, by making them aware of these roles.

Children and Self-Worth

Every person is born with inherent self-worth, a God-given value and dignity that can be neither earned nor taken away. Children whose parents help them to discover their true dignity are likely to grow into healthy adults who are capable of loving and being loved.

Children whose parents are present and responsive to their needs find the home to be a safe, nurturing environment. They learn that life is worth living and that everyone, including them, is in this world for a specific purpose—to contribute in some way to making it better. When a child is hurt or when he feels burdened or overwhelmed by problems, he will instinctively know that home is a haven where he can recover, be comforted and return to his friends and the world a stronger and finer person. Since the family has such enormous importance for the child, devastating problems arise when its relationships are violated by abuse, neglect, desertion by one or both parents, or preferential treatment of a particular child. Parents are always carefully observed by their children. Youngsters are very sensitive and apt to be deeply hurt if they are not given equal and adequate love, attention and affection.

Even in families hurting from a broken marriage, the committed love of one or both parents helps the children. Separated or divorced couples may not be able to live with each other, but they can maintain a deep relationship with the children—one that enhances their own self-worth and that of their children. This does require, however, that playing one parent against the other be avoided.

Using imagery that is very relevant to our later discussions about life, sexuality, love and growth, Jean Vanier talks about what happens inside the hearts of children who are not valued or cherished by significant persons in their lives, especially parents:

> I personally know what happens when a child is not accepted as he is, when the child feels that he is not loved, when the child is so small and fragile that he feels that he is not wanted. At that moment, he closes himself up, he enters a world of fear, a world of insecurity; his little heart is wounded. What is true of the hurt child is true of each of us; we all need tender love, love that supports us. If we have the impression that nobody loves us, all kinds of things happen inside our hearts which lead us to a form of anxiety. The parents' fertility after the birth of a child is a deeply human spiritual fertility. The child has to be loved; he

has to be helped to live in peace; he has to be made to feel that he is protected, encouraged to grow and to trust himself so that he can walk softly, according to the rhythm of nature, according to his ability, toward a maturity of love where he himself can become fertile, with that same spiritual fertility. The fertility of love comes from the united body, from man and woman united. When man and woman are divided, the child is plunged into insecurity.

Fertility is not only a person giving life to another, but a community, man and woman, who help the child to grow by giving him the tenderness, reassurance, the support, the relationship he/she needs to grow toward maturity. The same thing goes for every human and Christian community. In order to grow, the child needs a love that is not possessive, but liberating; a love that lets him grow and accomplish his mission.[1]

An irreplaceable impact in the life of a child is made by the reliable presence and unconditional love of his parents. These exert a powerful influence from the time the child is in the mother's womb. From that moment and always, love is the best preventive measure parents can use to protect and nurture their children. If children receive love in the home, they are less likely to seek it elsewhere. They are also less likely to make harmful decisions that would sadden and disappoint their family because most individuals cannot bear the thought of hurting those they love.

Our sense of self-worth is an integral part of our relationships with others. Children discover their great dignity and worth primarily through their family life. Human beings are literally pre-programmed for interconnection with each other. People come into existence as a result of the union of man and woman and thus begin relationships immediately. We become functioning human beings because of this fact. Even the courage eventually to leave the family and become independent comes from healthy relations within the family; healthy family living produces individuals who feel secure enough in their own worth and ability to be able to establish a life for themselves without cutting the tie to their parents and siblings.

---

[1] Jean Vanier, "Family = Hope = The Fertility of Love," *Ninth International Congress for the Family* (Paris: Fayard Publications, 1987), pp. 104–5.

Human beings are born with inherent worth and value, but it is usually in and through relationships with others that people learn this about themselves. *This is, in fact, a primary purpose of the family—to love and care for each other in such a way that each member eventually learns to respect and value himself and others.* When a child does not have this initial experience of love, it is much more difficult to come to this realization later in life.

Absence in childhood of being loved and cherished frequently shows up in adolescence. Such young people attempt to find love and acceptance among their peers through sex and drugs. Often they do not understand that they are so motivated by a desire to feel important and needed. Parental affection during the early years is a strong deterrent to such behavior.

Mother Teresa recently remarked:

We know that the best place for children to learn how to love and to pray is in the family, by seeing the love and prayer of their mother and father. When families are broken or disunited, many children grow up not knowing how to love and pray. A country where many families have been destroyed like this will have many problems. I have often seen, especially in the rich countries, how children turn to drugs or other things to escape feeling unloved and rejected.[2]

To live satisfying, happy lives, children need to know that they are valuable and that their lives can make a difference—that the world is a better place because they are here. Without this, life becomes unattractive, desolate and hopeless. As a result of negative self-perception, many youths resort to "living for the moment" only, seeking whatever pleasure they can get out of a particular situation.

---

[2] Mother Teresa of Calcutta, message to delegates at the United Nations Fourth International Conference on Women, Beijing, Communist China, September 1995.

Love and Family

There could be no more vital lesson in family life and sexuality education than to know what love is. Through the ages people have agreed, although their choice of words might differ, that love is commitment to another's good. It includes caring, knowledge of the other, compassion, sacrifice and faithfulness.

Discussing the true meaning of love, Mother Teresa of Calcutta said:

It is not enough for us to say: "I love God," but I also have to love my neighbor. St. John says that you are a liar if you say you love God and you don't love your neighbor. How can you love God whom you do not see, if you do not love your neighbor whom you see, whom you touch, with whom you live? And so it is very important for us to realize that love, to be true, has to hurt. I must be willing to give whatever it takes not to harm other people and, in fact, to do good to them. This requires that I be willing to give until it hurts. Otherwise, there is not true love in me and I bring injustice, not peace, to those around me.[3]

Love is as important to the emotional and psychological well-being of children as food is to the physical. It implies a committed relationship in which children are accepted and cherished even when their behavior is unacceptable. Committed love says to the child, "You are a very important person, and I will always be here for you when you need me. I'll do everything I can to help you grow into a loving human being who will be compassionate, understanding and forgiving of others. We won't always get along and we're both going to make mistakes, but that's part of growing and learning; we'll just have to forgive each other. But no matter what happens, it will never change my love for you. I will always love you."

Philosopher and former college president Dr. Damian Fedoryka talks about the power of parental love:

---

[3] Ibid.

[T]he genuine formation of the child as a personality seems impossible without love. . . . Parental love must include the response of *reverence* —reverence for the mystery and dignity of the child as a human being, reverence before the intervention of the Almighty who descends into human affairs in response, as it were, to the challenge of the spousal act of the parents, finally, a reverence in response to the awesome fact that a person, who primarily belongs to God, has been entrusted to us who are called upon to be the child's first introduction to the Sovereign. . . .[4]

Needs of the Child

The helpless young child, at least in the earliest stages of development, seems to be just a bundle of needs. Yet the child is more than this; he is a spiritual being. What later proves decisive, therefore, is whether or not the child was loved and whether the filling of his needs was accompanied by love. Indeed, it is more important that the child was loved than that his objective needs were met.

At the center of this consideration stands the real yet mysterious power of love to touch and nourish another person. If the child is not loved, even if he is otherwise cared for or if he senses the self-centeredness of his parents, he will turn inward. The self-centeredness of the child can be established as a pattern in the earliest years.

The need for parents to communicate love when children make mistakes or deliberately disobey is crucial to healthy development. When a child neglects his schoolwork and earns a failing grade on a report card, it would be damaging for the parents to belittle the child for his lack of responsibility. The child already knows, without being told, that he has been negligent. Rather, the parents could say that they are disappointed because they know the child can do better. They might then ask the child, with their help, to work out a plan to improve his work at school. *It is important that the child understand that he is not a failure (although he*

---

[4] Dr. Damian Fedoryka, "Reflections on Christian Parenthood," unpublished paper submitted to Family of the Americas Foundation, Inc., pp. 4–5.

has failed to be responsible in his work) and that such problems can be corrected. Parents must be sensitive to the child's need to feel loved even when he has failed. Discipline should be loving and directed to the correction of the problem rather than to the destruction of the spirit of hope within the heart of the child.

Sometimes parents are not aware of the needs of their children because they are busy with work or fail to understand how overwhelmed young people can feel when they have a problem. Parental obligations will, at times, require that parents set aside their own plans in order to be available for their children. This commitment cannot be compromised because of the inconvenience or difficulty of a particular situation. Parents must be willing to do whatever is necessary to help their children, even when it is not easy or convenient.

Mother Teresa has addressed this topic, saying:

I was surprised in the West to see so many young boys and girls given to drugs. And I tried to find out why. Why is it that way, when those in the West have so many more things than those in the East? And the answer was: "Because there is no one in the family to receive them." Our children depend on us for everything—their health, their nutrition, their security, their coming to know and love God. For all of this, they look to us with trust, hope and expectation. But often father and mother are so busy they have no time for their children, or perhaps they are not even married or have given up on their marriage. So the children go to the streets and get involved in drugs or other things. We are talking of love of the child which is where love and peace must begin, here in our own family.[5]

Love is more than just a feeling of care or concern. Love must be tangible; it must be expressed in action to be real. Love is the ability to recognize someone else's needs and the willingness to use one's resources to respond to those needs. It requires that everything else, including one's desires, be put aside for the good of another.

---

[5] Mother Teresa of Calcutta, "Whatever You Did unto One of the Least, You Did unto Me," speech at the National Prayer Breakfast, Washington, D.C., February 3, 1994.

Yet love produces an attitude of fulfillment rather than sacrifice! That is because when we love another, nothing we do for them is too much. Loving others brings out the best in us and makes us realize that the pleasure of giving surpasses that of receiving. One instance of this is that, as children mature, they derive more and more pleasure from giving gifts to their parents and grandparents. You can see their joy as they prepare a surprise gift for someone, especially if it is something they have made.

Spoiling vs. Loving

The attitude of love differs from "spoiling" children by giving them all that they want and demand. *The child's need is for love, not things.*

Sometimes parents feel guilty because they have not spent enough time with their children, and they try to compensate with material gifts. This is not done for the child but to make themselves feel better. When families are materially wealthy, parents will have to discipline themselves in order not to give too much to the child. Children learn appreciation and gratitude best when they must plan and wait for something they want rather than have it given to them without any effort on their part. With some planning, parents can include a child in the purchase of something he would like by having the child contribute a part of his allowance or other money he has earned.

The problems of spoiled children tend to carry over into adult life and are often expressed in marital problems, including infidelity. Adults who were spoiled as children were rarely required to be thoughtful, considerate and responsible. When they marry and have children they often expect the spouse to take on the total responsibility for the family. This is evident in situations where the wife continues to tolerate the husband's lack of involvement rather than incur his wrath over being asked to share in the care of the children. Many wives tolerate "spoiled husbands" because of an insecurity about the relationship and a fear of risking the judgment or disapproval of their spouse. If we carefully assess who makes a man "macho," it is often the woman who actually encourages it.

Frequently, the responsibility for arranging child care before and after the work day, as well as regular household chores, falls on the working mother. Many husbands think their obligation to the family consists mainly (or even exclusively) in providing financial support. By tolerating this attitude and excusing husbands from involvement with the children on a daily basis, many women reinforce this attitude. As a result, such women end up with three jobs: family, housework and work outside the home. This is why the so-called woman's liberation movement has often resulted, not in emancipation, but in encumbrance with three times as much work.

Parents who are committed to the well-being of their children are guided by questions such as, "What does our child need in this situation?" and, "Is what we are doing helping or hurting our child?" Children who receive this kind of concern tend to respond well.

Affection and Praise

Committed parental love includes obligations to provide one's children with affection *and* discipline. Both are essential to the healthy development of children.

Affection is the easy part of love that comes naturally to most parents. It includes loving touches, such as hugs, kisses and caresses, as well as nonphysical signs, such as praise, listening and so forth—all of which communicate "on the spot" acceptance. Children who experience affection have good feelings about themselves and their membership in the family. This goes a long way in developing each child's ability to care for others as he has been cared for by the parents and family. Baby-sitting for a younger brother or sister or visiting grandparents instead of going out with friends can help children learn the joy of choosing others over themselves, even if they don't recognize the joy in it at the time.

Children continue to need affection, even during the teen years, when they experience a natural tendency to distance themselves from parents and family. Parents should tell and show their children that they love them, even when they are testing their independence and becoming rebellious. Parents may need to remind themselves to be affectionate with their teenagers—an arm around the shoulder, a pat on the back, a hug; such expressions will vary within each family. Likewise, parents need and want expressions of affection from their children. After all, mothers and fathers are people too and never outgrow the need for affection. Parents should remember, though, that a normal component of the maturation process often involves distancing on the part of the child.

Sometimes parents are quick to discipline and slow to give recognition for good behavior. On the one hand, they want their children to behave and act maturely, but on the other hand, they tend to forget that good behavior is learned and needs reinforcement.

Praising can be an excellent way to reinforce acceptable behavior. For example, when we say "thank you" for something we like, we are teaching proper manners and also reinforcing them. It is even better to be specific by labeling the desired action. As an example: "Thank you for helping me with the dishes. That gives me the extra time I need to finish mending your costume for the school play."

It is never a good idea to give praise if it is not truly deserved, because the one receiving undue praise will be able to see the insincerity and the other's credibility will be lost. For example, if a child performs badly in a school contest or local sporting event, it would be false to praise his performance by saying the rules were harsh or unfair. It is better to praise the child for his determination and hard work while, at the same time, encouraging him to learn from the experience and to look forward to the next competition.

As with discipline, when praise is due it is best to provide it immediately. Since it is easy to become critical, parents will have to learn to think more positively and to recognize and encourage praiseworthy behavior. Here is an example of how to make a negative statement into a positive one and still accomplish the same goal:

Negative statement: You cannot go out with your friends now!

Positive statement: When you finish your chores you may go out with your friends.

Discipline and Self-Worth

Discipline is a much misunderstood and frequently misused word. Many people equate discipline with punishment. Actually, the word means receiving instruction from another, correcting, molding and strengthening. In short, it means "to teach." Discipline is an expression of love and an education in justice.

Children with a sense of personal worth come from families where there are adequate amounts of affection and discipline, as well as a healthy combination of the two. These are not opposites but different ways of expressing love. When parents need to be tough and firm with their children, this is very loving—as much an act of love as affection is because firmness is what the child needs at the time.

Parents who expect their children to become more responsible and emotionally mature as they grow older will need to allow for growth along the way. This is not to say that principles of discipline no longer apply but that youth need increasing opportunities for freedom and responsibility in order to build self-confidence. For example, it would be appropriate to allow an older child to begin dating, but not a twelve-year-old. Similarly, parents should be reluctant to allow a teenage son or daughter the privilege of obtaining a driver's license when the teenager shows little or no responsibility with schoolwork or at home.

The foundation for self-discipline during the teen years is established by the parents in the earliest years of childhood. Parents cannot afford to delay in helping their children develop self-discipline—to teach them how to manage themselves, their emotions and their behavior. This discipline must start early in life and be administered out of love and a desire to protect children from harm.

Discipline should be directed toward the development of responsibility, a most important value. Think of it as "response-ability"—the ability to respond appropriately to the different situations of life. Taking responsibility means considering the consequences of an action, both to ourselves and others, and making a decision for which we are willing to be held accountable. Young people enhance their feelings of self-worth when they behave responsibly and make loving decisions that help rather than hurt themselves and others.

CHAPTER FIVE

Responsibility, Sexuality and Self-Worth

Giving, beginning within the family and extending outward into society, is the moral center of the system.

George Gilder
Men and Marriage

While every person is obviously an individual human being, he is part of a family and community as well. *Our personal choices affect not only ourselves but also others.* One of today's biggest lies is that people, even teenagers, can go into a bedroom and do whatever they want and the rest of society should have nothing to say about it. While current trends make even the use of the word "fornication" sound old-fashioned, the fact is that such sexual misconduct has many harmful consequences for individuals, couples and society. For instance, if illicit sexual activity results in pregnancy, often the mother will need to use the services of a hospital provided and financed by the community. If not pregnancy but an illness results—such as venereal disease—affected individuals will go to parents, friends or public facilities for assistance. Our interconnectedness is something that must be discovered and the family is the primary place where children learn that personal choices and behavior do affect others.

According to Dorothy Wallis, chairwoman of Louisiana's Adolescent Pregnancy Commission, forty-two Louisiana high-school students become pregnant and eighteen more are treated for a sexually transmitted disease every day. Government expenditures (state and federal) related to teen pregnancies amounted to $335 million for the 1991–1992 fiscal year. In Mississippi, 21.4 percent of all pregnancies reported in 1992 involved girls between the ages of ten and nineteen. Just one year earlier, state expenditures for social programs related to these teen pregnancies totaled ninety-two million dollars.[1]

Adolescents often go through periods when they want more freedom without additional responsibility. Granting a request for greater freedom should be based on the child's willingness and ability to accept the increase in responsibility. Although a teenager may have reached the minimum age required to obtain a driver's license, the parents should grant this *privilege* only after the teenager has shown responsibility in other areas (such as schoolwork, chores, consideration for others) and has an understanding of the consequences of abusing this privilege. When a parent acts irresponsibly and grants this privilege before the teenager is prepared, it is a disservice to the community as well as to the youngster.

Some ways for young people to learn and demonstrate self-discipline and responsibility and enhance their self-worth are:

1. doing things for others—friends, the elderly, the ill or handicapped;

2. being helpful and thinking of family members, especially elderly family members;

3. taking personal responsibilities seriously—homework, personal hygiene, household chores, and so on (don't let a child be a guest in his own house);

4. being true to themselves—standing up for their values and beliefs despite peer pressure to do the opposite; and

5. accepting responsibility for their own behavior and decisions.

---

[1] "High Cost of Teen Pregnancies," editorial, *The Times-Picayune* (New Orleans), January 13, 1994.

An awareness of personal worth is essential to the development of a positive, healthy attitude toward sexuality. All of our choices in life reflect how we feel about ourselves. Illicit sex, for example, indicates a lack of respect for oneself and others.

Decisions and Solutions

Strength of character does not grow out of a problem-free life. Having problems is part of being human. Rather, a strong character is the consequence of a willingness to work toward solving the inevitable problems with which one is confronted. Doing this and making decisions are disciplines that parents can begin teaching in the early years of childhood. Consider the example of a three-year-old child who is having a temper tantrum. Using an approach known as "benching" or "time-out," the parent tells the child to sit in a chair until the child is in control of himself and is able to come up with another way of handling the problem, or is willing to let the parent help with a solution. This kind of approach is a stepping-stone to responsibility and problem-solving because it:

1. sends the clear message that having a temper tantrum is not acceptable behavior;

2. teaches emotional management (self-control) and provides the opportunity for parents to teach the child how to talk out rather than act out feelings; and

3. forces the child to find an acceptable, appropriate solution to a problem or disappointment.

Adolescents and Growing Up

As a parent, you have firsthand knowledge of the fears, hopes and experiences that adolescents face. You know what they worry about most: who they are, where they're going, how they're going to get there. You also can recall what it is like to experience many changes in the anatomy and physiology of your body as well as in your feelings and attitudes. This insight will help you become more comfortable in talking with your teenager. This is the teen's first experience of adolescence; you have *already* been there and have a lot of wisdom to share—and stories, too!

Remember, being an adolescent and growing up are not the easiest things, but they need not be overwhelming. You know that it is not easy, but you also know it can be done.

Growing and maturing can be compared to the beginning of life and birth. At first the baby is cozy, warm and protected in the mother's womb. However, the baby cannot remain there; he must be forced out into the world. Becoming an adult can be just as uncertain, scary and painful, but something better lies ahead—the freedom to contribute and to care for others, to pursue one's vocation and perhaps to have a family of one's own. This process does not happen suddenly.

Adolescence comes from the Latin word *adolescere*, which means "to grow up." It is the exciting but challenging journey from childhood to adulthood. As parents, you can explain to your children that you have made this journey and you stand ready to encourage them and to caution them against wrong turns—that you are eager to help them accomplish their unique goal and mission in life.

The Minnesota State Planning Agency has compiled a list of factors that contribute to risky behavior in teenagers. Among these factors are:

- unclear parental values

- poor communication with parents

- a parent who abuses drugs or alcohol

- an unstable family

Teens who find themselves in such situations can often develop low self-esteem and so engage in risky behavior.

Self-Worth and Inferiority

One of the dangers of adolescence is the possibility of falling into a hard-to-overcome sense of inferiority. Such feelings can lead to self-destructive behavior such as we have previously described.

To avoid developing a sense of inferiority, children need to know that they are loved and to hear the message: "You were born with dignity and worth that no one can take from you. Not even you can take it from yourself! You are an individual—a precious, unique gift. Life does have meaning, and it is your task and challenge to discover it. You have an irreplaceable contribution to make to your family and society, which no one can make for you. Your life can make a difference, if you let it."

Teens may struggle with feelings of inferiority because of their concerns about their physical attractiveness, intelligence, money and the changes that accompany puberty. Adolescent feelings of personal worth are also strongly influenced by how others—notably, their parents and peers—think about them. The key to overcoming the ups and downs of such feelings is to be proud to be oneself.

If teens are to live satisfying lives, they need to feel that they are valuable and that the world is a better place because they are here. If parents and other adult family members act positively toward them—conveying the message that they are important and valuable—adolescents will tend to feel this way. However, if parents and relatives devalue teenagers by saying unkind things or by treating them with indifference or rejection, their self-worth can be diminished or confused.

Of course, always worrying about what others think can make a person shallow and self-centered while causing feelings of self-doubt and insecurity. It is important to remember that we are unique and valuable even when positive feedback is *not* received from others. Even while our perception of self-worth changes, we can never lose the intrinsic gift of self-worth.

Eight Reminders about Self-Worth

Here are some important reminders that you can share with your children about self-worth:

1. A person's self-worth never changes. Every human being is created with innate, God-given dignity and value. A strong sense of our inherent worth can help when others don't affirm or value us as we would like. This is especially relevant to a teen's ability to resist pressure from peers who want him to behave irresponsibly (such as encouraging illicit sexual behavior or the use of alcohol or drugs). The young person who has both strong ideals and a good sense of self-worth will be able to withstand the rejection or teasing of peers when he decides not to participate.

2. Teens are not alone. One needs only to observe others to realize that everyone has times when he feels shy, quiet, angry, mean, silly, or distant and aloof. People often act this way when they are feeling insecure. Everyone experiences such times.

3. Don't compare yourself to others. This is at the root of any sense of inferiority. It is folly because people tend to compare their greatest weakness to another person's greatest strength, or their innermost feelings of inferiority to another person's outward appearance. There will always be people who are better or worse at some things. When people accept who they are, they don't have to compare themselves to others. Instead of comparing, make the most of what you have by concentrating on your strengths. Accentuate the skills that you have, and work to develop new ones based on what you observe and admire in others. If you respect yourself, others usually will, too.

4. Establish genuine friendships. Instead of comparing yourself *to* others, care *for* others. The best way to have good friends is to be a good friend, first, by doing things for others and by expecting nothing in return. Father John Powell explains:

> Love rejects the question "What am I getting out of this?" Love understands by direct experience those often-quoted words of Francis of Assisi: "It is in giving that we receive". . . .
>
> Giving the gift of myself in love leaves me with a deep and lasting satisfaction of having done something good with my life . . . of having used well the gifts which God has invested in me. . . . [Love] supposes a willingness to struggle, to work, to suffer, and to join in the rejoicing. . . .
>
> It is, of course, the paradox of the Gospels: satisfaction and fulfillment are the by-products of dedicated love.[2]

5. Be your own person. This requires knowing your values and being faithful to them. It helps to know what you want and to have a plan for achieving it. Keep a journal of your goals, ideals, priorities and values. Otherwise, you will be tossed around by every distraction that comes along.

6. Pay attention to prayer and spiritual growth. Study what really matters in life. Spiritual needs must be taken care of in order for the whole person to remain healthy. Remember that men and women are spiritual as well as physical beings.

7. Stay in touch and communicate with parents. Parents are constant, faithful friends who are interested in the well-being and happiness of their children. They have a lot of wisdom and love and can be the strongest support in times of difficulty. Communicate your problems to them, seek their advice, and pray for them. It is also good to stay in touch with grandparents, as they have many years of experience and wisdom to share.

---

[2] John Powell, S.J., *Unconditional Love* (Allen, Tex.: Tabor Publications, 1978), pp. 56–57.

8. Face your problems. Ignoring problems does not make them go away. Instead, it tends to lower one's feelings of self-worth. When you train yourself to avoid procrastination and to face problems head on, you will find that it gets easier to meet challenges in the future.

Eight Tips on Friendship

Regarding the fourth item mentioned above, here are some tips for young people (and adults alike) on how to be a genuine friend:

1. Be accepting and respectful of others.

2. Be a good listener.

3. Avoid gossip. People tend to trust and confide in someone who doesn't gossip.

4. Avoid sarcastic or other insulting remarks and teasing. Build people up, don't tear them down.

5. Be sensitive to others—their desires and needs. Don't pursue a friendship only for your own benefit.

6. Don't be unreasonably critical of others, but don't be afraid to speak up when a true friend would do so.

7. Give others the benefit of the doubt.

8. Remember the Golden Rule: "Do unto others as you would have them do unto you."

Test Yourself and Discover Your Goodness

Here is a short checklist to help your children feel good about themselves. With your help, your children can make a list of all of their good points and things they like about themselves. They can put it where they will see it often, add to it when they can, and invite you to do so as well. Here are a few examples of what they might include on this list (They can check off what is true for them and add others.):

☐ I help with work at home or on the farm.

☐ I help my brothers and sisters with some of their projects.

☐ I spend time with my grandparents.

☐ I give some of my time to help the poor.

☐ I try to stay healthy by eating good foods, exercising and getting enough sleep.

☐ I am usually polite and practice good manners.

☐ I don't drink alcohol or use other drugs.

☐ I am a responsible driver.

☐ My parents can trust me to be home on time when I go out and to be where I tell them I will be.

☐ I often try to think of others' needs and interests before my own.

☐ I try to be kind to people, even to those I don't particularly like.

Write down at least one problem that concerns you:

_____

_____

Trust your parents and talk to one or both of them about what you have written. With their help, plan a strategy to solve those problems that can be solved. You may want to work on one problem a week or month. Here's a guide to use, just to give you an idea.

My problem is

_____

I've decided on this goal for dealing with this problem. Here are some steps that I will take to reach this goal.

_____

_____

Periodically review these steps to see if you are accomplishing them.

Your children are now on their way to solving at least one of their problems. However, there may be some that cannot be solved at present. What about those? Tell your children, "The best way to have a healthy mind is to learn to deal with those things which you cannot change." If you can't solve a problem, learn to minimize its negative effects/consequences. Have your children tear up a paper listing their "unsolvable" problems, but first see which one you can help them solve and then encourage them to stop worrying about the others. Also, be sure to tell your children, "Substitute prayer for worry."

CHAPTER SIX

The Importance of Communication in Solidifying Family Life and Individual Self-Worth

The person is a being for whom the only suitable dimension is love.... Love for a person excludes the possibility of treating him as an object of pleasure.

Pope John Paul II
Crossing the Threshold of Hope

Communication is of utmost importance in the development of the person. It is especially important to foster conversation in the family. Patrick Fagan writes:

> Conversation can be a great form of giving, the giving of self-revealing and the giving of patient listening and understanding. The great need of today is for plenty of conversation, and the great danger of today is the dearth of conversation because of too much television and related technologies. They drive out talk. Conversation is the life blood of family life, of strong child development, of marital unity, of deep friendships. Without plenty of conversation all the ills earlier listed are more and more likely to happen!
>
> How much children love conversation. It is the greatest gift a parent can give a child and the family. . . .[1]

---

[1] Patrick Fagan, "The Social Teaching of John Paul II on the Family: Towards a More Generous Gift of Self in the Family," unpublished and undated paper (circa 1990), p. 13.

We usually think of communication as words, spoken or written, but most communication is nonverbal and includes things like gestures, facial expressions, voice inflection and posture. We cannot stop communicating. Even when silent we are communicating nonverbally. This kind of communication often provides a more accurate picture of what we are feeling because we are not able to control it as well as we can verbal communication. Our feelings often come through despite our best efforts.

Touching is a good way to communicate nonverbally and to reinforce love. It can be a sign of acceptance of a person as an equal. Parents relinquish no authority when they acknowledge their children as persons of equal value and worth. When parents and children come through for each other, they give one another an encouraging pat on the back, a hug or a squeeze of the hand.

A word of caution. Since nonverbal communication speaks louder than words, young people need to be aware of how they communicate with their bodies. While it is only natural to want to look and feel attractive (especially at the time when one first becomes interested in dating), wearing suggestive clothing and otherwise acting seductively should be avoided because these give a bad impression and could lead to illicit behavior. It is important to send clear, consistent messages about one's intentions. This will minimize any misunderstanding. When the nonverbal message is clear, there is less of a need to clarify further with words. (*Moreover, it is important to remind young people that true attractiveness comes from within and that nothing is more beautiful than goodness.* That is the lesson of favorite children's tales such as *Cinderella* and *Beauty and the Beast*, and it is the wisdom found in Proverbs 31: "Charm is deceitful, and beauty is vain, but a woman who fears the Lord is to be praised.")

Since family values are often in conflict with those of society, parents have to take a stronger stand for their own beliefs and make sure that they communicate them to their children through word and deed. Today, many people, including some parents, believe it is healthy and unavoidable for young people to engage in sexual experimentation. This attitude exists despite the tragic consequences around us, such as the high incidence of teen abortion and sexually transmitted diseases. Parents must emphasize to children that normal, healthy adolescent relationships do not include fornication.

You will save your children untold grief and many severe problems by showing them that a promiscuous relationship is an inappropriate and unhealthy substitute for other kinds of communication. You can help them recognize the dangers mentioned above and also remind them that:

1. When sex comes before marriage, the relationship loses its potential for true intimacy and becomes solely physical.

2. Through premarital sex, the couple bypasses the important steps of getting to know each other. Their physical contact becomes a poor substitute for authentic communication.

3. Once people become involved physically, it is difficult (even though necessary) to return to the gradual sharing of thoughts and interests that form solid relationships. (These points are discussed in greater detail in Part Three.)

Listening is the most frequently used communication skill. About 70–80 percent of a person's waking hours are spent in some form of communication. Of that, some 9 percent is spent writing, 16 percent reading, 30 percent speaking and 45 percent listening. More than 90 percent of what is learned throughout a lifetime comes through the senses of sight and hearing, through the eyes and ears.

Listening is a way of validating the worth of another person. In fact, it is one of the most powerful ways of loving another. Good listeners like and esteem themselves and others and, in turn, are liked and esteemed *by* others. Studies reveal that people are efficient listeners only about 25 percent of the time. Failing to listen sends the message, intentionally or unintentionally, that neither the person speaking nor what he has to say is important.

At one time or another, all of us have had the experience of not being listened to. We can probably recall quite easily our feelings of frustration and anger. At other times, we have caught ourselves not listening and have felt embarrassed and guilty. How often do parents and children say to each other, "You're not listening!"

Eight Tips for Good Listening

The following suggestions will help you become a better listener:

1. concentrate and make eye contact

2. try to learn

3. hear the unspoken feelings, as well as the stated words, of the speaker

4. respect the speaker's opinions

5. do not "tune out" the conversation when it becomes dull

6. do not think about what to say while the other person is speaking

7. lean toward the person

8. respond with appropriate comments (feedback) such as, "Yes, that's interesting"

Eight Bad Listening Habits

If you have any of the following habits, work to break them:

1. changing the subject

2. avoiding eye contact

3. interrupting

4. interpreting instead of accepting a statement

5. appearing bored

6. laughing off the speaker's words or concerns

7. preparing a reply while the other person is talking

8. engaging in another activity, such as reading or doodling, while the other person is speaking

Communicating the Truth

The most essential requirement for honest communication between individuals is trust. This is no less true when it involves parents and their children. Parents must start to build a relationship of trust as soon as children are born and must maintain a consistent involvement in their youngsters' lives by participating together with them in family prayer and community worship, sports, school functions and other activities. Through this daily contact and interaction, children will come to value their parents not only as leaders and teachers, but also as their most trusted friends.

Another way in which parents can gain the trust of their children is by telling them the truth about the world in which they live. Children need to know that the world and people outside the home, while they may be interesting and beautiful, are not as unconditionally loving and accepting as one's family. Children must be prepared to resist outside efforts to undermine those values that were taught in the home. They should also be taught that prayer during the good times is excellent preparation for the bad times, when it may be our best, and perhaps only, help. If parents have been wise in preparing their children for the transition to a more complex and challenging environment outside the home, these young people will not be overwhelmed when the time comes, but will be able to make their own contributions in a more responsible and prudent manner.

Assertiveness and Communication

Assertiveness is another important component in communication. Assertiveness means being honest about your needs and expressing them in a direct manner that, at the same time, respects the dignity and equality of the other person.

A hostile or aggressive person is not assertive. Examples of hostile or aggressive statements may include:

- "This is another one of your dumb ideas."

- "You always mess things up."

- "You always think of yourself first."

Pouting or giving in for the sake of peace is not assertive, either. Some examples:

- "Well, if that's what you want."

- "Well, I guess I have no choice."

- "You always get your way."

Assertive talk is neither rude nor self-effacing; rather, it is straightforward. Examples:

- "I need to talk about this problem."

- "I can't go along with that."

- "I want you to know how that makes me feel."

- "I think that there is another way to look at this."

Notice that assertive statements are "I" statements. Assertive people are willing to state how they feel and to accept responsibility for their feelings and decisions.

Are You Approachable?

Since communication involves "give and take," it is important that parents be approachable in the eyes of their children. Take this test to find out whether you are an "askable" parent. Score yourself on a scale of 5–1 (5 = Strong, 4 = Good, 3 = Fair, 2 = Weak, 1 = Poor).

A parent or guardian who is askable:

_____ really listens

_____ takes adolescents seriously (does not ridicule)

_____ does not avoid answering difficult questions

_____ is willing to search out answers, look up information

_____ is not easily embarrassed

_____ is honest

_____ is not suspicious, does not jump to conclusions about adolescent's behavior when questions are raised

_____ brings up issues or concerns with a teenager who does not talk much

Talking with Adolescents

How well do you know these guidelines for talking with adolescents?

1. Communication between parents and children is important at all ages. It will be easier during adolescence if it has taken place consistently during earlier years.

2. Adolescents need, want and value your opinions. They may appear to reject them at times, but this is only an unconscious test to see if you really mean what you say.

3. Talk with adolescents about your areas of concern. Give examples: statistics, case studies, newspaper articles, TV shows, and so on. This is taking advantage of teachable moments. It will enhance your credibility as a teacher.

4. Be willing to listen to your adolescent's concerns (at his moment, not your own) and to take them seriously. It is far better to be told something that you disagree with than to have no communication at all. Always be able to guide without being disagreeable.

5. Discourage one-on-one dating until the child reaches the maturity of dating age, and be sure to discourage dating when significant age differences are involved.

6. Encourage entertainment at home.

7. Make sure your adolescent is capable of being faithful to the values you have taught, and make clear that you are willing to give trust where trust is due. (When trust is given and the child acts responsibly, this begets even more trust.)

8. Be strong in your own ideals, values and beliefs.

Self-Worth and Your Family

In this chapter we have reviewed the effects of one's sense of self-worth and of the ability to communicate on the development of healthy sexual attitudes and behavior. We have also listed "do's" and "don'ts" and ways to foster strong self-worth and communication skills in your children. The more you make these efforts a priority, the better the example you set and the more you let your children know of your love and concern for them.

PART THREE

Educational Warfare

CHAPTER SEVEN

Knowing the Normal Growth and Development of the Human Person

Sexual maturity . . . requires and fosters many other virtues per-fective of the human person, for instance, thoughtfulness, charity, and responsibility. . . . Indeed, it [self-mastery] is the very char-acteristic that enables us to make the kinds of choices that are worthy of our personhood, worthy of our human nature.

Janet E. Smith, Ph.D.
"Humanae Vitae": A Generation Later

For a young person the proper understanding of sexuality does not occur because a parent has "explained sex well" in one discussion. Chastity is part of a youngster's identity formation and begins long before the teenage years. Psychotherapist and author Erik Erikson studied the development of children and adolescents and identified eight stages:

1. trust vs. basic mistrust

2. autonomy vs. shame and doubt

3. initiative vs. guilt

4. industry vs. inferiority

5. identity vs. role confusion

6. intimacy vs. isolationism

7. generativity vs. stagnation

8. integrity vs. despair[1]

In this chapter we will examine a child's maturation and the importance of parental guidance and example, building on these basic stages.

Basic Trust vs. Basic Mistrust

While in Mother's womb, a baby is safe, secure, comfortable and warm. Suddenly, at birth, the child is thrust into the outside world of coldness, light and different sensations. At birth, a baby does not realize that he is part of the world. For him, everything is himself. He knows only that he feels comfortable or uncomfortable; he cries and someone comes and takes care of him—he feels good again. When Mother picks him up, he is close again to the conditions that he enjoyed for nine months in her womb. The gurgling of her stomach and her heartbeat are all familiar and comforting to him. This is why it is possible for an inexperienced mother to be able to comfort her baby when the older, experienced grandmother cannot do so.

Gradually, the baby begins to discover his hands, feet and objects around him. Everything goes into his mouth. He soon begins to differentiate. Some things are a part of him and some are not. He then makes a very important discovery; he knows now that he is part of a world bigger than himself! As he gets older, he crawls around and later walks. Into the cupboards he goes and pulls out all of the pots and pans. He must figure out something about the world in which he lives. Will he learn that this is a good world—trustworthy and safe—or will he not? Will he learn that the world will take care of him or that it is precarious and scary? It is to be hoped that he discovers a wonderful world full of trust and happiness.

---

[1] Paula Vandegaer, S.S.S., "The Psycho-Sexual Development of Young People," unpublished paper submitted to Family of the Americas Foundation, Inc., part 2, 1984.

Autonomy vs. Shame and Doubt

At age two, the child reaches another milestone—he starts to make choices. Mother has begun to demand things of him. She wants to toilet train and keep him out of the cupboards. She says, "Don't touch this, don't do that." He learns to say "No." He discovers that he is an autonomous human being who can cooperate or not.

Two-year-olds practice saying "No." It is a standard response to just about any request. At this stage there is no true conscience, except for that which the parents have been able to instill at this early stage of development. When they say, "Don't touch the flowers on the table," he will not touch them. If Mom and Dad leave the room, though, he is likely to get into the flowers. Complex mechanisms are involved in the development of shame and doubt. A child becomes full and free within a set of boundaries and limitations. For a child, having to wake up each morning and make his own decisions about everything is neither liberating nor good. However, when he wakes up in the morning knowing that he is to put on his clothes and brush his teeth, he doesn't have to think about these things. Instead, the habits and values taught by his parents make him feel comfortable.

For a small child with a newfound sense of identity, consistent guidelines are a necessity. If Mom and Dad are too strict in their training, or if they are erratic and leave the child with too much freedom and decision-making, the child will have no sense of security. Either extreme can produce emotions of doubt, uncertainty and shame. If a child goes through this stage successfully, the opposite will be true.

Initiative vs. Guilt

Between the ages of three and seven, a significant change occurs—the child begins to see that he is an individual living in a safe world. He learns that he can take the initiative in relationships—that he can try to entertain others or be quiet, that he can hug Aunt Suzy or not. This is an age when children can be very charming. They will snuggle up in your lap, want to hear stories and want to make you like them (as though they need to do so).

True conscience formation occurs during this time as Mom's and Dad's teaching gradually becomes internalized. The child begins to think, "Mom and Dad wouldn't like that," and eventually, "I know that this is wrong." Take the example of a small child who draws with crayon on the living room wall. When he finishes, he realizes that his mother is not going to like what he did, and he feels guilty about having done something wrong. This is an early experience of conscience. Mother has never told the child directly not to do such a thing, but the child knows better. Mother responds by explaining to the child that one should not draw pictures on a wall and that there are paper and other proper materials for drawing. She shows the child where these are and tells him to use them and not the wall. The child then knows for certain that he has done something wrong and that Mother is upset, yet he also knows that he has been forgiven.

Many years later, this same mechanism will operate in all areas of his life, including the area of sexuality. In the meantime, children need consistent, loving guidance from their parents as their conscience begins to be formed.

A special word of concern. During these early formative years, youngsters engage in highly imaginative thinking. Young children do not have a clear understanding of fantasy and reality. If a child thinks there is something scary in his room, as far as he is concerned there *is* something scary in his room and only turning on the light or some other intervention by Mom and Dad will make it go away. Similarly, a child will weep if the characters in a story are hurt; they are very real to him. Parents should be very careful about monitoring what kind of television programs and commercials their children see at this age. This responsibility should be taken very seriously at a time when even many *daytime* television programs contain sex and violence (particularly offensive are daily "soap operas" and "shock/talk" shows).

Respected film and television critic Michael Medved has analyzed the negative impact on society by those divisions of the entertainment industries in his book *Hollywood vs. America*. He notes:

> In 1988 the Planned Parenthood Federation of America commissioned an exhaustive study by Louis Harris & Associates which found that in the prime afternoon and evening hours the three largest networks broadcast a total of more than 65,000 sexual references every year. This means hourly averages of twenty-seven instances of sexual content, with between one and two depictions or discussions of intercourse or "deviant and discouraged sexual practices." The study determined that the average American TV watcher now views 14,000 references to sex in the course of a year.[2]

Medved writes that in 1981, the *Journal of Communication* published a study on sexual behavior on prime-time television:

> Researchers . . . monitored one episode of each of the major network series—fifty-eight programs in all. In those shows they found forty-one instances of sexual intercourse outside of marriage, and only six references to intercourse between married people—a ratio of almost seven to one![3]

Parents should not ignore what is labeled by the media as children's or family programming. While the program content itself might be suitable for children, commercials may be aired that flash scenes unsuitable for young viewers. For example, a commercial may include excerpts from a violent or sexually explicit movie that is to be shown later that evening. Another commercial may feature scantily clad models and other sexually suggestive images in order to sell anything from beer to perfume. Once you begin monitoring the content of television programs and commercials, you may be surprised by how often you'll seek alternative entertainment for your children and family.

---

[2] Michael Medved, *Hollywood vs. America* (New York: HarperPerennial, 1992), p. 110.

[3] Ibid., p. 111.

Industry vs. Inferiority

From about age seven to the age of puberty, a child will be involved in learning more and more about the world, in developing his muscles and skills, and in exploring interests from sports and dancing to music and books. A common question will be "Why?" Why does this happen? Why is that so? Children of this age also learn how to work and to be productive. If they live on a farm, they will be closer to nature, learning skills directly from their parents. Dr. Melvin Anchell, a fellow in the American Society of Psychoanalytic Physicians and Life/Fellow in the American Academy of Psychosomatic Medicine, describes this phase of a child's development as the "latency period":

> It is a period in which Nature causes direct sexual energies in the 6 to 12 year old to become dormant. There is nothing hypothetical about the latency period. It has been shown to exist throughout the world—in primitive as well as civilized people. . . .
>
> Though direct sexual energies become quiescent during latency, these energies do not disappear, but are redirected by the 6 to 12 year old mind and are used to serve other purposes. For example, some redirected sexual energy is used for acquiring knowledge. This is why the 6 to 12 year old child is most educable.[4]

By this time parents hope their children will begin to discover their own talents, what they are good at and enjoy. They also hope that, through the years, their children will find fulfillment in being industrious, successful participants in our world.

---

[4] Melvin Anchell, M.D., *What's Wrong with Sex Education?* (Selma, Ala.: Hoffman Center for the Family, 1991), pp. 16–17.

Identity vs. Role Confusion

Now we come to puberty, adolescence and adulthood. Puberty can occur at anywhere from eight to sixteen years of age. (Generally, girls are a couple of years ahead of boys.) Youngsters may go through profound growth spurts. They will grow more during puberty than at any other time, except the first two years of life. Growth may be uneven; that is, the extremities may grow first and the trunk last and an ungainly appearance may result. (Internal organs also grow at an uneven pace.)

A child's social life is unstable at this time. At this age, he will love his best friend one week, be bitter enemies the next, and be good friends again a week later. If he is in a youth group, he will have high ideas and big plans but will usually have difficulty following through on them.

The main task now is to form an adult identity. A new sense of sexuality is emerging along with a different looking body. Society, too, is starting to have different expectations of children in this age group. They are capable of more responsibility and better judgment; they are becoming adults. It will take them time to assimilate and name their new feelings. As young people try to become adults, they will take on many new identities. They unconsciously identify with and imitate heroes and heroines. Girls will find new hairstyles, new dresses, and even new attitudes.

This is the age when positive sex education is more important, and welcomed, than ever. Youngsters are eager for high ideals. They want to know how to be good, positive adults and how to think ahead rather than simply react to circumstances. A discussion with parents often means a great deal to them. Adult conversation coupled with acceptance of their newly emerging adulthood is a positive experience. Words of advice and your best wisdom will be listened to carefully.

Sometimes puberty-aged youngsters appear to be scoffing and not listening, but that is often a smoke screen to hide their true feelings and interest. Do not be dismayed; just impart what you want them to know as lovingly and as carefully as you can. If you feel clumsy, don't worry. Due to their curiosity, your children are probably more accepting of your attempts than you realize.

The best safeguard during this period of emerging sexuality is a young person's relationship with his parents. Parents who support their child and demonstrate total, unconditional love for him find that this is the best motivation for young people not to be promiscuous. True love and friendship between parents and children is a powerful force that will, quite often, stop the latter from engaging in actions that would disappoint their parents. Children of all ages seek to please their parents. If it appears impossible to win their parents' love and respect, they will try to get it elsewhere. No one can live without love.

Share Yourself

Even when parents do everything right (as if that were possible), rejection of parental values sometimes occurs. Strong cultural forces or bad companions seduce children into experimenting with sex or drugs. However, if parents have been consistently, unconditionally loving during the early years, children almost always return to the right path after a time of maturing. Share yourself—the most important gift that you can give to your children. Love them through whatever they do, even when love requires showing discipline and reproach.

In addition to the values taught by parents, there are usually natural safeguards to the emerging sexuality of pubescent children. They tend to be shy, body-conscious, moody and erratic. While curious about sex, they usually do not experiment; natural modesty, shyness and an extreme sense of privacy are their prime characteristics. When these natural safeguards are not present, parents must find out why.

The problem will be located either within the family or outside of it. If a girl is unhappy at home, she might fantasize about pregnancy conferring independence and adulthood on her and making her loved. Otherwise, the problem may be in school. The norm set by her peers might lead to promiscuity and childbirth. Or an older promiscuous boy or girl whom the younger teen admires and seeks to emulate could be the cause.

If the problem is in school, group discussions about chastity can be helpful. Teens need to understand that premarital intercourse and other illicit sexuality are neither "cool" nor a sign of maturity; just the opposite, in fact. Parents, with the support of teachers and other adults, can help young people develop this attitude.

If you suspect your teen is promiscuous, be sure you find out if something is troubling him at home. What is he worried about? Does he feel loved and respected by you? Who is influencing your child? Now you must talk directly to your teen about sexual morality, appropriate behavior, the advantages of chastity and the catastrophic consequences of premarital sex —in particular, the grave health risks and emotional consequences. Most girls are profoundly affected when they hear that many boys admit they often use promiscuous girls as mere objects, disregarding them after—never considering any of them as the future mother of their children. Girls tend to be willing to trade "a little bit of sex" in return for a lot of love and affection, whereas boys often give "a little bit of love" in return for a lot of sex.

Intimacy vs. Isolation

After puberty, the period of adolescence occurs. This generally begins around age fifteen or sixteen and may last into the twenties. During this time, young people begin to mature, develop a sense of meaning and gain an idea of what they want to do with their lives. They either accept their parents' values and ethics or reject them.

Teens will ask other teens: "What do you think of what I said?" "Here is what I think about this." "This is what I think about that. Let me tell you what happened," and so forth. They will spend hours in discussion with them. In so doing, they are solidifying their newfound identity. We know what our personality is by the reactions we get from other people.

A young woman is going to be quite curious as to what her personality looks like to a young man, and vice versa.

Dating at this age is very important. A young woman wants to be loved for herself—for her ideas, values and personality. A young man wants to be valued for all of the manly qualities he possesses. If sexual relations become part of the relationship, uncertainty sets in. Teens may wonder if they are loved for themselves or for their sexual availability. This question can only be answered by abstinence. *To solidify truly a genuine relationship, abstinence is absolutely necessary.*

There are many sexually immature young men and women today—individuals who have no self-control. It is assumed that sexual maturity means dropping sexual discipline rather than controlling actions. This discipline should be taught from early childhood as a preparation for the future. When a young man and woman are dating, deeply in love and planning on marriage, both of them have a vested interest in and learn from each other's sexual maturity.

Adolescents and Sexuality

Much research has been conducted on sexual activity and attitudes among adolescents. Regarding promiscuity, several factors have been identified:

1. low degree of participation in and identification with organized religion

2. absence of love in the home and subsequent need for affection

3. pressure from peer group coupled with permissive attitudes toward sex

4. low self-esteem

5. tension between parent and child

6. little emphasis on educational achievement; low educational aspirations

7. deviant attitudes

8. drug and alcohol use

This research identifies eight major problem areas to avoid and/or solve in our family life. It also suggests a positive way to encourage adolescents to examine the rationales for sexual promiscuity. Young people tempted to have sexual relations before marriage should ask themselves, "Can becoming a sex object, using contraceptives and undermining both my health and my relationship with my parents really satisfy my need for love, affection and self-respect?"

In one recent study, the four leading predictors of early sexual activity were alcohol use, having a girlfriend or boyfriend, poor monitoring by parents and more permissive parental attitudes. Other factors included a history of abuse, poor academic performance and feelings of limited opportunities for socioeconomic advancement.[5]

Youngsters are being tempted daily to break the natural laws that protect their innocence, purity and modesty. Deep down, they know that to do so is folly, that they need to be challenged and disciplined. They need to hear from their parents and other adults that self-control is a virtue and the obligation of all responsible human beings. Adolescents should know the tremendous dignity and beauty of married love and aim for that goal, rather than sell themselves short. Sex before marriage *is* less—much less. Dr. Josef Seifert comments on the goodness and sacredness of spousal love:

> [T]he sexual act is such a profound and intimate mutual self-donation and creates an extraordinary and intimate union between two persons. Hence it is morally legitimate only when it is the expression of an exclusive, lasting and irrevocable union which the two persons enter into formally through the act of consent. Otherwise, the sexual act has the character of throwing oneself away.[6]

---

[5] Stephen A. Small and Tom Luster, "Adolescent Sexual Activity: An Ecological, Risk-Factor Approach," *Journal of Marriage and the Family* 56, no. 1 (February 1994): 181–92.

[6] Josef Seifert, "The Moral Difference between Natural Regulation of Conception and Contraception," unpublished paper submitted to Family of the Americas, Inc., p. 7.

Adolescents will also gain appreciation for sexuality the more they understand the gift of fertility and see the tremendous potential of sexuality. Couples will come to realize that chastity and saying "No" are decisions based on mutual respect. At various times each will have to make the decision and be the strong one. This is contrary to the notion among the promiscuous that chastity is for women and men have no responsibility for it. Every young man must be willing to acknowledge that, even though the consequences of early sexual activity are more apparent for the young woman, he bears equal responsibility for engaging in premarital sex and should be equally responsible for the results.

Sex and Responsibility

In a letter to Dr. Joseph A. Califano, then secretary of the United States Department of Health, Education and Welfare, Dr. John Brennan of the Medical College of Wisconsin wrote, "Of far greater value to the health of our teenagers would be your leadership role in a national program to protect their inner reproductive organs by the most effective and least expensive form of birth control, sexual abstinence." Brennan wrote that, along with the "rights of reproductive freedom comes responsibility and within responsibility come rewards." He offered specifics, stating that persons choosing to be abstinent would enjoy freedom from:

1. unwanted pregnancy

2. complications of the Pill and intrauterine device (IUD)

3. venereal disease

4. early sterilization from venereal disease or complications of pregnancy

5. complications of abortion

6. forms of genital cancer

7. the sorrow that befalls a family with an unmarried pregnant daughter

8. an inability to explore all the dimensions of personality

According to Brennan, "The need for self-discipline in sexuality is no different from the need for that trait in every other aspect of our daily lives."[7] He had another suggestion as well:

Teenagers should be taught that the thousands of little eggs in the ovaries of young girls are their gift of life to be protected until the right environment is present to produce children.

Nature has dictated that young people are physically able to reproduce as soon as they become teenagers. They must be taught that intelligence and self-control are essential. Social, economic, and educational standards dictate that they must wait for a period of time of perhaps ten years before it is to their advantage to reproduce. Total success in avoiding unwanted pregnancy, abortion, venereal disease, complications of the Pill and IUD depends not upon further advances in technology but upon a strong national program stressing the advantages of discipline.

It would be a strange society indeed if the government said cigarettes are wrong, alcohol is wrong, drugs are wrong, lying, stealing, and all forms of violence are wrong, but in sex you can do no wrong.[8]

Youth and Ideals

As we have seen, young people respond to high ideals. They need to be challenged to form a strong character. Most often, they will react positively. These comments are typical of those heard from teens who are not challenged or guided properly: "Don't treat us like we are animals who

---

[7] John Brennan, letter to then Secretary of the United States Department of Health, Education and Welfare Dr. Joseph A. Califano, as cited by Mercedes Arzú Wilson in *The Ovulation Method of Birth Regulation* (New York: Van Nostrand Reinhold, 1981).

[8] Brennan, personal communication with Mercedes Arzú Wilson, 1981.

cannot control our emotions. Don't insult us by throwing pills and condoms at us. That is telling us, 'We know you are weak and cannot control your sexual impulses. Here, take this and we parents and society don't have to worry about your promiscuity.' "

Mother Teresa challenges young people by telling them that the greatest gift a young man and woman can give to each other on their wedding day is their virginity. She tells of an incident that beautifully illustrates the ability of young people to deny themselves for the good of others. One day two young people came to her house and gave her lots of money. She asked them, "Where did you get so much money?" They answered, "Two days ago we got married, and before getting married, we decided not to have a wedding feast, not to buy wedding clothes, to give you the money instead." Mother Teresa knew well what a big sacrifice that was, so she asked the couple, "Why did you do this?" They replied, "We love each other so much that we wanted to share the joy of loving with the people you serve."

These young people had matured to the intimacy stage of development. In contrast, young people who are promiscuous at this age are still in the identity stage. If a young woman decides to become sexually active and take birth control pills, she identifies herself, not as a good girl who is simply experimenting, but as someone who is intentionally promiscuous. Unwittingly or not, this is an identity formation—albeit an unstable and undesirable one. The decision to begin taking these pills is psychologically destructive as well as detrimental to her body and morally wrong.

Parents, Youth and Sexual Promiscuity

What can parents do if they suspect that their teen is sexually promiscuous? Should they accept the situation in order not to lose their son or daughter? Tragically, that is not an unusual reaction in today's permissive society, which condones this kind of behavior. Yet we know that real love has nothing to do with "sexual liberation," which has made sex today's *number one article of consumption* via television, movies, books, "fashion" magazines and hard-core pornography, including porn traded on computer floppy disks.[9] Today's "sexual liberation" has, in fact, meant the exploitation and cheapening of human sexuality—the unleashing of instincts that need to be controlled, just like any other appetite.

Parents are often reluctant to disapprove of a teen's sexual activity and other moral errors, thereby tacitly approving them. A parent may even feel compassion toward young people who are promiscuous because he thinks it is impossible for teens to control their sexual impulses or not to follow when "everyone else is doing it." Parents who were able to control their sexual desires before marriage should not allow themselves to be deceived into believing that this generation of young people cannot do the same. However, if parents themselves do not practice self-control, they will believe their teenagers cannot either. Confused, misguided parents encourage promiscuity when they provide condoms and pills to their adolescent children. They do so without realizing that they are also promoting irresponsible behavior, adolescent immaturity and further difficulties in later years.

The consequences of promiscuity are severe, especially for women. For example, in addition to the threat of contracting sexually transmitted diseases (STDs) such as herpes, chlamydia and the human immunodeficiency virus (HIV), research shows that women who are at high risk of developing cervical cancer are those who were sexually active before age twenty, who have had sexual intercourse with three or more partners before age twenty-five or who have intercourse with someone who has had three or more partners. "As a direct result of early sexual relations," one New York physician observed, "a woman runs a greater risk of getting cancer of the cervix at a relatively early age (late twenties, early thirties). If there were still any doubt that there is an epidemic of cervical cancer among young women, this doubt has disappeared." An Oxford University study among women using oral contraceptives showed a relationship between prolonged use of birth control pills and the incidence of cervical cancer;[10] thus, young women who are sexually promiscuous *and* contracepting are intensifying

---

[9] "Kids Now Swap Hardcore Porn on Computer Floppy Disks," *Europe Today*, no. 3 (November 23, 1992): 14.

[10] "Studies Link Pill to Higher Cancer Rate," *The Lancet* (London) 2, no. 8356 (October 22, 1983): 930–34, citing studies by the University of Southern California and Oxford University.

their risk. (In addition, teenagers of *both* sexes are much more susceptible to STD damage because they have a lower level of antibodies than adults.)

Increased risk of some forms of cancer is not the only negative consequence of early sexual activity:

> Teen-age sex, especially at 15 years old or earlier, is especially dangerous to physical and psychological health. Several researchers have found high correlations between early sexual experience and alcohol and marijuana use. Early sexual experience has been linked with cigarette use, minor delinquency, and school difficulty. Nonvirginal girls are also over 6 times more likely to report having attempted suicide, are at slightly greater risk for reporting feeling lonely, feeling upset, and having difficulty sleeping, as well as experience lower self-esteem.[11]

In light of these facts, the development of your daughter's sexual identity can be immeasurably enhanced if, as author George Gilder writes, you help her to see everything at stake when society pressures her to deny, through contraceptive sex, her unique, feminine potential for later childbearing.[12] Mother Teresa is not alone in calling mothers "the heart of the family," and as Gilder says, even in two-career families the father admits that the mother's role is more indispensable, no matter how they divide child-rearing duties. Young women should be taught early on, as part of their identity formation, that one's femininity, virginity and fertility are precious gifts not to be squandered or denied. In talking with young people who may be living together before marriage, parents must not try to remedy the situation by being accusatory; rather they must challenge such a choice by asking questions such as, "What are your reasons for not making a commitment to each other? What will you do if a baby comes along? How do you envision your long-term future?" The couple may try to rationalize that it is "more moral" to live with one person instead of moving from partner to partner.

---

[11] Bradley P. Hayton, Ph.D., "The Risky Business of Adolescence: How to Help Teens Stay Safe," testimony before the Select Committee on Children, Youth and Families, United States House of Representatives, June 18, 1991, p. 5.

[12] George Gilder, *Men and Marriage* (Gretna: Pelican Publishing Company, 1986), pp. 5–7.

What can you do in order to protect your children? First, tell your son or daughter that there is a high incidence of divorce among couples who have lived together before marriage.[13] After reviewing fifty years of research, Jeffry Larson of Brigham Young University concluded that couples who cohabited before marrying have a 50 percent greater likelihood of divorcing than those who do not. The Washington Post reports that research by two sociologists, William G. Axinn and Arland Thornton, showed similar results: "Axinn and Thornton did not compare divorce rates in their study, but cited other studies that found that couples who live together before marriage have divorce rates 50 to 100 percent higher than those who don't. Living together 'may reinforce the idea that intimate relationships are fragile and temporary' and this might 'reduce the expectation that marriage is a lifetime relationship,' they said."[14]

Robert R. Bell, author of *Premarital Sex in a Changing Society*, explains that premarital sex "increases the chance of extramarital sex, which often leads to divorce." Bell suggests that, "A man who was sexually active before marriage may often find himself driven by his fleshly desires after the wedding. Because sex is not that special an act to him, he is more open to having problems with lust. . . ."[15]

"Conventional wisdom suggests cohabitation serves as a filter to get rid of those who are not compatible, and as a test to see if couples will stay together," says Jeffry Larson. "We find strong evidence that the marriages of those who have cohabited are less satisfied and more unstable" than those who did not. According to the U.S. Census Bureau, more than six million unmarried, opposite-sex partners are involved in such an arrangement.

Larson found several factors commonly working against cohabitation. Among these are: feeling among the couples that they had "violated their moral standards"; friction caused by opposition of parents to the living arrangement; and disappointment that the experience of living together did

---

[13] Jim Abrams, "Until Marriage Us Do Part," *The Washington Post*, February 2, 1993, p. C5.

[14] *Demography*, August 1992, as cited by Abrams.

[15] Josh McDowell and Dick Day, *Why Wait? What You Need to Know About the Teen Sexuality Crisis* (San Bernardino: Here's Life Publishers, 1987), pp. 80–81.

not make the marriage successful. He also found that when marriage does follow, partners who may have originally cohabited because they were not suited to marriage may feel constrained by a relationship that is more difficult simply to walk away from. Larson emphasizes that cohabitation is not a trial marriage; the two relationships are inherently and dramatically different.[16]

The incidence of divorce is 33–100 percent higher among couples who lived together before marriage.

Study Participants	Increased Incidence of Divorce or Separation
13,000 adults in the United States	33%
5,300 women in Canada	54%
4,300 women in Sweden	80%

[Sources: Jim Abrams, "Until Marriage Us Do Part," *The Washington Post*, February 2, 1993, p. C5. Cites study by sociologist William G. Axinn (University of Chicago) and Arland Thornton (University of Michigan), as reported in *Demography*, August 1992. Karen S. Peterson, "Couples Who Cohabited More Likely to Divorce," *USA Today*, October 7, 1993. Cites study by Jeffry Larson (Brigham Young University) presented to the American Association for Marriage and Family Therapy. Lauren Schlessinger, "The Cohabitation Trap," *Cosmopolitan*, March 1994, pp. 92–96H. Cites psychologist David G. Myers, *The Pursuit of Happiness: Who Is Happy—and Why* (New York: W. Morrow, 1992).]

As a concerned parent, you should share with your children the common-sense insights that were affirmed during an April 1995 conference of

---

[16] Karen S. Peterson, "Couples Who Cohabited More Likely to Divorce," *USA Today*, October 7, 1993.

the Population Association of America. More than a half-dozen demographers presented papers at the conference making strong arguments against cohabitation and offering research showing that people who live together before marriage have higher divorce rates, are more likely to be incompatible and sexually disloyal, and generally less happy than married couples. Marriage, on the other hand, is shown by research to have dramatic emotional, financial and even health benefits over cohabitation.[17]

Finally, ask your children whether they truly believe, deep down, that living together is a genuine expression of love and giving—especially when neither has made a binding commitment to the other.

Women who were sexually active before age twenty, who have had sexual intercourse with three or more partners before age twenty-five, or who have intercourse with someone who has had three or more partners, are at high risk of developing cervical cancer.

[Source: "Medical News," *The New York Times*, March 15, 1984. Similar findings are reported by Drs. Jane and Julian Chomet, *Cervical Cancer* (Wellinborough, U.K.: Thorsons Publishing Group, 1989): "The overall incidence of the invasive disease . . . has fallen slightly, but a disturbingly high proportion of cases now occurs in women under 35 years of age with an increase of six percent within the last ten years. . . . The younger a woman has intercourse, the greater the risk of developing cervical cancer. Some statistics indicate that having intercourse before the age of 21 poses the greatest risk. . . . It was also shown in the study that the risk of cervical abnormalities increased with the number of sexual partners."]

---

[17] Jennifer Steinhauer, "Studies Find Big Benefits in Marriage," *New York Times*, April 10, 1995, p. A10.

Marriage or "Relationship"

After such a discussion, a girl will talk to her boyfriend, whose reaction will confirm whether he loves her or is just using her. If the young man says that he will marry her if she becomes pregnant, why does he not marry her now? (The unspoken answer might well be, "Why should I marry her? She is giving me everything I would get if we were married and I don't have to contend with the responsibilities of marriage.")

A relationship will often break up after a candid, realistic conversation of this kind. Both young people may once again embrace the virtue of chastity.

On the other hand, when a young couple has been having intimate relations for some time, they develop a firm set of rationalizations. It will be difficult for them to see any wisdom in avoiding intercourse. "We have a wonderful relationship. We're close to each other and our sexual behavior is just like in marriage. The only problem for us now is to prevent pregnancy from occurring since we can't be married until we finish college in two years."

You, as a parent, friend, teacher or relative, must share your best wisdom with them at such a time, loving them through everything. It is quite possible that this situation will end with a "parting of the ways" and/or a pregnancy. The best that any of us can do is to share our knowledge and experience regarding these matters, including, in the case of pregnancy, our loving willingness to help our daughter choose life for her child (who, after all, is our grandchild) through either adoption or keeping the baby, either in marriage or as a single parent.

After a certain point, young people make their own decisions. Sometimes they have to learn for themselves. Usually, before one reaches this level, there are some expressions of concern on the part of either the young man or woman about their relationship, such as possible feelings of being used or about the insecurity of the whole thing. These would be opportune moments for you to talk about sexual maturity, authentic human love and what those virtues mean.

Generativity vs. Stagnation

Generally, young people will come through puberty and adolescence successfully with the help and guidance of parents and other family members. These children now have an idea of who they are and what their abilities and values are. They become confident that they have something to share, and they experience themselves as loving persons.

This is the time when young people are ready for marriage and for raising a family. You may want to encourage your child to say to himself, "I want to give to this world, to impart my values and ideas to others. I want to have children and to help others. I want to give of myself." Unfortunately, some people never reach this point. Instead, they spend excessive time and effort on themselves, overly preoccupied with their self-interests. Those who reach for the ideal, though, are the ones who find fulfillment.

In Dr. Viktor E. Frankl's words:

Being human always means reaching out beyond oneself, reaching out for something other than oneself—for something or someone, for a meaning to fulfill, or for another human being to love. In other words, being human always means transcending oneself, and unless this self-transcendent quality of human reality is recognized, psychology degenerates into some sort of monadology. After all, self-transcendence is the essence of existence.[18]

We undergo many changes in order to become the persons we were created to be. Many times throughout our adult years we encounter issues of identity, intimacy and fertility. These issues reemerge particularly in our thirties and again in mid-life crisis. We continue to ask, "Who am I?" as we

---

[18] Viktor E. Frankl, M.D., Ph.D., "The Meaning of Love," Ninth International Congress for the Family, World Organization for the Family, September 1986, as published in *Ninth International Congress for the Family: The Fertility of Love* (Paris: Fayard, 1987), p. 40.

constantly examine our progress and as our abilities and strengths continue to grow. This is where faith takes on the most vital role in our lives. When crises occur, faith and prayer are essential to remaining sound in mind and spirit and to overcoming those events which, at times, may seem unfair and/or endlessly difficult. How often we hear others say, "How lucky you are to have so much faith." One then wonders: But didn't their parents teach them to pray and believe? The reality is that many people take God for granted, forgetting that faith is a gift from God that must be requested. This is why it is frequently difficult for young people to pray often. Things are usually going well, and when crises strike, they tend to despair and suffer much—if they have not been trained to pray and to rely on God's plans for their ultimate good.

Raising teenage children will certainly challenge your maturity, identity and abilities as a parent. In fact, it may challenge everything about you, but faithfulness and dedication to your children will be important parts of your personal growth. It may not be easy, but God does give special help to parents. You are co-creators with Him and He, too, has a vested interest in your children.

Integrity vs. Despair

We hope that by the time we reach our advanced years, we will have arrived at some acceptance of life and be able to look back on our years with happiness and contentment. If, by then, we have not achieved a sense of ourselves and who we are—which is consistent with God's plan for us—we may despair. However, it is never too late to grow and change, to recognize that time, love and forgiveness are great sources of healing.

This completes our look at the stages of development in childhood and adolescence. Now we turn to specific discussion of sexuality and self-control for young people.

CHAPTER EIGHT

Adolescents and Healthy Sexuality: Self-Respect and Self-Control

Young adults are offended by the idea that we cannot control ourselves. Those that believe this have no hope for us or our future. They believe we are slaves to our instincts, and we reject that as anti-youth. Chastity is the only pro-youth lifestyle. Those who believe in us, including parents, must promote and live by it.

Christopher P. Tyrrell
President, American Collegians for Life

Sexuality is natural and good. This is a statement your children need to hear as you help them see that adolescence is a time for learning to enjoy and get along with members of the other sex. The task is to become an individual who is reasonably self-sufficient and independent yet also engaged in healthy relationships with others.

The development of wholesome sexuality includes not only the physical but also the spiritual, intellectual, emotional, creative and decision-making dimensions of human reality. It includes the understanding that sexuality is designed for married love. As Professor Alfonso Lopez Quintas emphasizes, such love is much more than the mere eroticism that is so often promoted today, seeking only immediate gratification—bringing, as a result, deception, sorrow and desperation.

Even as his body becomes able to transmit life, every adolescent needs to be able to understand the meaning of life. Sexual activity at this age, as

127

Dr. Viktor E. Frankl observes, hinders spiritual and mental development, causing adolescents to lose higher interests. Like all of us, to maintain an even keel, adolescents need to be interested in the spiritual meaning of life, to exercise their mental abilities, to learn creativity and enjoyment in every area of living, and to have a full but self-controlled emotional life leading to greater caring and empathy for others. In these aspects of life and in sexuality itself, self-control brings peace, progress and happiness, while lack of control brings their opposites.

Self-Control: Healthy and Healthful

Adolescents need to understand that in emotionally laden situations, chemical changes occur in our bodies. When a young man and woman become physically intimate, they open up not only new emotions but also new physiological experiences. These experiences are meant for a mature, committed relationship in marriage.

Responsible adolescents must postpone sexual involvement until they are married and can face the emotional and physical consequences, including conception. This is part of the self-restraint that comes from self-respect and increasing maturity. It is something that does not come easily but must be learned.

The foundation of self-control is laid in early childhood by parents as they teach reasonable limits through loving discipline. Self-control during adolescence and adulthood is simply a continuation of the discipline learned as a child. Without this early training, the teen will be at a great disadvantage. Indeed, it is not surprising that, according to the latest research, "High school students who get into fights are more likely to engage in a number of other risky behaviors, including sex with multiple partners and unprotected intercourse."[1]

---

[1] D. M. Sosin et al., "Fighting as a Marker for Multiple Problem Behaviors in Adolescents," *Journal of Adolescent Health* 16 (1995): 209–15, as reported in "Sex and Fisticuffs," *Family Planning Perspectives* 27, no. 3 (May/June 1995).

The following tables can help adolescents to recognize some of the excuses that people use for lack of self-control as well as some of the ways that many people, including teenagers, are able to keep control of themselves and the situations into which they enter.

Excuses People Use to Engage in Premarital Sex

The following is a list of some of the most commonly used excuses for becoming sexually active before marriage:

1. afraid he will lose the relationship

2. imagines "everyone is doing it"

3. wants to prove that he is a real man or that she is a real woman

4. thinks that he "owes" it to the other person

5. feels guilty for making the other person sexually excited

6. feels pressured or intimidated

7. is curious

8. does not want to appear old-fashioned or "square"

9. thinks it is the next step in the relationship

10. seeks to gain affection and warmth

11. wants to "prove" love

12. thinks he will find security

13. can't "help himself"

You Can Always Change Your Behavior

While young people are bombarded with the "everyone's doing it" message from some adults and peer pressure is intense, many are choosing to remain chaste. True Love Waits is an organization dedicated to presenting the chastity message to as many young people as possible. More than one hundred thousand young people have taken the organization's chastity pledge.

Young people who are not virgins may feel that they are hopelessly lost in an actively sexual world and they cannot get out. It may interest them to know that the chastity pledge is for anyone who wishes to practice the life-affirming lifestyle *from this day forward* and has little to do with the past. Anyone who has been sexually active may choose, at any time, to change his behavior. While it is impossible to get back one's virginity, it is always possible to return to such a mindset.

Figure 1

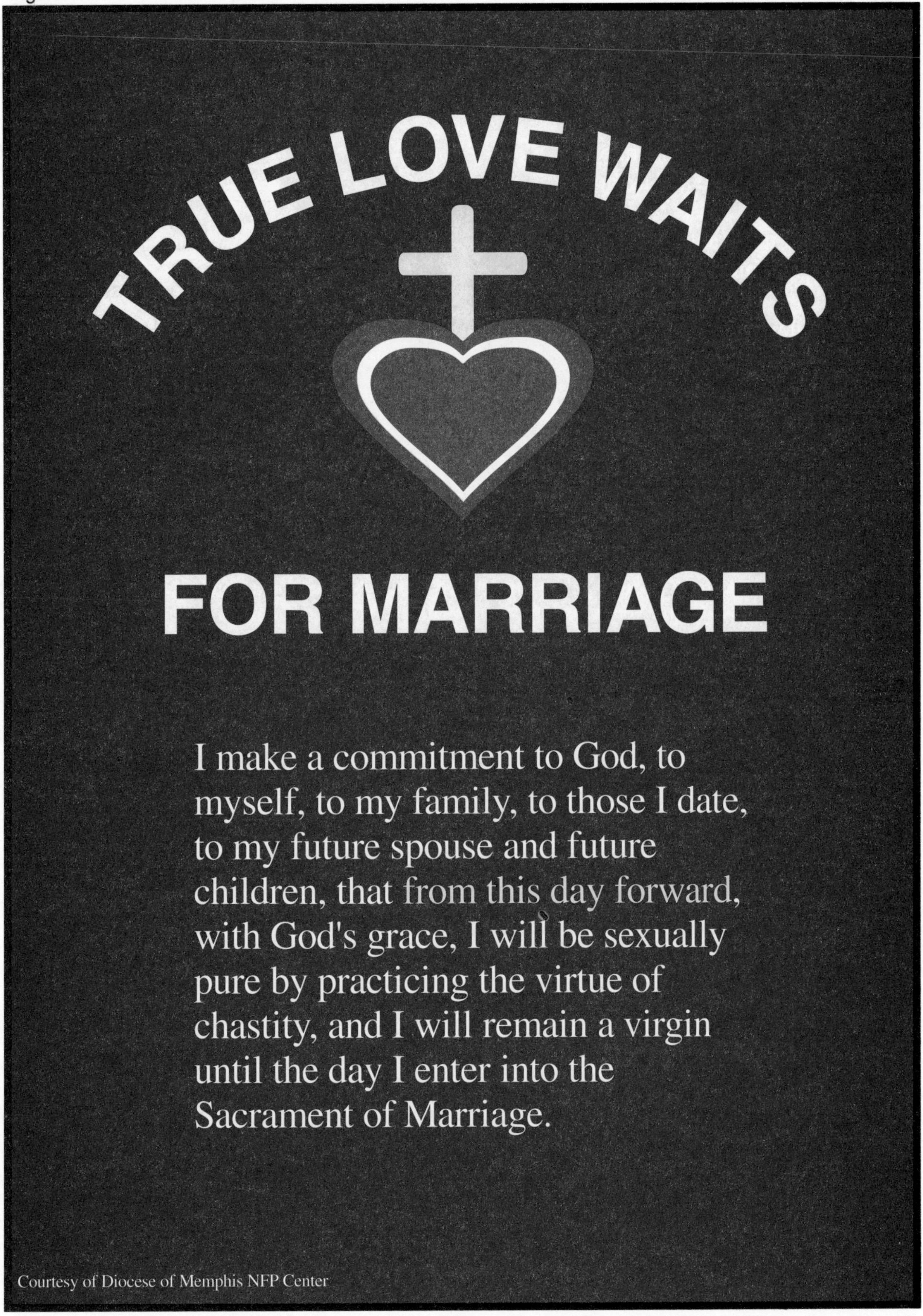

TRUE LOVE WAITS

FOR MARRIAGE

I make a commitment to God, to myself, to my family, to those I date, to my future spouse and future children, that from this day forward, with God's grace, I will be sexually pure by practicing the virtue of chastity, and I will remain a virgin until the day I enter into the Sacrament of Marriage.

Courtesy of Diocese of Memphis NFP Center

Figure 2

Second Chance   You CAN start over!!!

Do you feel hurt and empty?
Do you feel used and ashamed?

Did you just want to be loved?
Did you think that sex was love?

Do you wish you had waited until marriage?
Do you want to be free?

Do you want to start over?
Then DO IT because YOU CAN!!!

It's never too late to change!

TURN TO GOD . . .
who loves you with REAL love. Allow Him to love you. Ask to be forgiven and let Him forgive you. Forgiveness will free you from your sin and guilt and give you back your self-respect. Accept His grace to forgive yourself and to live a chaste life.

REGAIN YOUR VIRGINITY . . .
(spiritually and emotionally) and make the commitment from this day forward to save yourself for your future husband or wife.

DECIDE ON CHASTITY . . .
say "Yes" to the goodness of God's plan for your sexuality: SEX IS SACRED! YOU DESERVE THE BEST!

MAKE NEW FRIENDS . . .
who will love you, encourage you and support your decision to remain chaste.

AVOID TEMPTATIONS . . .
(persons, places and things – especially alcohol) that will weaken your resolve to be chaste.

PRAY . . .
to do God's will every day of your life.

YOU ARE PRECIOUS TO HIM . . .
He wants you to spend eternity with Him. THERE IS HOPE! You don't have to hurt anymore.

Courtesy of Diocese of Memphis NFP Center

Questions to Ask Yourself When You're Tempted

When a person is tempted to have sexual relations outside of marriage, he should ponder the following questions:

1. If this is good, why do I have to lie to my parents in order to get away with it?

2. If this is bad, why am I doing it?

3. Why should I violate my conscience and my belief in right and wrong?

4. Do I really want to get a sexually transmitted disease? (They are very common and some, like genital herpes, are incurable. Moreover, HIV always causes AIDS and that is always fatal.)

5. Do I want to risk my ability to have children? (Venereal diseases, many artificial birth control methods and abortions can cause sterility and related health problems.)

6. If this is supposedly so natural and normal, why do I need to use these artificial, unnatural birth control devices or pills?

7. What am I going to do if my birth control fails? (It often does!)

8. What will it do to our relationship when my birth control fails?

9. Am I prepared for the possibility that I might very well become pregnant? Am I ready to be a mother at such an early age? Will I ever be able to finish my education? Am I ready either to get married or to become a single parent? If I choose neither, will I be pressured into having an abortion; can I live with the guilt of having killed my own child? If I choose adoption, which is the only kind alternative, will I be able to live my life without knowing my baby or what he will be like as a child, an adolescent, a teenager, an adult and a friend? Will I disgrace my parents?

10. Do I really want to become a parent while I'm still in junior high school? In high school?

11. Do I want to jeopardize my plans for college or other goals that I may have?

12. Do I want to be able to keep on respecting myself?

Good Ways to Say "No" to Temptation

There are many good ways to tell someone you don't want to be sexually active. Here are five of them:

1. *Be Direct:* Say "No."

2. *Give a Reason Not to:* "That's for married people." "I'm not ready for this." Better yet: "I want to show my future spouse my love and fidelity by waiting for him."

3. *End the Situation:* "I have to go now." "Let's go somewhere/do something else."

4. *Mention Parents:* "My parents won't let me do that—and yours shouldn't either."

5. *Witness to the Truth:* "That's against my conscience and all of my beliefs."

Remember, it is best to take preventive measures by deciding beforehand how you will conduct yourself. Before dating, decide the limits that you must set on affection because we can't always know our strength or that of the other person to resist temptation. Our strength also varies from person to person and from situation to situation. With new feelings and experiences, we won't always know how we will react and whether we will have the strength to stay in control. Repeated temptation tends to weaken rather than strengthen us to hold off or set limits. Therefore, prolonged kissing, intimate caresses and so on should be avoided because they undermine self-control.

Finally, at a time when we are witnessing the bitter fruits of the "sexual liberation" movement of the sixties, seventies, eighties and nineties, it is important that your teen remember these words of Pat Socia, a sexuality education consultant from the state of Texas in the United States:

> The safe-sex message "is destroying our communities," says Xavier Flores, an AIDS-prevention counselor in East Chicago, Indiana. "They are telling our people that using a condom will save them from AIDS. That is simply not true." A burly, yet genial Hispanic, Flores is visibly angry. Stressing that there is an 18 to 20 percent failure rate among teenagers using condoms to prevent pregnancy, he argues that the "safe sex" message lulls young people into a false sense of security: "If we can have so many condom babies, imagine how many condom AIDS cases we're getting? A sperm is 500 times larger than the AIDS virus. Also, you can only get pregnant during a few days each month, but you can get AIDS any day. Why are we asking our children to trust their lives to a piece of latex?"[2]

Dangers

Premarital sex is not the only situation about which adolescents need your counsel. You will want to explain to them that masturbation is to be avoided because our sexual capabilities are meant for expressing love with our spouse and for bringing new life into the world. Masturbation can be a symptom of underlying problems such as a tendency toward isolation and concentration on self rather than others. Being careful not to cause excessive guilt or worry in this matter, parents can instead encourage their children to look outward toward others—toward social activities that include friendships with members of the opposite sex and toward partici-

---

[2] Andres Tapia, "Abstinence: The Radical Choice for Sex Ed," *Christianity Today*, February 8, 1993, p. 27.

pation in sports teams, youth groups, religious organizations or volunteer service clubs that help others.

You must warn your children at all costs to avoid pornography, the depiction of persons in sexually suggestive or explicit acts and poses. By its very nature, pornography destroys human dignity. It degrades and dehumanizes both "model" and reader alike. In both young and old, pornography creates or reinforces voyeurism, the disorder of seeking sexual gratification by sight. Pornography is addictive for some people. It also stunts and twists personality growth and causes deep problems in many marriages.

Do not be misled by those who claim that only violent pornography is harmful or those who try to distinguish between "hard core" and "soft core." Such individuals are sometimes financially involved, to one degree or another, with the pornographer. Others have simply accepted the flawed argument in order to defend a political position.

Reputable researchers know that all pornography perverts its readers. This includes the well-known magazines that, tragically, can often be found at the corner market in communities where citizens have not yet legally forced them out. This refers to publications that traffickers try to pass off as innocuous despite having explicit photographs focusing on the genitals and on sex acts, as well as cartoons and articles that make light of crimes such as prostitution, child pornography and rape.

Warn your children that the pornography they may be tempted to view is dangerous—that it is the same filth that law enforcement officers have found time and again in the homes of child molesters, sex murderers and serial killers. Be sure to remind your children of the true nature of sex by showing them, for example, the happiness of the loving, responsible married couple and the beautiful, innocent baby who live down the street. Sex is meant for love, joy, life and family—not for solitude, perversion, sickness and crime.

One sexual disorder is homosexuality, which is a desire for sexual intimacy with people of the same sex. Homosexual behavior is clearly the misuse of the sexual act. Indeed, one writer has sagely noted: "The way that gay men sometimes treat each other we call liberation. If it were men treating women that way, we would call it degradation." This inversion of the personality is much less common than many homosexuals and their apologists in the sex and population control lobbies would have us believe.

The frequently cited Kinsey Report that claims some 10 percent of the population is homosexual was written in the late 1940s and has since been shown to be seriously flawed. The more likely figure is well below 2 percent.[3]

A June 1991 report of the National Opinion Research Center states that, "Two percent of sexually active adults reported being exclusively homosexual or bisexual during the year preceding the [1989] survey."[4] According to a four-year study funded by the National Institute of Child Health and Human Development and conducted by the Battelle Human Affairs Research Center in Seattle, Washington, only 1.1 percent of participating males in their twenties and thirties reported being exclusively homosexual.[5]

Homosexual advocates also argue that homosexuality is ingrained rather than learned, but the experience of reformed homosexuals and organizations, such as Courage and Exodus, that help them demonstrates that many people do overcome the homosexual orientation and go on to lead chaste lives. Of course, even if homosexuality were ingrained from birth, no one is "forced" to lead an unchaste, high-risk lifestyle.

A useful analogy might be that of the person who is an alcoholic. Some studies indicate that there may be a genetic basis for alcoholism; however, just because the addiction may be an inborn tendency does not mean society can condone *behaviors* such as excessive drinking, even though we can and do admire the dignity and self-control of alcoholics who no longer drink. Rather, society condemns drunkenness while seeking to help problem drinkers and perhaps even find a cure for alcoholism.

---

[3] Survey of the National Center for Health Statistics, U.S. Centers for Disease Control and Prevention, January 6, 1993.

[4] National Opinion Research Center, June 1991, as cited in "Even New Republic Admits that Homosexuals' 10% Claim Is Wrong," Family Research Council, February 3, 1993.

[5] Boyce Rensberger, "Sex Survey: What Men Do and How Often They Do It," *The Washington Post*, April 15, 1993.

One reason why homosexuality has seemed to increase is that homosexual groups—whose members are often financially well-to-do and are free of the responsibilities and demands of family life—have been very vocal in influencing the government and the media. Homosexuality has spread like a disease because of the efforts of these groups to make "gay" behavior acceptable, confusing many people and encouraging them to experiment and become addicted to it. For example, homosexuality is rare in poor countries because most people are busy working just to survive. In contrast, homosexuality is more widespread in the richer nations of the world because affluence brings an abundance of leisure time—a situation that is conducive to experimentation with various addictions, especially when young people have not had the moral upbringing that would help them to reject immoral behavior.

The rising incidence of anal cancer in recent decades is also alarming. It is "probably tied to the increase in sexually transmitted diseases (STDs), including AIDS." Data from a seventeen-year program show increases of 24 to 34 percent among men and 10 to 13 percent among women, with the sharpest jumps seen among never-married men and those living in the San Francisco Bay Area.[6]

You can reassure your adolescent that homosexuality is rare and that, in the sometimes cruel adolescent world, even continued rejection by the opposite sex does not mean a propensity to this disorder. Instead, it simply means that people bloom at different stages; their time will come. You can remind them as well that some people are meant to be single and that many single persons live full, happy lives contributing to their communities and country. For those meant for marriage, it takes only one partner—the right one—after all the other rejections. Emphasis on love and other-directness is an excellent way to foster normal, healthy sexuality.

---

[6] M. Melbye et al., "Changing Patterns of Anal Cancer Incidence in the United States, 1940–1989," *American Journal of Epidemiology* 139 (1994): 772–80, as reported in *Family Planning Perspectives* 27, no. 3 (May/June 1995): 148.

HIV/AIDS

Acquired immunodeficiency syndrome (AIDS) is a fatal disease that shows no symptoms for long periods and is usually spread or contracted unknowingly. Contrary to claims that condom use during intercourse makes for "safe sex," even their most glowing advocates must admit that these flimsy devices work, at best, only 88 percent of the time—that users have more than a 10 percent chance of catching a 100 percent fatal disease. Other studies indicate a mere 70 percent success rate for condoms—a nearly one in three risk of contracting HIV. Condoms have an annual failure rate of 18.4 percent for girls under age eighteen. Among unmarried minority women the annual failure rate is 36.3 percent. Among unmarried Hispanic women it is as high as 44.5 percent.[7] It is not surprising, therefore, that most people are now using the phrase "*safer* sex" rather than "safe sex."

During homosexual acts, condoms often tear or slip off completely. "The breakage rate for anal intercourse among survey respondents was one condom in 105, which was much higher than that for vaginal sex (one in 165)," according to the authors of *Contraceptive Technology*.[8] (The Family Research Council cites this fact: "In 1984, 7 percent of San Francisco's homosexuals were HIV positive; seven years of safe sex later, the figure is 50 percent.")[9] Another expert notes that it is important to realize "there exists direct evidence of voids in condom rubber. Electron mi-

[7] "Quick Facts on 'Safe Sex,'" (Colorado Springs, Col.: Focus on the Family, 1994). Cites Mark D. Hayward and Jonichi Yogi, "Contraceptive Failure Rate in the United States: Estimates from the 1982 National Survey of Family Growth," *Family Planning Perspectives* 18, no. 5 (September/October 1986): 204. Also cites Elise F. Jones and Jacqueline Darrock Forrest, "Contraceptive Failure in the United States: Revised estimates from the 1982 National Survey of Family Growth," *Family Planning Perspectives* 21, no. 3 (May/June 1989): 103.

[8] Robert A. Hatcher et al., *Contraceptive Technology* (New York: Irvington Publishers, 1994). Cites "Can You Rely on Condoms?" *Consumer Reports*, March 1989, pp. 135–42.

[9] *Washington Watch*, Family Research Council, October 1991.

crographs reveal voids 5 microns in size (50 times larger than the virus), while fracture mechanics analyses, sensitive to the largest flaws present, suggest inherent flaws as large as 50 microns (500 times the size of the virus)."[10]

Over the course of a year, the average woman whose partner uses condoms has a one in six chance of becoming pregnant. The chance of contracting AIDS is even higher since HIV is five hundred times smaller than a human sperm and one-tenth to one-third the size of the smallest detectable hole in a condom.[11] Moreover, while a woman can become pregnant only one hundred hours each month, due to the nature of her ovulatory cycle, HIV can be transmitted at *any* time.

Approximately five thousand people around the world are infected with HIV each day, bringing the current number of infected adults to some ten million. While AIDS is primarily a heterosexual disease in many less developed countries (75 percent of reported cases worldwide are among heterosexuals), in the United States a much smaller percentage of men and women contract the disease through heterosexual activity. However, the United States Centers for Disease Control and Prevention reports that the incidence of HIV infection among heterosexuals, including teenagers, is rising.

Whether among heterosexuals or homosexuals, AIDS is clearly linked to promiscuous and/or unnatural sexual activity, such as sodomy (anal intercourse), as well as intravenous drug use. Consider the following breakdown:

---

[10] C. M. Roland, editor of *Rubber Chemistry and Technology* for the National Research Laboratory, "Letters," *The Washington Post*, July 3, 1992.

[11] "Quick Facts on 'Safe Sex'" cites Nancy E. Dirubba, "The Condom Barrier," *American Journal of Nursing* 87, no. 10 (1987): 1306. (Facts on smallest detectable hole in condom confirmed by U.S. Centers for Disease Control and Prevention and the U.S. Food and Drug Administration.)

male homosexual/bisexual contact	61%
intravenous (IV) drug use (female and heterosexual male)	21%
male homosexual/bisexual contact and IV drug use	7%
heterosexual contact	5%
receipt of contaminated blood transfusion or tissue	2%
other/undetermined	3%[12]

It is estimated that 1–1.5 million Americans have been infected with HIV—that's one in every 250 Americans. More than three hundred thousand people have been diagnosed with AIDS, and more than two hundred thousand have already died from it. The number of deaths is expected to increase dramatically. Nearly 80,000 people in the United States aged thirteen and older were diagnosed with AIDS in 1994. Some 18 percent of these persons were women; over a third of them were infected via heterosexual contact with an infected partner.[13]

The late Dr. Jérôme Lejeune discussed AIDS and its causes:

AIDS is a very interesting disease for epidemiologists. In countries such as America, France and other parts of Europe, it is a different condition from what is happening in Africa. The epidemiology is very simple, the virus that causes AIDS is very fragile, it cannot survive when it contacts air, and it can only be transmitted by direct injection, either through the blood stream, that is, through intravenous injection, or directly through the mucosa of the anus. It is important to note that there was no provision in science for such a virus to exist. A virus which could, on the one hand, destroy the immune function of a person so that he would die from any infection or any type of cancer and, on the other, a virus that would be so fragile that it could be transmitted only by intravenous injection or by intrarectum injection. Since sodomy between homosexuals has become so widespread and a large population is exchanging drugs

---

[12] Hatcher et al., *Contraceptive Technology*, p. 71. Cites "Distribution of AIDS Cases in the United States, through September 1989, by Exposure Category," U.S. Centers for Disease Control and Prevention, HIV/AIDS Surveillance Report, October 1989.

[13] "Update: AIDS among Women—United States, 1994," *Morbidity and Mortality Weekly Report* 44 (1995): 81–85.

through intravenous use, there is great danger that AIDS can become a worldwide epidemic.

For the moment we cannot cure people affected by the virus and who get the full disease, but we can prevent and eradicate entirely this disease without spending one dollar in research. We know everything about the epidemiology; we just have to say, sodomy is counter-natural and intravenous drugs are counter-natural. If people were properly informed and would refrain from practicing sodomy and the use of intravenous drugs, AIDS would vanish and disappear.

You may ask why understanding the consequences of sodomy is so important:

a. Nature built two very different systems of operation for the two openings—the vagina and the anus. The vagina is normally open to the outside world so that the sexual cells can be deposited inside the female body through sexual intercourse. The vagina is totally impermeable to viruses, because nature has provided that the vaginal mucosa has no lymphatic network, and the lymphatic network is made in our body to absorb substances.

b. On the contrary, the rectum is designed to absorb up to the last possibly useful nutrient that we have eaten. There is an enormous lymphatic network in the mucosa of the rectum. Therefore, the rectum is made to absorb and the vagina is made to receive nothing.

This is very obvious because the vagina is opened to the outside world, and if it could accept viruses, no woman would survive. They would die of every viral disease going around. Women survive because nature has decided that this is the way in only for the sperm and not for viruses, and the rectum is the way out for the waste and not for introducing anything. Therefore, when people say that using the anus for intercourse is counter-nature they are telling the truth, it is against nature. It is using nature in the wrong sense.

When people are not homosexual but practice sodomy with their wives, the wife could get AIDS just like homosexuals do. The rectal system is the same for a man or a woman.[14]

---

[14] Jérôme Lejeune, Ph.D., M.D., in a television interview for Family of the Americas Foundation, Inc., at the Thirteenth International Conference for the Family, Vienna, October 23, 1988.

Figure 3

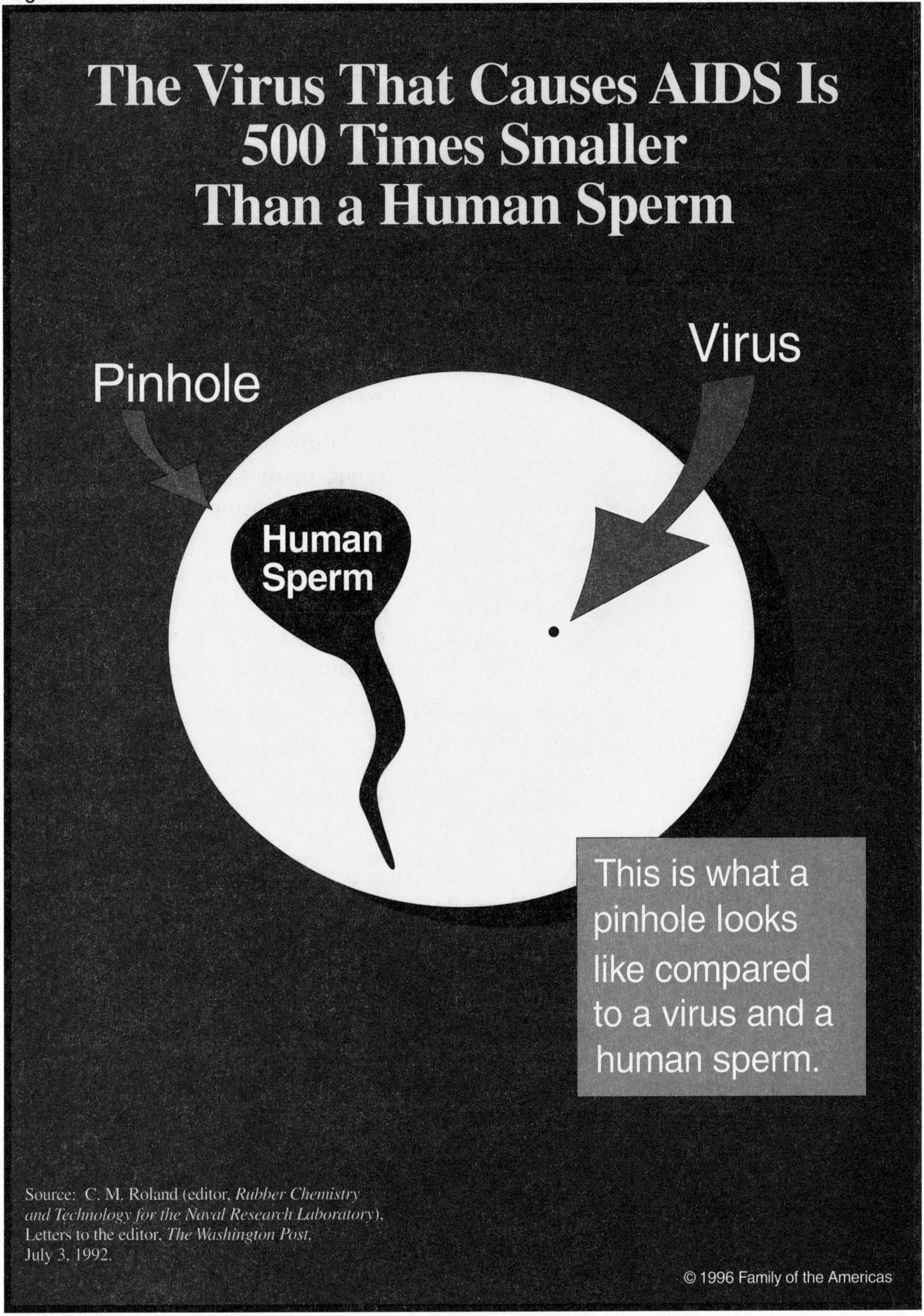
The Virus That Causes AIDS Is 500 Times Smaller Than a Human Sperm
Virus
Pinhole
Human Sperm
This is what a pinhole looks like compared to a virus and a human sperm.
Source: C. M. Roland (editor, Rubber Chemistry and Technology for the Naval Research Laboratory), Letters to the editor, The Washington Post, July 3, 1992.
© 1996 Family of the Americas

More Dangers

Be sure to warn your children about the dangers they face both from other young people and from older individuals who are bent on seduction, molestation, kidnapping and sexual assault. Teach your children to exercise extreme caution when approached by strangers and warn them *never, never* to accompany a stranger to his car, home or elsewhere.

You should also tell your children of the realities facing young people who run away from home. In order to survive, many runaways turn to prostitution with older people who, in addition to exposing them to grave health risks such as HIV, may also cheat, injure or kill them outright. Such victimization often leads youngsters into child pornography. Stress to your children that you love them and want to do your best to solve any and every problem in your family and that, in the unlikely circumstance they should run away, you would welcome them home at any time with open arms.

Drugs, Alcohol and Loss of Control

Taking drugs, including alcohol, is a decision to block out reality. It is impossible for us to make an intelligent decision when our brain and thoughts are distorted by an ingested chemical. Drugs are imminently dangerous to one's physical and mental health and, in the long term, can affect one's fertility and the well-being of future children.

The teen years are normally a time of tremendous growth and change —spiritual, physical, emotional and intellectual. Drug use can so interrupt the normal growth of these years that teen drug-users risk the possibility of entering their twenties with the emotional and intellectual maturity of a thirteen or fourteen-year-old. Those who numb themselves with alcohol and other drugs face the adult world at a level of maturity and life skills far below their chronological age. These young people will experience a great deal of stress during adulthood because they lack coping and problem-solving skills that are usually learned during the teen years.

Many people may not be aware of the strong connection between the use of drugs and promiscuity, yet the link is significant. Taking drugs clouds judgment, diminishes decision-making abilities and lowers one's defenses—making teens more likely to engage in practices such as fornication that they might otherwise avoid. Indeed, a five-year study for the United States Department of Health and Human Services found a clear correlation between alcohol use and sexual activity rates."[15] Similarly, a study published in *Pediatrics* found, "Compared with virgins, non-virgin girls were 2.5 times more likely to have used alcohol, 6.2 times more likely to have smoked marijuana, and 4.3 times more likely to have attempted suicide. . . . Boys engaging in premarital sex were 2.8 times more likely to have used alcohol, [and] 6.3 times more likely to have used marijuana. . . ."[16]

Imitations of Love

You can do your children a big favor by telling them that infatuation and crushes happen to young people constantly and these situations can have positive effects in helping young people to grow and understand themselves. However, it is very important to know what infatuation is, so as not to mistake it for love.

Two characteristics of infatuation are: (1) the teen has unrealistic expectations (storybook romance, marriage, living happily ever after, etc.), and (2) the teen is blind to any faults in the other person. These characteristics usually cause a relationship to become strained after several weeks,

---

[15] "Final Report to the Office of Adolescent Pregnancy Programs," Project Respect, #000816, Title XX, 1985–1990, p. 28.

[16] *The Times-Picayune* (New Orleans), April 26, 1991. Cites a *Chicago Tribune* story reporting on the study.

as reality sets in. Hence the experience of infatuation can help show how quickly strong feelings about another person can change. Time is the best test of whether an experience is infatuation or the beginning of real love.

You will want to point out to your children that true married love is reciprocal and realistic, wholehearted and unconditional. Conditional love is counterfeit and withholds from the other. That is, the other person must *do* something to receive love. ("I will love you if you give yourself to me . . . if you spend all of your time with me.") Similarly, the other person must *be* something to receive love. ("I love you because you have such an important and exciting job or status in school.")

Impress upon your children that looks are not as important as what is inside the heart. Is he generous, kind-hearted, joyful, good and considerate with parents, siblings and the elderly? Is he hardworking, with no serious vices?

Spousal Love

Be sure to stress to your children the sublime nature of love in marriage. Intimacy is the ability to share one's whole self with another person; it is a gift of one person to another. It means becoming completely honest and letting the other know who we really are.

Intimacy cannot be rushed or forced. It develops through a gradual process of sharing one's dreams, hopes and fears. It matures through patience and needs the protection of confidence. Intimacy is neither genuine nor complete without love. As Dr. Frankl states:

> By and large, family life is based on love. This brings up the question: What is the relation between love and sex—more specifically, human sex? As far as the latter is concerned, it is truly human only to the extent that it serves as an expression of love. Human sex is always more than mere sex because it functions as the physical expression of love—or, let me say,

as the "incarnation" of love! However, human sex must become human and it does so by ever more becoming self-transcendent.[17]

In this connection, Frankl goes on to explain four stages of "psycho-sexual maturation." The first and second stages are concerned with the mere satisfaction of sexual urges. The third stage is an improvement on these because in it the partner is seen as a fellow human being rather than a sex object. The fourth stage is the highest. In it, the partner is seen not only as human but also as unique and incomparable. This is the realm of marriage.

Dr. Josef Seifert has spoken beautifully of the sacredness of spousal love, and his comments are a virtual recipe for a happy marriage:

> Love is a free response to another person because of the preciousness that the other possesses. Love is not exclusively the response of the will to the preciousness of the other person—which is revealed to us as a gift —but also a response of the heart. The essential traits of love as such find their culmination in spousal love. The innermost preciousness and the irreplaceable nature of the other person become transparent to us and touch our heart in such a way that is different from any other kind of love.
>
> In a similar fashion, the desire to make the beloved happy and to see him/her achieve the highest good finds a singular expression and achieves a unique summit in spousal love. Our yearning for the happiness of the beloved is not simply more intimate and personal than our desire for the happiness of friends and relatives. Rather, we are filled with an ardent interest in his/her spiritual and physical well-being, and, what is more, we long for their happiness in the most intimate spiritual and bodily di-mensions into which no other form of human love can reach. . . . Here we discern a basis for the fact that spousal love is possible only between a man and a woman. For this complete spiritual and bodily self-donation presupposes the difference between the sexes and their mutual ordination for each other.

---

[17] Viktor E. Frankl, M.D., Ph.D., "The Meaning of Love," Ninth International Congress for the Family, World Organization for the Family, September 1986, as published in *Ninth International Congress for the Family: The Fertility of Love* (Paris: Fayard, 1987), p. 40.

The most profound significance of the marital bond, as well as of sexuality and procreation, discloses itself in the light of spousal love. With such a love as the foundation, marriage and the bodily union of man and woman in marriage are filled with the most personal meaning and happiness. Understood in its deepest dimensions, marriage is a unique community of love, which possesses a high value.[18]

---

[18] Josef Seifert, "The Moral Difference between Natural Regulation of Conception and Contraception," unpublished paper submitted to Family of the Americas, Inc., p. 7.

CHAPTER NINE

Healthy and Unhealthy Education in Sexuality

There is no school sex program given anywhere at any grade level that does not disrupt normal sexual growth processes.

Melvin Anchell, M.D.
What's Wrong with Sex Education?

Parents have the wonderful opportunity to give their children a thorough education in normal development, family life and sexuality that goes beyond the one-dimensional sex education courses that are now prevalent. These courses disregard moral considerations as they detail the "mechanics" of sex (even sexual perversions, which have been renamed "alternatives") and promote birth control and abortion—all while supposedly aiming to reduce or eliminate, not the illicit sexual activity, but the innocent unborn babies who are conceived as a result. Advocates of such amoral sex education would destroy youth's innocence early in life and encourage them to engage in sex long before marriage.

In October 1991, a privately funded task force proposed guidelines for a national sex education program. These guidelines included the use of innocuous terminology such as "sexual orientation," "sexually transmitted diseases," "masturbation" and "abortion." William Yarber, chairman of this National Guidelines Task Force, said, "Schools at last have national direction in developing their own sexuality programs" for kindergarten through twelfth grade. These guidelines have been embraced by the

Sex Information and Education Council of the United States (SIECUS), the leader of which has publicly stated that their goal is to provide sex education starting with preschoolers.[1]

Children are not prepared to hear information about sex in the explicit, amoral context that is proposed today. To begin with, the proponents of these programs—members of what can only be called the sex education lobby—often instigate and infiltrate seemingly objective school panels that are considering sex education curricula. They then use educators, social workers or self-styled "sex experts" who ignore the most important element in this delicate matter—parents.

So contrary is this approach to reality, human nature, spiritual values and common sense that wherever it is tried, in the United States and throughout the Western world, premarital sex, teenage pregnancy and abortion rates climb. They do not fall as its proponents claim. Indeed, as one thoroughly documented study shows:

> What has been the price? Between 1970 and 1987 the total number of births to women under the age of twenty has gone down, but only because the annual number of abortions has gone up by a much larger amount—250,000—and the number of female teenagers themselves—partly because of abortion—has declined by nearly 400,000. . . . The pregnancy rate for teenaged girls, despite increased exposure and access to contraceptives, rose by 10% from 1974 to 1985. Sexual activity rates for both sexes have soared. In 1987, 302,500 children were born out-of-wedlock to girls age fifteen to nineteen; a generation ago, fewer than 150,000 children were born out-of-wedlock to *all* American women.[2]

Such trends have only stimulated the market for those who profit from others' misery, such as abortionists, manufacturers of birth control pills and devices, the sex education industry, pornographers, and so forth.

---

[1] For additional reading on the history and aims of SIECUS, see Robert G. Marshall and Charles A. Donovan, *Blessed Are the Barren* (San Francisco: Ignatius Press, 1991), chapters 3 and 4.

[2] Ibid., p. 96. Cites "Teenage Pregnancy: National Policies at the Crossroads," *Family Policy* (Washington, D.C.: Family Research Council, 1989), p. 1.

Today's sex education is not "value-neutral", as its promoters insist. Rather, it is anti-values, especially values of parents. Such sex education encourages children (even during the "latency period," from about ages five to twelve, when they are emotionally and psychologically unprepared for detailed sexual knowledge) to live according to their impulses rather than the conscience that you have strived to help them form. Sex educators subtly (and not so subtly) mock moral restraint and suggest that any possible sexual act is permissible.[3] "When they say 'abstinence-based,' they also teach foreplay, or what they call 'outercourse,'" notes Reyn Archer, M.D., former deputy assistant secretary for population affairs for the United States Department of Health and Human Services. "Safe sex" practices that SIECUS has listed for teens include: "Flirting, dancing . . . undressing each other, masturbation alone, masturbation in front of a partner, mutual masturbation. . . . Teens could surely come up with their own list of activities."[4]

There is a price for the activity that occurs after children have been told how to have intercourse, how to try to ward off pregnancy and how morality is somehow "old-fashioned." It is often girls and young women who pay the highest toll; they are sexually exploited and often left with a child to take care of or to place for adoption. Still more young women will suffer agonizing guilt and other complications of abortion or, as has been proved by increasing rates of infertility, risk permanent damage from contraceptive use or abortion.

Valerie Riches reports similar consequences from England:

The young are under constant pressure from various interest groups to indulge in sexual activity. Parents have been ostracized; we cannot be surprised at the consequences. The number of underage children seen in family planning clinics has doubled between 1976 and 1982. Abortion in the 11–15 age group and in the 16–19 age group has tripled between 1969 (the first full year of legal abortion) and 1982. There is growing

---

[3] Marshall and Donovan, *Blessed Are the Barren*, p. 68.

[4] Debra W. Haffner, "Safe Sex and Teens," *SIECUS Report*, September/October 1988, p. 9, as cited by Douglas R. Scott, *Bad Choices: A Look Inside Planned Parenthood* (Franklin, Tenn.: Legacy Communications, 1992), pp. 80–81.

concern about the increasing incidence of cancer of the cervix in younger women related to early sexual intercourse. Child prostitution, which had been almost unknown for the past half-century or more has begun to reappear. Sexually transmitted diseases in the under 25's, so commonly followed by pelvic infection and sterility, have now become commonplace.[5]

In the United States, nearly five thousand centers, including school-based "clinics," provide birth control methods or refer for sterilization and abortion. The evidence is clear about their effects—many teenagers having intercourse. A 1986 Lou Harris poll commissioned by Planned Parenthood itself showed that teens who received comprehensive sex education were far more likely to engage in intercourse than teens who did not receive any sex education: 46 percent versus 34 percent.[6] More recently, responses to a survey of readers by *Seventeen* indicate that approximately 51 percent of teens have had sex, with the average age of the first experience being 15.8 for females and 15.4 years for males.[7]

Assuming that such a survey is plausible, it is important to note that, while half of all teenagers may have had sex, another half have not. This is a key fact for your teenager to know when faced with pressure from peers and even from some sex educators who claim that "everybody's doing it."

In order to create a demand for its services, the sex education lobby and its friends in the United States government are, as Kristi Stone of the Family Research Council reports, "working hard to convince Americans that 80% of teens are actively engaged in sex and pursuing many alternative lifestyles." As an example, Stone cites a report issued by a committee led by U.S. Congresswoman Patricia Schroeder (D-Colorado), which concocted the 80 percent figure by adding twenty-year olds among teens. "In fact," counters Stone, "a study by the Department of Health and Human

---

[5] Valerie Riches, "No Entry for Parents: The History and Consequences of Birth Control for Children" (Royston, England: Nightingale Press, 1984).

[6] Andres Tapia, "Abstinence: The Radical Choice for Sex Ed," *Christianity Today*, February 8, 1993, p. 29.

[7] "Love and Sex in the 90s: Our National Survey," *Seventeen*, November 1991, p. 64, as cited by Scott, *Bad Choices*, p. 50.

Services found that among girls under age 18, almost 65% were virgins. In ages 15–19 (a group said to be swarming to the bedroom), almost 50% were still waiting."[8]

Basing its actions on another lie from the purveyors of sex in our society, since 1970 the United States government has spent some two billion dollars of taxpayer revenue on programs that promote contraceptives and so-called "safe sex." The supporters of these programs claim abstinence is impossible. Have their efforts been successful? Hardly. During the same period (1970–1990), nonmarital teen births have risen a dramatic 61 percent. According to the National Center for Health Statistics, in 1990 the number of births to unwed mothers (including nonteens) reached a record high in the United States: 1,165,384 as compared to 667,747 such births in 1980—a 75 percent jump.[9] The Center also reports that "more than 36 out of every 1,000 women aged 15–17 gave birth in 1989." This figure is up 8 percent over 1988 and over 19 percent since 1987.[10]

The current teenage birth rate is the highest in this country since the so-called sexual revolution of the 1960s. Dr. Robert Kistner of Harvard Medical School, developer of the oral contraceptive, came to the conclusion that the use of contraceptives among teenagers stimulates promiscuity: "About 10 years ago I declared that the pill would not lead to promiscuity. Well, I was wrong."[11]

---

[8] Kristi Stone, "Teens, Big Business and the Politics of Sex," *USA Today*, April 30, 1992, p. 13a.

[9] Charmaine Crouse Yoest, policy analyst for the Family Research Council, in testimony before the Committee on Energy and Commerce, Subcommittee on Health and Environment, United States House of Representatives, hearing on the Reauthorization of Title X of the Public Health Service Act, March 19, 1991, p. 2.

[10] National Center for Health Statistics, "Vital Statistics of the United States," Centers for Disease Control and Prevention, *Morbidity and Mortality Weekly Report* 39, no. 46 (November 23, 1990), and earlier; also Congressional Resources Services, as cited in "Relation between Unwed Births, Abortions and Title X Funding," newsletter of Family Research Council, February 3, 1993.

[11] *Family Practice News*, December 15, 1977, as cited by James H. Ford and Michael Schwartz in "Birth Control for Teenagers: Diagram for Disaster," *Linacre Quarterly* 46, no. 1 (February 1979): 76.

Family-Centered Education in Human Sexuality

We are living in a world which is tempting its youth to break every natural law and to violate every traditional principle and moral value. The so-called "sexual liberation" [or sexual exploitation] has become the number one article of consumption today. This is not real "love," but cheap exploitation of human instinct that sees men and women as soul-less bodies to be exploited at will. Never in the history of man have there been such scientifically destructive and politically vicious attacks on the family —methodically destroying our youth—designed to divert them from their natural desire to be challenged to be pure, chaste, modest, faithful, capable of a life-long commitment to their spouse.

The principal aim of this book is to impress upon parents what a profound impact they can make on their children. Their example is the *primary influence* in a child's life. Parents will understand that the love and affection they give their children is the greatest deterrent against promiscuous behavior, as well as other rebellious conduct often encountered in the adolescent years. They will realize that a strong and disciplined family produces more responsible citizens and, consequently, a better world. The parents' good or bad example will leave an indelible mark on the behavior of their children and will most likely determine the path they will follow in future years.

The Family of the Americas Foundation, a nonprofit, educational organization, is dedicated to the promotion of family-centered values through the training of parents. Figure 4 shows the effectiveness of its Fertility Appreciation for Families program, funded by a $1.2 million grant from the U.S. Department of Health and Human Services (HHS) from 1983–1987. This program for parents and adolescents promoted family-centered sexuality education, helping parents to assume their role as the principal educators of their children in matters of human sexuality.

Figure 4

Comparison of Sex Education Programs to Reduce Teen Pregnancy

Number of Pregnancies per Thousand Adolescents aged 15–19

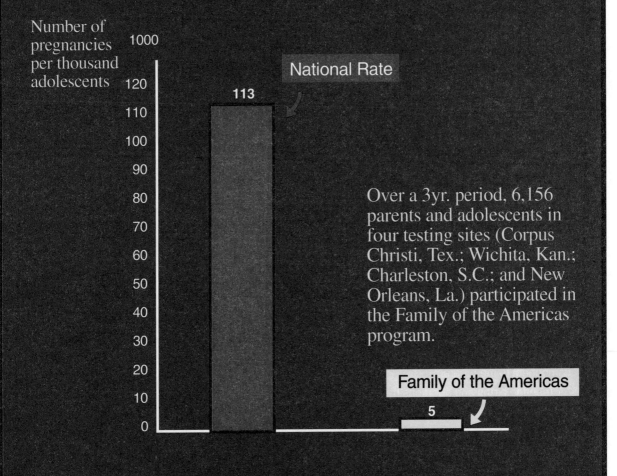

Number of pregnancies per thousand adolescents

National Rate

113

Over a 3yr. period, 6,156 parents and adolescents in four testing sites (Corpus Christi, Tex.; Wichita, Kan.; Charleston, S.C.; and New Orleans, La.) participated in the Family of the Americas program.

Family of the Americas

5

Evaluations based on:
Weed & Olsen, 1986 evaluation;
The National Center for Health Statistics 1980 national rate;
and the independent evaluation of the University of New Orleans for Family of the Americas program,
Fertility Appreciation for Families.

Figure 5

Relation between Unwed Births, Abortions and Title X Funding

This graph of Title X funding clearly shows that family planning enrollment, unwed births and abortions are remarkably correlated.

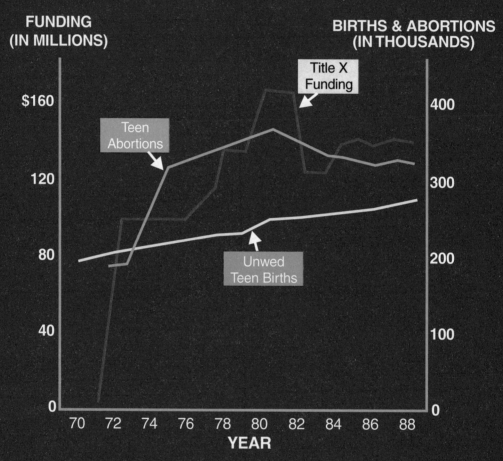

FUNDING (IN MILLIONS)

BIRTHS & ABORTIONS (IN THOUSANDS)

Title X Funding

Teen Abortions

Unwed Teen Births

YEAR

Title X, the U.S. federal family planning program, has an estimated 1.5 million teenagers as clients, one-third of the program. Parental notification is not required for receipt of services, and there is no evaluation component to the program.

- Teenage births and abortions have increased at the same time Title X funding has increased.
- When Title X funding decreased, the number of increasing teen births and abortions leveled off.
- Between 1975 and 1980, as funding built up to its highest level, teen births increased 16%.
- Between 1980 and 1983, when funding was cut by $38 million (-23%), births increased only 3%.
- Between 1983 and 1987, funding increased by $18 million (+14%), and births sped up again, increasing by 12.3%.

Sources: National Center for Health Statistics, *Vital Statistics of the United States Annual*: Centers for Disease Control, *Morbidity and Mortality Weekly Report*, Nov. 23. Graph used with permission of the Family Research Council.

By the end of the program, 2,478 parents and 3,678 adolescents had been reached. *Family of the Americas Foundation's program participants had a pregnancy rate of only five per one thousand.* With the national rate at 111 per one thousand adolescent females, this rate was *approximately twenty-two times lower than the national average.* In a similar study by the Alan Guttmacher Institute, approximately ninety-six pregnancies per thousand were typical, while another Planned Parenthood program reported about 113 pregnancies per thousand teenage females. These numbers represent a marked difference in adolescent sexual activity. The data directly indicate that the number of adolescent pregnancies experienced by Family of the Americas participants was only a fraction (*less than one-twentieth*) of national and regional averages. The evaluators concluded that the Family of the Americas program was successful in reaching large numbers of participants of diverse ethnic origin and that program benefits appeared to be long-term in nature.[12]

There are two basic reasons why "safe sex" is not what it is touted to be. First, as Planned Parenthood's own data show, educating teens about sexuality and contraceptives does not lead to increased contraceptive use.[13] Currently, less than half of sexually active teens use condoms.[14] For those who do use condoms, the device often fails. One-third of teenage pregnancies occur while a contraceptive is being used. Condoms have an annual failure rate of 18.4 percent for girls under eighteen years of age.[15] This means that in a one-year period, the chances of getting pregnant while using a condom are one in six. A study of married couples in which one partner was infected with HIV found that 17 percent of the partners who used

---

[12] Peggy C. Kirby and Louis V. Paradise, "Fertility Appreciation for Families: Prevention Services Demonstration Project: Evaluation Report," October 1, 1987, p. 23.

[13] Marion Howard and Judith Blarney McCabe, "Helping Teenagers Postpone Sexual Involvement," *Family Planning Perspectives* 22, no. 1 (January/February 1990): 21.

[14] "Sexual Behavior among High School Students—United States, 1990," *Morbidity and Mortality Weekly Report* 40, nos. 51 and 52 (January 3, 1992): 886, as cited in "Quick Facts on 'Safe Sex,'" Focus on the Family, undated (circa 1991).

[15] Cites Mark D. Hayward and Jonichi Yogi, "Contraceptive Failure Rate in the United States: Estimates from the 1982 National Survey of Family Growth," *Family Planning Perspectives* 18, no. 5 (September/October 1986): 204, as cited in "Quick Facts on 'Safe Sex,'" Focus on the Family, undated (circa 1991).

condoms for protection still contracted the virus within eighteen months. In another study that would almost be laughable if the AIDS epidemic were not so deadly, the United States Food and Drug Administration tested the "Effectiveness of Latex Condoms as a Barrier to Human Immunodeficiency Virus-sized Particles under Conditions of Simulated Use." The study found that "leakage of HIV-sized particles through latex condoms was detectable . . . for as many as 29 of the 89 condoms tested." (That's about one out of three!) However, "This test did not incorporate motion." As Dr. Lorraine Day writes, "Can you believe it? Their simulated-use condition is SEX WITHOUT MOTION!" Dr. Day asks, if 30 percent of condoms allow leakage of the AIDS virus during "use," then what is the leakage rate during sex if the participants *do* move?[16]

If Your Children Are Sexually Active, Talk to Them

Pregnancy is possible only for the few fertile days in a woman's cycle. Sexually transmitted diseases (STDs), on the other hand, may be transmitted any day of the month/cycle. AIDS is only one of the many serious dangers facing persons who are promiscuous. There are more than twenty dangerous STDs. Sadly, two-thirds of all reported STD cases are among people under the age of twenty-five,[17] infecting some eight million teenagers annually.

What appears to be an epidemic of STDs is only the beginning. In a December 1992 article that appeared in *The Washington Post*, former U.S. Secretary of Health, Education and Welfare Joseph Califano, Jr., warns of "a sinister combine" of AIDS, substance abuse and new drug-resistant

---

[16] Lorraine Day, M.D., "Condoms Don't Work!" (Palm Desert, Calif.: Rockford Press, 1992), p. 4. Cites Carey et al., U.S. Department of Agriculture, Rockville, Maryland.

[17] U.S. Department of Health and Human Services, 1991 Annual Report of the Division of STD/HIV Prevention, as cited by Abigail Van Buren, "Dear Abby," *The Washington Times*, January 28, 1993, p. B4.

forms of tuberculosis (TB) that is becoming "an American Cerberus" (the three-headed dog from Hell in Greek mythology).

Citing drug use and illicit sex in spreading HIV, Califano notes that the incidence of tuberculosis—a disease that was once virtually eliminated in the United States—has increased "relentlessly" since 1985, particularly in large urban centers.

According to Califano, the incidence of TB among children has jumped 40 percent. (Tragically, however, Dr. Califano joins the sex education and condom lobbies in recommending a solution that is essentially the "hair of the dog that bit 'em"—more capitulation by parents to the self-styled "sex experts," more condoms in the schools and, yes, even "clean needles" for intravenous drug users.)[18] Dr. Helene Gayle, AIDS coordinator for the United States Agency for International Development (USAID), reports a similar trend in Africa, where, if current projections hold true, between 30 and 40 percent of the population may be infected with HIV by the end of this century.[19]

Obviously, teenagers are not being told the facts about premarital sex, and they will suffer the consequences for the rest of their lives. Despite the failure of "safer sex" and contraceptive education, these continue to be promoted. With statistics proving the failure, it is criminal to deceive people into believing that they are "safe." Doctors take extraordinary precautions in order to avoid contracting HIV. They never rely on a thin piece of latex, upon which our teens are being told to rely (especially when surgical gloves made of latex *three times* thicker than condoms have been known to leak blood).[20]

---

[18] Joseph A. Califano, Jr., "Three-Headed Dog from Hell," *The Washington Post*, December 21, 1992, p. A24.

[19] Dr. Helene Gayle, AIDS coordinator for U.S. Agency for International Development, interview with Jim Fisher-Thompson, staff writer for USIA Wireless File, U.S. Information Agency, January 7, 1993.

[20] Richard Smith, "The Condom," October 1990, p. 13; also Nancy E. Dirubba, "Condom Barrier," *American Journal of Nursing* 87, no. 10 (1987): 1306.

Words Can Do Harm

Advocates of sexual license cleverly manipulate terminology in order to disguise the evil nature and effects of illicit sex. The public is misguided by euphemisms such as "sexual activity" instead of fornication, adultery, statutory rape, and so forth. Such panderers coldly refer to the killing of an unborn child as "termination of pregnancy." They urge children to be "responsible" and "protected" while engaging in fornication, but in reality, they mean the opposite—be promiscuous and obstruct the normal functions of the body.

The sex lobby—which is made up of organizations such as Planned Parenthood, the American Civil Liberties Union and others—devotes its intellectual energy and tremendous economic power primarily toward the destruction of the moral and legal foundations of the family. As Pope John Paul II has often said, everything passes by way of the family. He repeated this message by stating that "the health of a country depends on the health of the family within that country." Who would have thought, thirty years ago, that in the United States it would one day be legal to kill an unborn baby? Who would have thought that minors would be taught compulsory sex education without morals as enticement to sexual experimentation? Who would have thought that parents would be denied the right to know if their children are receiving chemical or mechanical forms of birth control, or whether their fourteen-year-old daughter undergoes an abortion?

The sex lobby presents itself as altruistic, but its fruits are evil and obvious. As author and Planned Parenthood expert Douglas R. Scott points out, Planned Parenthood has an innocuous name, but it thrives on half-truths, deception and euphemisms as it encourages destructive behavior by young people. The Alan Guttmacher Institute, which according to Scott has been "viewed and touted as an independent, reputable research organization," is actually "the research arm of Planned Parenthood."[21] The organization has admitted some of the organization's phony bill of goods—

---

[21] Scott, *Bad Choices*, p. 110.

that the artificial birth control that Planned Parenthood has promoted for decades has a failure rate far higher than previously thought. (Of course, Planned Parenthood is only too happy to assist in killing the unborn babies of clients who trusted its birth control advice.)

Can all human life be protected, from the moment of conception, if the source of human life—human sexuality working in union with God—is not protected? Since contraception in all times, and clearly in our own, has always led to abortion, is it not imperative that all forms of contraception be clearly condemned? Indeed, is it not almost worthless to condemn abortion if its root is not also condemned as well? It is the abuse of God's great gift of sexuality; abortion is the ultimate abuse.

The sex lobby also denounces parents and others who wish to defend morality, protect their children and exercise control over their children's education in sexuality. These groups, as Valerie Riches says, even smear opponents of their perverse brand of sex education as somehow being against sex itself rather than against its misuse.

CHAPTER TEN

The Sex Lobby: Lies about Population Growth

There is no population problem. Population growth is the result of the plunging death rate and increasing life expectancy world-wide. That is progress.

Sheldon Richman
CATO Institute

The sex lobby and the population control lobby are often one and the same, and so are their goals and rationales. To understand the dangers these groups pose for you and your family, let us examine the ideologies that motivate them and provide their arguments for promoting birth control, abortion, and so forth. Foremost among the rationales used by the sex/population lobbies is the now widely accepted notion that there are too many people in the world and that the number of people should be reduced, one way or another.

Discussing her work among the poor, Mother Teresa has said:

We are reminded that Jesus came to bring the good news to the poor. He had told us what is that good news when He said: "My peace I leave with you, My peace I give unto you." He came not to give the peace of the world which is only that we don't bother each other. He came to give the peace of heart which comes from loving—from doing good to others.

He gave up everything to do the Father's will—to show us that we too must be willing to give up everything to do God's will—to love one another as He loves each of us. If we are not willing to give whatever it takes to do good to one another, sin is still in us. That is why we too must give to each other until it hurts.

When I pick up a person from the street, hungry, I give him a plate of rice, a piece of bread. But a person who is shut out, who feels unwanted, unloved, terrified, the person who has been thrown out of society—that spiritual poverty is much harder to overcome. And abortion, which often follows from contraception, brings a people to be spiritually poor, and that is the worst poverty and the most difficult to overcome.

Those who are materially poor can be very wonderful people. One evening we went out and we picked up four people from the street. And one of them was in a most terrible condition. I told the Sisters: "You take care of the other three; I will take care of the one who looks worse." So I did for her all that my love can do. I put her in bed, and there was such a beautiful smile on her face. She took hold of my hand, as she said one word only: "thank you"—and she died.

I could not help but examine my conscience before her. And I asked: "What would I say if I were in her place?" And my answer was very simple. I would have tried to draw a little attention to myself. I would have said: "I am hungry, I am dying, I am cold, I am in pain," or something. But she gave me much more—she gave me her grateful love. And she died with a smile on her face. Then there was the man we picked up from the drain, half eaten by worms and, after we had brought him to the home, he only said, "I have lived like an animal in the street, but I am going to die as an angel, loved and cared for." Then, after we had removed all the worms from his body, all he said, with a big smile, was: "Sister, I am going home to God"—and he died. It was so wonderful to see the greatness of that man who could speak like that without blaming anybody, without comparing anything. Like an angel—this is the greatness of people who are spiritually rich even when they are materially poor.[1]

---

[1] Mother Teresa of Calcutta, "Whatever You Did unto One of the Least, You Did unto Me." Speech at the National Prayer Breakfast, Washington, D.C., February 3, 1994.

Many people simply assume that these population control notions are valid because they have heard them so often, especially in the media, and because poverty and want exist in many regions of the world. However, the statistical evidence starkly contradicts the assumption that the cause of poverty is too many people and that reducing the number of people will reduce poverty.

In 1967, Nobel Prize winning economist Simon Kuznets published the results of a study in which he compared population growth rates and economic growth rates of a group of countries over the last hundred years to see if high rates of population growth correlated with low rates of economic growth. He found that there was no connection.

Later, both Kuznets and Richard Easterlin studied a much larger group of countries for which data were available from World War II. Again no connection was established between population growth and economic growth. Other studies have supported this conclusion. In his review of the literature for the International Union for the Scientific Study of Population in 1983, Ronald Lee wrote: "Dozens of studies, starting with Kuznets', have found no association between the population growth rate and per-capita income growth rate. . . . These studies control for other factors such as trade, aid and investment to varying degrees."

While there is no connection between population growth and economic growth, research indicates there is a connection between population density and economic growth. Numerous studies support Danish economist Ester Boserup's theory that populations must grow beyond a certain minimum level before they can get into the process of economic development.

The United States, England and Hong Kong, and other countries became rich during unprecedented growth in population. The most densely populated nations are among the richest.[2]

The economically dynamic countries of Japan, Germany and South Korea are each much *more* densely populated than India, Haiti and Somalia—countries that are known today for their struggles with dire poverty.

---

[2] Sheldon Richman, CATO Institute, testimony on International Population Stabilization and Reproductive Health Act (S. 1029), July 20, 1995, p. 1.

The population density rates (per square kilometer) in 1990 were as follows:

South Korea	432
Japan	327
Germany	254
India	252
Haiti	215
Somalia	12[3]

Robert L. Sassone, J.D., notes that the American states of Massachusetts, Connecticut and New York are three times more densely populated than Communist China,[4] the population of which is often described as "teeming." According to United Nations data, the population of Communist China is 129 per square kilometer.[5]

Economist Julian L. Simon refers to the use of such emotionally laden terms as the "germs in a bucket" approach—they evoke negative images of people crowding and elbowing one another in a small space, thereby garnering support for "population control."[6] Simon also notes that history, since 1800, shows *no negative correlation between population growth and economic growth.* "In 1986 the National Research Council of the National Academy of Sciences completely reversed the earlier 'official' world view it expressed in 1971," Simon wrote. "It noted the absence of any statistical evidence of a negative correlation between population increase and economic growth."[7]

---

[3] Surface density area (per square kilometer) 1990 *Demographic Yearbook*, United Nations, pp. 141, 144–48.

[4] Robert L. Sassone, "A New Way of Looking at World Population and Food Supply," as reprinted in *Europe Today*, no. 3 (November 23, 1992): 15.

[5] Central Intelligence Agency, *The World Factbook 1995*, pp. 88–89.

[6] Julian L. Simon, *Population Matters: People, Resources, Environment, and Immigration* (New Brunswick N.J.: Transaction Publishers, 1990), p. 163. See also Simon, *The Ultimate Resource* (Princeton N.J.: Princeton University Press, 1981), pp. 175–87.

[7] Julian L. Simon, "Population Control: Bush at Home in Rio," *The Detroit News*, May 31, 1992, p. 3B.

As stated by Sheldon Richman in his testimony as previously cited:

The increases in population and wealth have not been merely coinciden-tal. They are causes and effects of each other. Today, with few exceptions, the most densely populated countries are the richest. Any mystery in that is dispelled by the realization that people are the source of ideas. . . . As the Nobel laureate and economist Simon Kuznets wrote, "More popu-lation means more creators and producers, both of goods along estab-lished production patterns and of new knowledge and inventions." . . . Those who wish to stifle population growth would condemn hundreds of millions of people in the developing world to abject deprivation that characterized the West before the Industrial Revolution.

. . . As Carroll Ann Hodges, of the U.S. Geological Survey, wrote in the June 2, 1995, issue of *Science* (pp. 1305–1312), "Yet, despite the specter of scarcity that has prevailed throughout much of this century, no sustained mineral shortages have occurred. . . . Minerals essential to industrial economies are not now in short supply, nor are they likely to be for the next several generations." (The only thing getting more expensive is labor, an indication of the scarcity of people.) . . . Natural resources, in other words, do not exist in fixed supplies.[8]

For example, fertility rates in Brazil have fallen sharply in recent years as a result of aggressive population policies and propaganda imposed by the industrialized West; however, poverty and unemployment continue to plague the country.

Further complicating the issue is a point raised by Nicholas Eberstadt in "Population Policy: Ideology as Science." Eberstadt writes, "Indicative of the uncertainties attendant on measuring world population is the lag time between the estimated peaking of world population growth and the an-nouncement of that event by demographers. It is now widely believed that the world rate of natural increase reached its maximum between 1960 and 1965, and has declined since then. Demographers, however, did not begin to suggest with any confidence that the world rate of population growth might have peaked until 1977."[9]

---

[8] Richman, testimony, p. 7.

[9] *First Things*, Religion and Public Life, January 1994, p. 33.

We need to understand these realities and to move beyond the false and misleading claims that the population control and sex education lobbies wield in their bizarre campaign to separate sex from fertility, family from parenthood and, in the case of sex education, child from parent.

The Population Controllers

When discussing population, it is critical to acknowledge the difference between family planning and population control:

- **Family planning** implies that decisions are made by couples, taking into account their own beliefs and circumstances, regarding the number and spacing of their children.

- **Population control** measures, in contrast, are implemented by governments and international agencies after they have determined the number of children couples ought to have.

These two concepts are fundamentally different. Family planning gives couples control over their reproductive behavior. Population control forces them to relinquish this control to governments and international agencies.

As we see in the report from the Committee on Population and the Economy, there are many types of coercion:

There are different types of coercion built into population programmes. At the simplest level is the anti-natalist propaganda using advertising campaigns and third world broadcast media outlets to promote the ideal of the small family and to portray parents of large families as irresponsible and anti-social.

The next stage is the manipulation of tax and welfare structures to bribe people to have small families and to punish those who dare to exceed the limits. For example the 1984 World Bank report *Population Change and Economic Development* contained the following examples:

TANZANIA

Working women in the government service are allowed paid maternity leave only once every three years.

SINGAPORE

Children from smaller families are given priority in school admissions.

KOREA

Free medical care and education allowances to two-child families providing one of the parents has been sterilised.

THAILAND

Technical assistance in farm production made available to contraceptive users. Participants in the programme provided with the services of a "family planning bull" to impregnate their cattle. . . .

The World Bank's *World Development Report 1980* described the so-called "village system of family planning" developed in Indonesia.

[INDONESIA]

"A new policy . . . is that couples of reproductive age need to have a family planning card if they want an official letter from the government. An official letter is needed if a person wants to sell or buy land, to get a bank loan, to get permission to organised circumcision, hair cutting rituals and important events."[10]

Brazil is not alone among developing countries that have been flooded in the past quarter-century by the industrialized West with population control measures such as birth control pills, intrauterine devices, sterilization programs and abortion with total disregard for the impact on the dignity and cultural heritage of her people. The peoples of Latin America, Asia and Africa have suffered physically from the effects of such "remedies,"

---

[10] Committee on Population and the Economy, "Population and Freedom of Choice," undated (circa 1995).

and they have suffered spiritually as well from the violation of their religious beliefs and cultural norms. As Sheldon Richman reports:

> Government programs in the area of reproduction are particularly fraught with danger. By now the horrendous cases of China, India, Bangladesh, and other nations that carry out population control by force should have taught us that the state has no place in this most personal area of life.[11]

The issue here is whether the power and funds of governments should be used, successfully or unsuccessfully, to pay for campaigns to change people's desire for children and their childbearing behavior.

Population controllers claim that 120 million women worldwide have "unmet needs" for family planning services. By definition, a woman with "unmet needs" does not immediately desire additional children and is not using contraception. This includes women who are infertile, who are not very sexually active, or who do not wish to use contraceptives for religious or cultural reasons. These women do not believe they have a need for contraceptives; population controllers disagree.

Lant Pritchett, a senior economist at the World Bank, explained in an article in the March 1994 issue of *Population and Development Review* that, "Desired levels of fertility account for 90% of differences across countries in total fertility rates." That is to say, people in developing countries have large families because they want large families. In many cultures, such as those with agricultural economies, large families mean more people to work on the family farm. Children are considered a great asset. These people are neither stupid nor irresponsible as population control groups would have us believe. Family planning programs frequently decree that there is a need for population control, a need that they are then in a position to satisfy, without regard for the cultural traditions and desires of their "clients."[12]

In addition to the aforementioned organizations, United Nations bodies such as the World Health Organization (WHO), UNESCO and UNICEF

---

[11] Richman, testimony, p. 8.

[12] Committee on Population and the Economy, "Population and Freedom of Choice."

are involved in population control. The United States is engaged in population control through the United States Agency for International Development and through powerful private foundations and groups such as the Population Council, Pathfinder Fund, Population Institute, Ford Foundation, Rockefeller Foundation and others. The International Planned Parenthood Federation, which is headquartered in London, wields immense influence around the world, just as its member group, Planned Parenthood Federation of America, does in the United States (and with hefty government contributions of taxpayer dollars). It seems that Planned Parenthood is particularly determined to reduce population at any cost even if it means legitimizing sexual aberrations and wedging itself between children and parents in the matter of sex education.

In a number of less-developed countries, the commitment of public funds to family planning efforts is striking. In 1980, the World Bank estimates government expenditure per current contraceptive user was sixty-eight dollars in Ghana and sixty-nine dollars in Nepal. These figures compare with World Bank numbers suggesting that the total governmental expenditure on all health programs worked out to be about twenty dollars per family in Ghana, and eight dollars in Nepal. As a matter of fact, in Nepal the country was so inundated with condoms that it cost the government fifty thousand dollars to dispose of them.

In 1987 alone, USAID spent some 231.6 million taxpayer dollars on population control activities. Money spent on population control programs has exceeded USAID's total worldwide health-related expenditures since 1969. In some years, spending on contraceptive "re-education" has been almost three times the expenditures on health assistance.

Today the United States government spends more than 400 million dollars annually on international population programs. Additional funding for population programs comes from the World Bank, the International Monetary Fund and the United Nations Population Fund (UNFPA). Under a policy established by the administration of President Ronald Reagan in 1984, the United States government refused to provide funds for UNFPA and other groups that were known to offer abortion counseling and/or to support coercive population control programs. The Reagan policy was continued during the term of his immediate successor, President George Bush, but pro-abortion President Bill Clinton has since moved to reverse the ban.[13] The Ford Foundation and Rockefeller Foundation have spent hundreds of millions of dollars over the years and worked closely with governments in anti-population programs.

These powerful entities use both coercion and deception as their stock in trade. For instance, the U.S. forces foreign governments to accept population control funds as a condition for receiving development assistance. Moreover, in case after case, public and private agencies have victimized the poor by deceiving them about the nature and effects of the pills and devices that are thrust upon them.

As stated by Julian L. Simon,

They are prepared to take away the power to procreate . . . [from] poor women in Virginia and India, by sterilizing them against their wills. We believe that a system that allows more people in any category to live is better for that category of people—including the poor, as well as people of all colors.

The pro-controllers say that they are for reproductive freedom. We say that interfering with people's freedom to choose and have as many children as they like—for example, the fines in China for bearing more than one child, and the forced sterilizations of poor black women in Virginia, programs supported by the population establishment—is the worst sort of offense against reproductive freedom. Our approach to reproductive freedom is to respect everyone's right to have as many or as few children as they wish, and to assist them with knowledge of how to do so.[14]

---

[13] "Abortion Forecast Renews Fight for Overseas Family Planning Aid," *The Washington Post*, March 9, 1996; also "U.S. Congress Cripples 1996 Fiscal Year Aid for Family Planning," World Population News Service, POPLINE, January–February 1996.

[14] Simon, *Population Matters*, p. 561. For additional reading in this area, see also Robert Whelan, *Choices in Childbearing* (London: Committee on Population and the Economy, 1992), and Jacqueline R. Kasun, Ph.D., *The War against Population: The Economics and Ideology of World Population Control* (San Francisco: Ignatius Press, 1988).

Indeed, in assessing trends in family planning, the authors of *Contraceptive Technology* note a shift from voluntarism to coercive family planning approaches. As if forgetting their earlier statements in support of the privacy and reproductive "rights" of women, the authors refer to coercion as being merely "unfortunate" but "well established."[15]

In recent years the formation of organizations such as Health Action International (HAI) in Amsterdam and Feminist International Network for Resistance against Reproductive Technologies and Genetic Engineering (FINNRAGE) has signaled a weakening in the alliance between feminists and population controllers. Women involved with these groups have pointed out that women's interests and health needs become secondary in population programs which stress the attainment of demographic targets.

The following quotations are taken from a 1995 British Broadcasting Company (BBC) interview with Sister Mary Pilar Verzosa. This interview was aired on the Canadian Television program *Horizon*. The narrator's words are in italics:

> *Contraceptive vaccines are being developed.... In the Philippines women believe they have been tested with a contraceptive vaccine, secretly....* Sister Mary Pilar Verzosa recounted, "The government would announce ... national immunisation days.... [O]nly women of reproductive age, that is from 14 to 45-year-old[s], should come to the health centres for their tetanus immunisation shots."
>
> *Records show two-thirds of tetanus deaths in the Philippines are amongst men, so why would they target women? She was even more suspicious when she discovered the jabs were to be given five times in three years, when usually a tetanus is given much less frequently....* "The Department of Health would send their teams into the schools, they would just tell the teacher in charge that this was a government programme, it's a service being given, it's good for the girls."
>
> *Then she started to hear disturbing reports from women when she was working in the slums.* "The women would say why is it that the tetanus shots that we've been getting have had effects on us? Our fer-

---

[15] Robert A. Hatcher et al., *Contraceptive Technology 1990–1992* (New York: Irvington Publishers, 1990), pp. 581–82.

tility cycles are all fouled up, some of the women among us have had bleedings and miscarriages, some have lost their babies at a very early stage. The symptoms could come soon after their tetanus vaccination—some the following day, others within a week's time. For those who were pregnant on [sic] their first 3 or 4 months the miscarriage was really frightening."

There are several research programmes around the world testing the contraceptive vaccine linked to tetanus which creates an immune response. The vaccine contains Beta HCG, part of a hormone necessary for pregnancy. This Beta HCG stimulates antibodies so that if a woman's egg becomes fertilised her own natural HCG will be destroyed and pregnancy will not occur. "I began to suspect that . . . [t]hey have laced the tetanus toxoid vials with the Beta HCG. The only way I could make sure that they hadn't done that was to examine the vials" . . . *unnoticed. The nuns packed them with ice and sent them to an independent laboratory.* . . . "Three out of those four vials registered positive for HCG, so my suspicions are affirmed that here in our country they are not only giving plain tetanus toxoid vaccination to our women, they are also giving anti-fertility."

Sister Mary was not alone. Many women and doctors reported similar findings. Dr. Vilma Gonzaga became suspicious when she had two miscarriages, both times after receiving the tetanus jab. She is now suing the government since tests showed she had very high levels of antibodies to Beta HCG.[16]

Writers from around the world detail violations of women's rights by population programs when women are coerced to have fewer children than they desire in order to meet government goals. Frequently, women in the Third World are not told of the side effects of the various contraceptive methods. These adverse reactions may be more severe for poor women than for women in the West due to malnourishment and their generally poor health.

---

[16] "The Human Laboratory," video documentary filmed by British Broadcasting Company, November 6, 1995, as broadcast on the Canadian television program *Horizon* (from a transcript, pp. 12–13).

Concern has also been expressed over what are called "provider dependent" methods. These are methods which must be controlled by medical personnel and not by the woman herself. Implants like Norplant and injectables like Depo-Provera promise protection against conception for months and even years. However, if a woman changes her mind and wants a child, she may be forced to continue use of these methods. If the government has set population reduction goals, she may be unable to find medical personnel willing to assist her by removing implants.

> [T]hrough [BBC's] moving filmed testimony, *HORIZON* uncovers a catalogue of claims that Norplant is destroying women's lives. Serious side effects have been reported. . . . The film follows the diminutive *Farida Akhter* on her mission of mercy through the slums of Dhaka to uncover what she believes is the truth of the [Norplant] trials: side effects often not reported; women pleading for removal of Norplant, but being turned away or asked to pay large sums of money; claims that they did not even know it was an experimental drug. And harrowing tales of bad science and coercion come from the poorest slums in the western hemisphere, in Cité Soleil, Haiti, which health workers believe has become America's offshore human laboratory. *Farida Akhter* says: "It's cheaper for them to use Third World women than to use an animal in a laboratory in the West."[17]

In the BBC documentary, the following dialogue discusses yet another contraceptive:

> *Narrator:* Norplant is at least an officially approved contraceptive. But there are other, less regulated methods already in use . . . there are . . . a whole range of private foundations that are funding the building of a population control movement. One private organisation is run by two doctors [Dr. Elton Kessel and Dr. Stephen Mumford] from America's southern states who believe they've found the answer for Third World women in a drug called Quinacrine.
>
> *Dr. Elton Kessel:* We have trials of the Quinacrine method going in some 17 countries like India, China, Bangladesh, and the trials are going very

---

[17] Ibid., introduction.

well. 10,000 women have had this method without a single fatality being reported.

Narrator: Dr. Elton Kessel was the founding director of Family Health International. He now researches Quinacrine in a worldwide operation, masterminded from Dr. Mumford's basement in Chapel Hill, North Carolina. Quinacrine is inserted into the top of the womb where it causes inflammation and scarring in the Fallopian tube, in theory blocking the tube with scar tissue and preventing the sperm from reaching the egg.

Stephen Mumford: It's a very simple procedure, takes only a few minutes. It can be done in very primitive setting by people who do not necessarily have a lot of clinical skills. . . .

Narrator: But some scientists believe the drug could put women's lives at risk—from cancer and ectopic pregnancy. And they question this entire approach to sterilisation.

Professor Shree Mulay: This method of producing scar tissue is extremely barbaric. To try to damage the tissue so that you produce inflammation and block the tubes that way I think is extremely crude. It is imprecise for sure because one does not know where exactly that is going to take place and it causes a tremendous amount of pain because of the inflammation. There has been a long history of chemical sterilisation research and this history is really an ugly one and it's quite a shocking one because all kinds of agents have been used—sulphuric acid, formaldehyde—all of these agents which actually burn the tissue and cause production of scar tissue. Chemical sterilisation was first tried out by the Nazis in their very first experiments in the death camps. That it has been picked up in the 60s, 70s and the 80s and been promoted as rescue for the women of the Third World I think is quite extraordinary.[18]

In a field trial prior to marketing it for general use, the previously mentioned fertility regulating vaccine (FRV) is being injected with tetanus toxoid into young women in India. According to a World Health Organization document, the vaccine, anti-human chorionic gonadotropin (hCG), is being injected without the strict controls imposed on such experiments

---

[18] Ibid., pp. 9–10.

by most developed countries where governments regulate the introduction of new vaccines to ensure that there are no serious, unwanted side effects.[19]

The motives behind such attacks on individuals and families—after all, real human beings are targets when "population" is criticized—often include unfounded opinions about economic reality. Yet, as many astute observers have pointed out, they also include the puzzling and sinister notion that other people are bad—that human beings are the problem, rather than social injustice, faulty distribution of goods and services and lack of economic opportunity and freedom. The population controllers never seem to see themselves as part of an "overpopulation problem," only the defenseless poor, whom they belittle, coerce and seek to reduce in number.

Population Controllers and Government

In contrast to what the population controllers would have us believe, most countries in the world have the natural resources to feed and provide a life with dignity for every citizen. According to a report of the United Nations Food and Agriculture Organization, every nation has the capacity to feed its people well.[20]

Based on their figures, between 1951 and 1992, food production rose by more than 30 percent. This has occurred despite the fact that Western farmers are paid millions of dollars a year to keep land out of production. If these European and American farmers were to produce to their capacity, there would likely be an overabundance of agricultural products.[21]

The fact is that social justice and a more equitable distribution of wealth, together with the natural incentive of free enterprise (including equal opportunity for all in education and economic life), are the true solutions to poverty. Jesus said "the poor you will always have with you."

---

[19] *JF Reports* 1, no. 2 (March-April 1995): 5.

[20] "The State of Food and Agriculture, 1990," as cited in *Europe Today*, no. 3 (November 23, 1992): 15.

[21] Committee on Population and the Economy, "Population and Food," undated (circa 1995).

Their presence is an opportunity and challenge to love—to become fit inhabitants of Heaven by acknowledging and fulfilling our obligation to help those who are less fortunate than ourselves.

Tragically, it is tempting to take the easy way out. Governments allow themselves to be persuaded or coerced into family planning programs detrimental to the physical and spiritual health of their people. Powerful governments from the developed world want to decrease the population of the Third World with whatever means available, without regard for the cultural and religious mores of targeted nations. Special interest groups and members of the birth control industry profit at the expense of poor women who are not made aware of the many side effects of artificial contraception and the promiscuity it fosters. As freelance journalist Elizabeth Sobo has written:

> This year, a record $350 million will be spent by the U.S. Agency for International Development (AID) for population-control programs in less-developed nations. A significant part of these funds will pay for birth-control "education" in nations where there is substantial moral and cultural resistance to Western family-planing methods.
>
> Birth-control "education" is not really education at all, but rather a measure of last resort, adopted by the AID Office of Population in places where interest in contraceptives is low. In fact, internal AID documents are more frank in describing the activities as "persuasion" or "motivation." They are intended, in other words, to change preferences for large families and to increase demand for contraceptives.[22]

We have reviewed the moral, spiritual and physical consequences at issue here, but what about the political factors? Even now, men and women in developing nations are beginning to recognize the "control" element in the population programs that are being forced upon them by the industrialized West. Many perceive racist overtones in the population control lobbies, as well as a long-term agenda to prevent the growth of developing nations and thus a shift in the global balance of power. As recently as the 1992 United Nations Conference on Environment and Development,

---

[22] Elizabeth Sobo, "Africa under Siege," *Catholic Twin Circle*, February 16, 1992.

which was held in Rio de Janeiro, serious concerns were expressed in this area. For example, a June 5, 1992, report of *The Washington Post* quotes Rosiska Darcy de Olivera, co-chairman of the Brazilian Women's Coalition, as saying, "To say that women from the South who have many babies are responsible for the environmental crisis—it's a scandal."[23]

Similarly, writing in *Issues in Reproductive and Genetic Engineering*, Farida Akhter of Bangladesh observes:

> One cannot separate their premises: racism, eugenics, and political and economic exploitation of the poorer countries by the Western world. This is one very strong reason why women should be critical of the slogan of reproductive rights. . . .
>
> In practice, reproductive right means the right to pick up a contraceptive produced by multinational corporations and provided by international agencies and the state in countries like Bangladesh, under population control programmes. . . .[24]

Leftist movements in many developing countries can only be aided by our failure to address the root causes of economic stagnation and poverty —that is, by Western funding of aggressive population control programs *at the expense* of meaningful democratic reforms, debt reduction measures and technical assistance and skills training (which are all aimed at promoting sustainable economic development and better standards of life in larger freedom).

Professor Julian L. Simon outlines the population controllers' motive and mode of operation:

> The most striking characteristic of the population movement—at least to me—is the willingness to decide upon life or death for others. . . .
>
> The population-control "establishment"—the fifty or so organizations whose names run from Audubon Society to Zero Population Growth, and

---

[23] Joel Achenbach, "At Summit, Dueling Hemispheres," *The Washington Post*, June 5, 1992, p. C1.

[24] Farida Akhter, "The Eugenic and Racist Premise of Reproductive Rights and Population Control," *Issues in Reproductive and Genetic Engineering* 5, no. 1: 1, 5.

include more than five-million members—claims the moral high ground for its point of view. . . .

The foreign governments that implement the U.S. population establishment's point of view—among others China, Indonesia, and India from time to time—engage in documented coercive practices that are unacceptable to most Americans. . . .

The pro-controllers redefine couples' wants in the interest of the population establishment's goal. They refer to a baby as "unwanted" if the woman says that before the baby was conceived she did not want it. The father's desire is excluded from this definition, as is the jointly decided desire of the couple. And a mother's change of heart after the baby is born does not count. . . .

The pro-controllers claim to be selfless and generous. But they justify reducing immigration "to help the working people" of the United States. And they support population control in foreign countries—the long-time director of the Office of Population of the Agency for International Development, physician Reimert Ravenholt, was especially vocal on this point—to assist our foreign trade. The proposition is economic nonsense, but the motive clearly is the purely selfish economic welfare of U.S. citizens. . . .

The pro-controllers urge building nature preserves, and caring for the environment, on behalf of future generations. But their population policy goes exactly the other way. It aims to take account of the welfare only of those who are alive right now, ignoring the benefits that additional people now will create for future generations.[25]

As we analyze the politics of population control, we come to the sad realization that the facts have been distorted and the truth hidden in order to increase funds for population programs and to decrease funds for public health. As Professor Simon reports, from 1968 on, funds for health programs dropped dramatically while expenditures on population programs increased.

---

[25] Simon, *Population Matters*, pp. 558–63.

Bigotry, Racism and Population Control

Many family and foreign policy analysts, as well as other observers such as missionaries, conclude that religious bigotry is part of the reason for population programs. (One wise religious leader in Kenya rightly describes population control programs as "contraceptive imperialism.") According to Professor Simon:

> The pro-controllers claim to help people get what they want by assisting couples avoid "unwanted" children. Actually, they attempt to foist off upon other people their own desires that fewer children be born into the world. They pressure couples to have fewer children than the couples desire because the pro-controllers believe that will speed economic development. And in their name, the U.S. government pressures foreign countries to pressure their citizens to reduce fertility below what couples would freely desire.[26]

Even in the recent past, Planned Parenthood's newspaper ads have directly attacked the Pope and Catholic moral teaching. Moreover, Planned Parenthood has not abandoned the bigoted views of Margaret Sanger, who founded the organization in the early twentieth century and who remains a heroine to radical feminists and other supporters of Planned Parenthood today. Consider these chilling facts:

> At a March 1925 international birth control gathering held in New York City, a speaker warned of the menace posed by the "black" and "yellow" peril. The man was not a National Socialist (Nazi) or a leader of the Ku Klux Klan. The Speaker was Dr. S. Adolphus Knopf, a member of Margaret Sanger's American Birth Control League (ABCL), which along with other groups became known as Planned Parenthood. . . .
>
> Not to be outdone by her followers, Planned Parenthood founder Margaret Sanger wired President Coolidge urging him to establish a

---

[26] Ibid., pp. 558–59.

"Federal Birth Rate Control Commission", which was to have "free access to all facts and statistics as to all customs and conditions now menacing the racial health of our country". . . .

Elsewhere Sanger spoke of her plan for sterilizing those she designated as "unfit" as the "salvation of American civilization". And she also spoke of those who were "irresponsible and reckless", among whom she included those "whose religious scruples prevent their exercising control over their numbers". She further contended that "there is no doubt in the minds of all thinking people that the procreation of this group should be stopped".[27]

Margaret Sanger advocated birth control not only to eliminate persons with disabilities and to combat those racial and religious groups that she deemed "unfit," but also to replace fundamental standards of morality with a new spirit of sexual license. The "aim of life," she wrote, "is to free all inhibitions . . . to direct one's controls [sic] from logic and reason—not from fear and morality."[28]

It is not surprising that among Sanger's early associates were individuals such as Lothrop Studdard, a white supremacist who described the eugenic practices of the Nazi's Third Reich as "scientific" and "humanitarian," and Dr. Harry Laughlin, whose proposals for "race betterment" apparently served as inspiration for the Nazi's compulsory sterilization law, which passed in Germany in 1933.[29]

Only after the Nazis gave eugenics a bad name did Sanger and her ilk go "underground" and resurface in the early 1950s with "overpopulation" as their new excuse.

Interestingly, one of the world's leading foes of Planned Parenthood and its insidious agenda is a Protestant, not a Catholic. Douglas R. Scott,

---

[27] Robert Marshall and Charles Donovan, *Blessed Are the Barren* (San Francisco: Ignatius Press, 1991), p. 1. For additional information about Planned Parenthood, read *Bad Choices: A Look Inside Planned Parenthood*, by Douglas R. Scott (Franklin, Tenn.: Legacy Communications, 1992), or contact Life Decisions International at P.O. Box 419, Amherst, N.Y. 14226–0419.

[28] Marshall and Donovan, *Blessed Are the Barren*, p. 59.

[29] Ibid., p. 2.

president of Life Decisions International, has long criticized Planned Parenthood for its anti-Christian rhetoric and activities. "Planned Parenthood is only opposed to those men and women who are *so* religious that they act upon their faith," Scott points out, "but if you claim to be a 'religious' person who supports its agenda, they will gladly embrace you and flaunt your 'religious' connections."[30]

Scott argues that Planned Parenthood has a long anti-Catholic history in particular. "If they can label someone as Catholic the attitude is that they no longer have to deal with the logic of the argument against them. They would much rather just dismiss their opponent as 'just another ignorant and blind Catholic.'" Scott calls the strategy "effective but based on deep-seated religious bigotry." He urges Catholics to continue standing against the Planned Parenthood agenda. "Too many of my Catholic brothers and sisters are falling victim to Planned Parenthood's bigoted attacks. Don't be intimidated by those who seek to silence you. That's what they want to see happen."[31]

The Myth of Overpopulation

The panicked cry of "overpopulation" is as factual as Chicken Little's exclamation that "The sky is falling!" The "population bomb" forecast by Paul Ehrlich in 1967 has proved to be a misconception.

Professor Ehrlich published *The Population Bomb* in 1968, eleven years into a nineteen-year decline in the U.S. fertility rate (average births per woman, ages fifteen to forty-four). During this period the rate dropped from 3.77 in 1957 to 1.74 in 1976, dropping below replacement level of 2.11 in 1972.

In 1973, Ehrlich and his wife Anne, writing in a college textbook titled *Population, Resources, Environment*, made the following statement in

---

[30] Douglas R. Scott, personal interview, May 7, 1996.

[31] Ibid.

regard to world population control: "Several coercive proposals deserve serious consideration, mainly because we may ultimately have to resort to them unless current trends in birth rates are rapidly reversed by other means." In spite of the failure of his dire predictions to materialize, Ehrlich continued to expound on his theory, publishing *The Population Explosion* in 1990 after eighteen straight years of population rate below replacement level.

In the last two decades, the developed nations have reached the point of demographic suicide. Instead of "exploding," birthrates in the United States, Western Europe and Japan have fallen below the replacement level of 2.1 children per family.

The Total Period Fertility Rate (TPFR) tells us the average completed family size at a given time. In developing countries the replacement level of fertility will be higher than 2.1, due to higher rates of mortality, especially infant mortality. In other words, Third World women need to have 2.8 to 3.0 children per family since fewer actually reach adulthood and reproduce.

Nearly all European countries are significantly below replacement level. French and British fertility rates have remained around 1.8 for more than ten years. Italy has the lowest TPFR in the world at 1.25 children per woman. In Eastern Europe, some countries are making concerted efforts to increase the birthrate.[32]

The less-developed world continues to grow at a normal level and the "limits to growth" predicted by the Club of Rome in 1972 have since been shown to be completely far-fetched. Indeed, despite being frowned upon by many population "experts" for their "dangerously high" rates of population growth, Bangladesh and Communist China actually grew much less rapidly between 1980 and 1990 than wealthy nations such as Kuwait and the United Arab Emirates (UAE). Consider the average annual growth of population in each country during that decade:

---

[32] Committee on Population and the Economy, "Population and Fertility Rates," undated (circa 1995).

Communist China	1.47%
Bangladesh	2.3%
Kuwait	4.4%
UAE	4.3%[33]

Here are some additional statistics from the United States Census Bureau:

- The world's population growth rate has "declined to about 1.5 percent at present," the lowest rate in fifty years.

- "Fertility levels have fallen so low in some countries, mainly in Europe, that no return to 'replacement level' fertility is expected in the foreseeable future."

- "Eighty-six countries . . . have low rates of 20 or fewer births per 1,000 population. Sixty countries are below replacement level. Countries with high birth rates represent only 21 percent of world population, while those with low birth rates represent 45 percent."

- Fertility rates throughout the world have been dropping so rapidly that the U.S. Census Bureau has just cut its three-year-old estimate of world population in the year 2000 by one hundred twenty million, and in the year 2020 by more than three hundred million.[34]

Moreover, despite the consensus of the media that the world has been heading toward an agricultural crisis, the mainstream view among agricultural economists is quite the opposite, and has been so for years. Most agricultural economists agree that the trend has been toward improvement in the food supplies of almost every main segment of the world's population.

---

[33] "Average Annual Growth of Population, 1980–1990," *World Development Report*, 1992, pp. 268–69.

[34] U.S. Census Bureau: World Population Profile, 1994.

In November 1993, the World Bank released "The World Food Outlook." Here are some of its conclusions:

- World food production has more than kept pace with population growth rates, and it shows few signs of slowing. During the 1980s, world cereals production increased by 2.1 percent per annum while population grew by 1.7 percent. Prospects are very good that the twenty-year period from 1990–2010 will see further gains.

- The World Bank's index of food commodity prices fell by 78 percent from 1950–1992 in constant 1990 currency.

- According to most estimates, both land and water are abundant. Only 11 percent of the world's land surface is currently used for agricultural crops and, by one commonly accepted estimate, land and water use for agriculture could more than double.

- The proportion of the developing countries' population suffering from chronic under-nutrition has declined from 36 percent during the late 1960s to 20 percent during the late 1980s.[35]

The truth is that population growth has important long-term benefits because, overall, individuals contribute more than they consume. As Professor Julian L. Simon states:

> The principal evidence for optimism is the record of food production, as represented by data collected by UNFAO from member countries and by the U.S. Department of Agriculture from 104 countries and from American agricultural attachés. Production of food (as measured by food's adjusted value on the market in a given year, divided by the world population) was either 28 percent or 37 percent higher in 1979 than in the 1948–1952 base period, according to UNFAO and the USDA respectively. . . .
>
> According to [D. Gale] Johnson, who has surveyed the documentary history of famine and reports the results in his monograph *World Food*

---

[35] World Bank, "Population and Food."

Problems and Prospects (1973), "It is highly unlikely that the famine-caused deaths [in the third quarter of the twentieth century] equal a tenth of [those for] the period 75 years earlier."...

Johnson states that many, if not most, of the 12 to 15 million famine deaths that have occurred in this century "were due to deliberate governmental policy, official mismanagement, or war and not to serious crop failure."[36]

Economist Jacqueline R. Kasun, of Humboldt State University, California, likewise debunks the "overpopulation" myth by pointing out two important facts: (1) cities, towns and villages cover far less than 1 percent of the earth's land surface, and (2) everyone on the planet could live in the state of Texas, even with about 4,500 square feet allotted to each three-person family.[37]

Robert L. Sassone, J.D., has reached a similar conclusion:

According to the UN, all of the world's buildings put together take up only about 20,000 square miles of land. Thus, all the world's buildings could easily fit into a smaller nation such as Ireland or Scotland, leaving the rest of the world vacant. Every parcel of land directly given over to human use, including all farmland, buildings, roads, etc., comprises only about 11% of the land area of the earth. The earth has a population density of about thirty people per square mile. This means that if we were spread evenly over the earth, the nearest person to you would be nearly 1,000 feet away, hardly crowded.

The UN projection for future population which in the past has proved to be the most accurate states that within fifty years the world's population will decline. In Great Britain and Europe this decline will begin in only about ten years. Once the population decline begins, it will have so much momentum that the population will continue to decline at increasingly faster rates. In fact, already the number of births in most areas of the world, including Latin America and East Asia, is declining.[38]

---

[36] Simon, *Population Matters*, pp. 96–98.

[37] Jacqueline R. Kasun, Ph.D., "Population Control of the Family" (Gaithersburg, Md.: Population Research Institute, 1988), p. 12.

[38] Simon, *Population Matters*, pp. 96–98.

Columnist Marilyn Vos Savant uses another analogy. If the entire population of the world stood together with each person given a 2 ft. × 2 ft. space, the total area covered would be smaller than one thousand square miles, or an area roughly the size of Jacksonville, Florida.[39]

While current concerns about urbanization (the mass migration of once-rural peoples to urban centers) may merit evaluation, it is obvious that the "overpopulation" crisis is a myth—just as it is obvious that today's population control methods are harmful to women, families and nations. In 1994, 45 percent of the world's people were living in urban areas.[40] Harmful birth control chemicals and devices that are forbidden or highly regulated in the United States and other developed nations (such as certain intrauterine devices and the drug Depo-Provera, which was only recently approved for use in the U.S.A.) are routinely foisted upon women in poor countries by the same population controllers who claim to have their "well-being" in mind. (More information about the harmful effects of artificial methods of birth control is provided in Part Four of this book.)

Too Few, Not Too Many

Having defused the so-called "population bomb," let us analyze some of the dangers of population depletion. In his 1987 book, *The Birth Dearth: What Happens When People in Free Countries Don't Have Enough Babies?*, Ben J. Wattenberg warns of a crisis emerging in the West due to the overpopulation myth:

> . . . I had occasion to carefully review the data and came to realize just how long it has been that America has maintained a fertility rate that was below replacement level, what I call here a "birth dearth" level. It began in 1972 and it's still very much with us in 1987—fifteen consecutive years. . . . [T]hese new rates in America (and Europe and Japan) have now gone so low as to be harmful and that they will likely last—

---

[39] Marilyn Vos Savant, *Parade*, September 1, 1991, p. 11.

[40] United Nations estimate, Population Division, Urban Agglomerations, 1994.

unless people understand the magnitude of the problem and respond by changing their reproductive behavior.[41]

The United States Census Bureau for the first time predicted in 1989 that the U.S. population would not replace itself in coming decades. Widespread economic and social problems will result from this trend, and Wattenberg mentions some of them:

[A]s we enter the second generation of the Birth Dearth, which is just about upon us, the shortfall is not just in babies, but in young adults as well. The earlier "missing" babies become "missing" producers and consumers, soldiers and sailors, mothers and fathers. And then, assuming only that fertility rates remain at their current level, the next generation of babies—the small families of these smaller number of maturing Birth Dearth babies—starts shrinking. That, too, will likely be with us within a few years. And all this family size change, of course, reflects itself sooner or later in actual population numbers. The nations affected by the Birth Dearth move inexorably from high growth rates, to slow growth rates, to no-growth rates, to negative growth rates that are already apparent in some of the West European nations. . . .

I believe the Birth Dearth will, in the near future, begin to cause turbulence at every level of our economy, from the counters of fast-food restaurants to major corporate board rooms. Modern capitalism has always been rooted in the economic fact of vigorously expanding domestic markets. That phase is ending. The ensuing turbulence will be difficult —though not impossible—to deal with. Ours, after all, is a responsive and flexible economy.

Indeed, the coming effect of the Birth Dearth may well provide great economic opportunity for some. (Invest in mortuaries, nursing homes, geriatric hospitals, and pharmaceutical companies, not in companies that manufacture baby food, tricycles, or little league uniforms—and not in suburban four-bedroom housing developments.)[42]

---

[41] Ben J. Wattenberg, *The Birth Dearth: What Happens When People in Free Countries Don't Have Enough Babies?* (New York: Scripps Howard, 1987), p. v.

[42] Ibid., pp. 7–8.

Figure 6

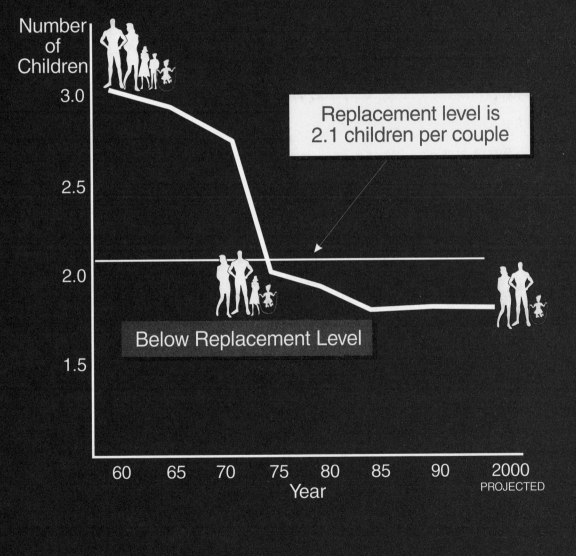

Fertility Decline of the Western Industrial Countries

Total Fertility Rate (number of children per woman)

Number of Children

Replacement level is 2.1 children per couple

Below Replacement Level

3.0

2.5

2.0

1.5

60   65   70   75   80   85   90   2000

PROJECTED

Year

Sources: *World Tables*, 3rd ed., vol. 2; World Bank, *Recent Demographic Developments in the Member States of the Council of Europe*, 1986. *World Development Report*, World Bank, various years.

See Appendix 1.

Population Density of Selected Countries with Indicators of Economic Strength

Country	Population Density (per sq. km.)—July 1995 Estimate[43]	National Product Real Growth Rate—1994 Estimate[44]	National Product per Capita—1994 Estimate[45]
Hong Kong	5599	5.5%	24,530
Bangladesh	957	4.5%	1,040
Bahrain	929	2.2%	12,100
South Korea	464	8.3%	11,270
Japan	335	0.6%	20,200
Germany	233	2.9%	16,580
United Kingdom	241	4.2%	17,980
Haiti	237	-15%	870
Nigeria	111	-0.8%	1,250
China	129	11.8%	2,500
Guatemala	101	4%	3,080
Kenya	51	3.3%	1,170
Brazil	19	5.3%	5,580
Peru	19	8.6%	3,110

Increased life expectancies and dwindling birth rates are already starting to have a dramatic impact on parts of Europe. Of the 340 million citi-

---

[43] Central Intelligence Agency, *The World Factbook 1995*, pp. 33–336.

[44] Ibid.

[45] Ibid.

zens of the twelve states of the European Union, about 20 percent are over age sixty. Demographers say that, as this trend continues, the ratio will also increase. Their projection is that by the year 2010 there will be "more Europeans drawing pensions than contributing to them."

Until recently, Europe has compensated for diminishing birth rates through immigration. As European countries seek to pursue more "closed-door" immigration policies, social researchers point out that rather than causing unemployment, immigrants from Turkey and North Africa perform jobs Europeans are unwilling to do, thereby adding to the tax base. The contributions of these immigrants helps to fund social welfare programs such as pensions and health care. Europe's "birth dearth" means that new means of subsidizing programs for the elderly must be explored.[46]

In the United States, it has been suggested that the time has come to privatize Social Security. Continuing the current government-controlled system "will require raising the payroll tax rate over the next 30 years to 18% from today's 12.4% rate, with a risk that it may have to be substantially higher." Such an increase would be necessitated by the lack of young workers paying into the system.[47]

[46] William Drozdiak, "Europe's 'Birth Dearth' Spawns Reappraisal of Immigration," *The Washington Post*, January 20, 1994, p. A19.

[47] Martin Feldstein, "Time to Privatize Social Security," *The Wall Street Journal*, March 8, 1996.

Figure 7

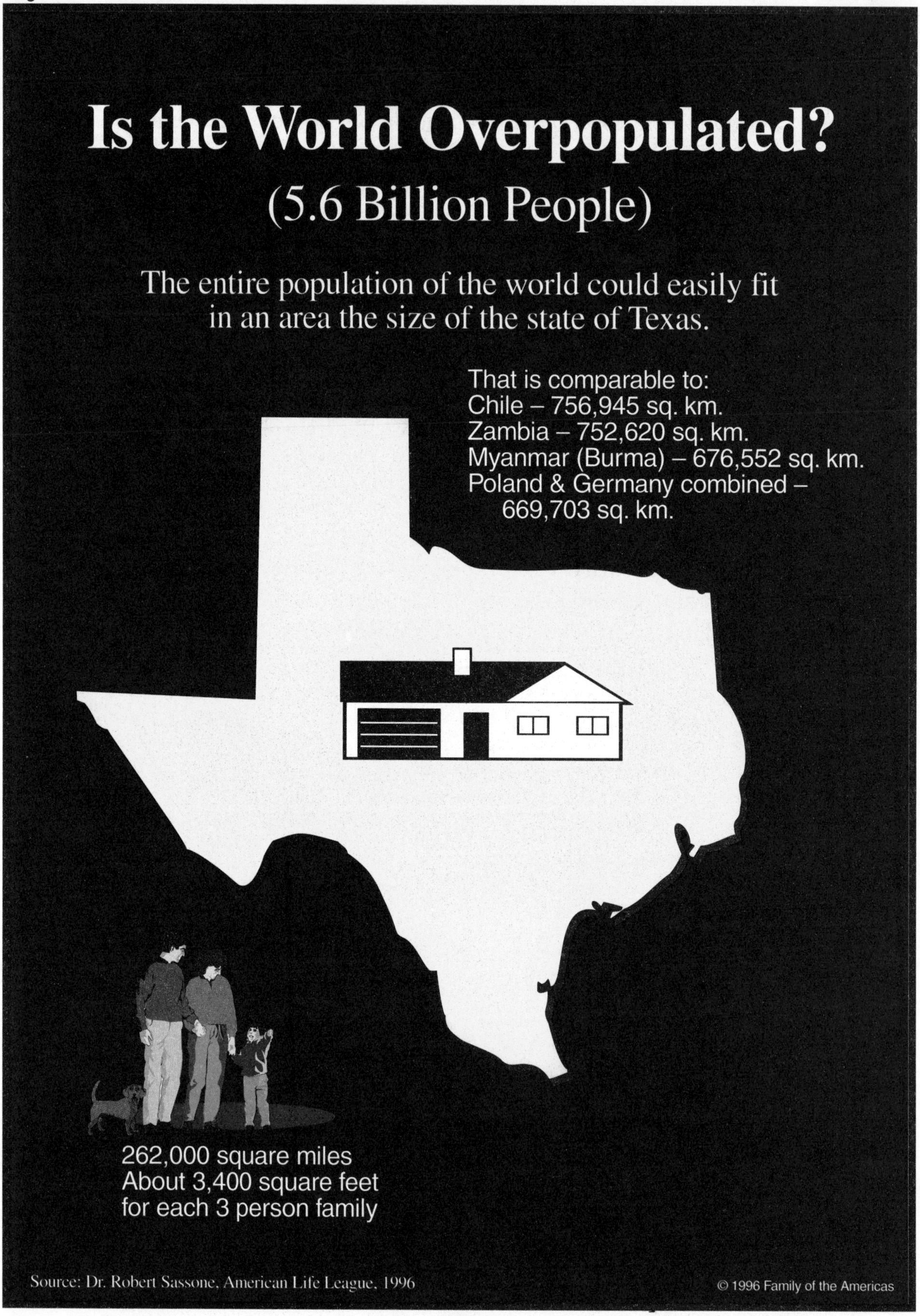
Is the World Overpopulated?
(5.6 Billion People)
The entire population of the world could easily fit in an area the size of the state of Texas.
That is comparable to:
Chile – 756,945 sq. km.
Zambia – 752,620 sq. km.
Myanmar (Burma) – 676,552 sq. km.
Poland & Germany combined – 669,703 sq. km.
262,000 square miles
About 3,400 square feet
for each 3 person family
Source: Dr. Robert Sassone, American Life League, 1996
© 1996 Family of the Americas

Figure 8

Is the World Overpopulated?
(5.6 Billion People)

If the entire world population stood together with each person given a 2 ft. by 2 ft. space, the total area covered would be smaller than 1,000 sq. miles or an area roughly the size of (or smaller than)

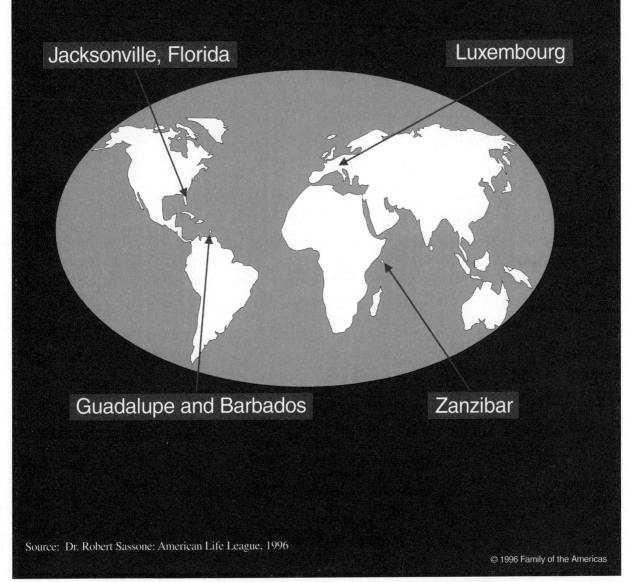

Jacksonville, Florida

Luxembourg

Guadalupe and Barbados

Zanzibar

Source: Dr. Robert Sassone: American Life League, 1996

Children Are Blessings

Until the anti-child propaganda of recent years, mankind has always considered children a blessing. "Lo, sons are a heritage from the Lord," says Scripture, "the fruit of the womb a reward." Likewise says the Proverb, "grandchildren are the crown of the aged."

While the joys of welcoming a new life into the world are obvious (and sufficient in their own right), Dr. Jacqueline Kasun reminds us of the economic rewards of children, as well:

> In the United States each child born in 1996 is expected to spend forty-seven years in the labor force, earn about a million dollars over his lifetime, and pay $400,000 in taxes. The discounted net present value in 1996 of the typical child's future earnings, over and above the cost of his own maintenance, amount to about $100,000. This sum would be available to support public services and to add to society's capital.[48]

As Dr. Kasun hints, the economic potential of children pales in comparison to the deeper rewards and blessings that they offer their families. Sadly, however, in a world attuned to self and affluence, it has become fashionable among many people to consider children as an inconvenience. Yet as a parent you know that the young ones you have brought into the world, nourished and protected are far dearer to you than your own life.

I have had the joy of listening to a mother and father of very humble means rejoice at the blessing of their large family. The couple raised carpenters, accountants, secretaries and housekeepers—all of them happy, respectful and loving toward their parents. Together their lives had been full, fruitful and blessed by God. All of their basic needs had been met through hard work, love and affection. They even had time to do volunteer work in association with their church. This is a common occurrence in the de-

---

[48] Jacqueline R, Kasun, Ph.D., personal communication with Mercedes Arzú Wilson, May 7, 1996.

veloping world. These people are materially poor, but they are spiritually wealthy. They feel and count their blessings every day. This is the way it should be, and I pray that those who attack the poor and their little ones will one day have the grace and good sense to understand and to make amends. In the interim, however, recognize the risks to your family and protect them from the unrelenting efforts of the "sexperts" and population controllers.

CHAPTER ELEVEN

You *Can* Protect
Your Family

One critical problem facing many of today's youth is that their parents have willingly accepted the fallacy that they cannot and will not adequately teach their children about sexual matters. This has allowed the state and its agents, such as Planned Parenthood and SIECUS, to fill the void—all to the detriment of children.

Douglas R. Scott
President, Life Decisions International

As we have seen, the population controllers' views of sexuality do not match reality or most parents' desires. You can do your youngsters a life-long favor by giving them the truth about a healthy appreciation of marriage, children and family in contrast to the dangerous deceptions of the sex and population lobbies.

As a result of the lies that sex outside of marriage has no harmful consequences and that birth control and abortion solve problems rather than create them, teenagers are often pressured into promiscuity against their deeper instincts. Another part of the problem is that teenagers often do not have sufficient support from their parents and responsible educators to *resist* temptation against illicit activity.

How can you as parents best respond to your children's needs and to the serious challenge posed by supporters of compulsory sex education and population control programs? First, tell your children that simply because someone else—a friend, teacher, celebrity, or "with-it" member of the clergy —says something that contradicts your family's beliefs, it need not be true. Answers to current challenges of time-honored beliefs do exist, and if they are not on the tip of your tongue, seek the help of someone who has them. In this program and in the writings of the authors and specialists listed herein, you will find answers to many of today's common false arguments.

It is important to remember that you are not alone; other families share their values with their youngsters. They, too, refuse to turn the development of their children over to strangers who are outside parental control and will undermine principles of morality, family cohesiveness and parental authority. You can join forces with these parents in your community who object to outsiders foisting amoral sex education on your children. Moreover, if the sex education lobby has already "won" in your school, you can demand the "opt in" option—that is, parents have to sign permission slips to put their children *into* such programs, rather than out of them, so that youngsters whose parents do not wish them to take part will not feel that they are the exceptions. You can also demand that your children be given solid alternative courses in other subjects, instead of being sent to study hall during the sex education time slot.

Most important, keep in mind that families are society's true shapers of the future—that families, including your own, have recourse against those who would take those rights away. Throughout history, the family has firmly resisted every attempt to modify or destroy it. As one leader in public policy and the defense of the family has said so eloquently, "It is as if the family, as the fundamental reality of human society, is the small but stubborn rock that breaks the ideologue's plow of abstractions about human nature."[1]

---

[1] Carl A. Anderson and William J. Gribbin, "The Solidarity of the Family," introduction to *The Family in the Modern World: A Symposium on Pope John Paul II's Familiaris Consortio* (Washington, D.C.: American Family Institute, 1982).

Parental Responsibility

Parents must be alert to dangers inside, as well as outside, the home. After all, parents are closely observed by their children, who frequently do things —right or wrong—because they see their parents doing them. Without even realizing it, children may talk, dress and behave like their moms and dads.

No one can take the place of parents. Mothers must remember that children grow quickly and that, in a flash, their youngsters will be in school full time (unless, of course, the children are home schooled). During these early formative years, one of the greatest gifts that parents can give to a young child is their time and attention. (Another is to have a brother or a sister.) Once the children are grown, mothers will have plenty of time to pursue careers or engage in the volunteer activities that they might have missed while their children were young and most dependent on them.

If the husband can afford to take care of the family with his salary alone, mothers should not work outside the home. When both parents do this, the time that families have together is limited, which in turn affects the development of children. Over the course of the 1980s, the average working parent spent five hours more per week at the job—five hours per week less with the family. As a result, parents and children have less time to get to know each other and children are deprived of the attention, affection and discipline that is expressed over time—a key building block of healthy personality. As Patrick Fagan writes, "Children who do not receive affection must learn early to defend themselves against loneliness and self-doubt, conditions which lay the foundation for defensive (noncooperative) ways of relating with others and with reality for the rest of their lives."[2]

When both parents are absent from the home, children must be entrusted to the care of others or left on their own. In fact, a comprehensive report issued in December 1992 by the Carnegie Council on Adoles-

---

[2] Patrick F. Fagan, "The Social Teaching of John Paul II on the Family: Towards a More Generous Gift of Self in the Family," unpublished and undated paper (circa 1990), p. 3.

cent Development cites one study that found that adolescents in the United States spend an average of just five minutes a day in one-on-one interaction with their fathers and just twenty minutes of such interaction with their mothers. According to another study, nearly 30 percent of all eighth-graders in the United States are home alone after school for two or more hours (children from low-income households were most likely to be alone for more than three hours). The Carnegie Council also reports that, on average, teenagers watch about twenty-one hours of television per week, compared to a mere 5.6 hours spent on homework.[3]

These disturbing statistics have been brought about, in large part, by a significant increase in the number of women who work outside the home. For example, between 1970 and 1988, the percentage of working mothers with infants age one or younger more than doubled, from 24 to 52 percent.[4] Sadly, in the Western world, many of these mothers do this, not to help pay for food and necessities as in the developing world, but to obtain luxuries (such as a second or third family car, VCRs and stereos, home computer games, and so on)—items that could be done without completely, or at least until children have grown and started school.

The most challenging task that any adult can undertake is the loving care of one's children—the formation of their minds and the protection of their bodies. This is too crucial a task to leave to any outsider or to an institution. Although many parents have rued the time that they "wasted" away from the family while their children were young, few mothers ever regret being at home at least during the early years of their child's life.

The German pediatrician and educator Dr. Theodor Hellbrugge speaks of the dignity of mothers and motherhood and of the importance of family structure if children are to "learn" security. He stresses the necessity of "close social linkage between mother and child" in children's socialization and cognitive development. He also calls a mother's "whole maintenance schedule" of caring for baby "the decisive factor" in personality formation (but notes that interaction with the entire family is essential, too).

---

[3] Barbara Vobejda, "Home Alone, Glued to the TV," *The Washington Post*, December 10, 1992, p. A3.

[4] Fagan, "Social Teaching," p. 4.

Clearly, it is not natural for a mother to place a very young baby in day care while she works. This action should be taken only if it is absolutely necessary, and this is rarely the case. No mother can possibly feel at ease at work when her whole body and mind are directed toward that special bonding between a mother and her newborn child, who cries in search of his mother's warmth, scent and soothing voice. (After all, the child had been accustomed to the security and warmth of the mother's womb for nine months!) It is a documented fact that children who receive little or no love after birth are usually very sad and sickly and that some even die of loneliness.

Certainly, we agree that women are equal to men in terms of inherent dignity and worth; they have equal potential to make outstanding contributions to their communities and the world. However, mothers fulfill both their potential and their solemn responsibilities by making the care of their children the primary concern. When the children go off to school, there will be ample opportunity to pursue or return to a career.

Of course, as we have said earlier, husbands/fathers also have a crucial role to play in family life; therefore, single-parent families have more difficulties when it comes to questions of work and child care. All of us should pray for and support the efforts of single parents who try to do the best for their children.

Love and Closeness

Our closeness to our children will help them develop the fortitude to avoid and resist temptation. Their strength will come from our love for them. They don't want to disappoint us, and if we train them to accept a certain degree of discipline, they will have the strength of character to resist temptation.

You as a parent will enjoy greater peace of mind when your children go away to college or move to homes of their own if you know that you have done your best to instill in them a strong sense of morality, virtue and family love. You should continue close communication with your children, even when they are away, by writing or telephoning. Continued interest in your children's new activities will make their time away from home more exciting for all of you. At the same time, they will be less likely to feel homesick or "disconnected."

Attention

Participate in your children's activities long before they leave home. If you love your children, this will not be a burden but a rewarding experience that you and they will remember and cherish for a lifetime. Know where your children are at all times—children can sense a parent's lack of interest and are deeply hurt by it. Among your duties as a parent is the obligation to help them learn at school and to attend school functions, monitor their homework and so forth. Your interest will heighten your child's interest. However, be careful not to put too much pressure on your children to excel beyond their abilities in academics or sports—such pressure can be just as harmful as lack of interest.

As your children grow into adulthood and reminisce about the past, you will discover the importance of your interest in their day-to-day activities. Young adults delight in telling stories that include you as the loving parent who was ever-concerned about their safety and happiness and who, as a result, often helped to avert disaster. This is a reward you won't forget. Indeed, parents rarely regret the time spent with their children and usually wish they had done more.

Always encourage your children to make the most of their opportunities—especially in education—and to develop their talents to the fullest of their abilities. If your children leave home to obtain a higher education, let them know that you are still very much concerned about them. *Don't hesitate to show your feelings of affection toward an older child.* Fathers should show affection toward their sons and daughters, as do mothers. Young men, especially, are eager to display affection toward their parents but often refrain from doing so because of prevailing social mores. Help them out by making the first move.

Sex Education

In addition to spending ample amounts of time with your children and showing your affection and interest, one of the most important things you can do to protect your children is to meet your responsibilities in the area of sex education. Too often now, parents are led to believe that they are ineffective teachers of sex education. Some may recall their own parents' omissions or discomfort in this area and thus allow the cycle to continue.

Today, children are exposed to the influence of the media at a very early age, and we can expect them to start asking questions of us earlier in life than we did of our parents. Therefore, parents must be knowledgeable about basic anatomy and physiology when it comes to human sexuality and fertility and be prepared to answer their children's questions simply yet accurately. Remember that your children admire and trust you more than anyone else in the world. What you say to them makes an indelible impression on their minds. Consider what happens when a child finds you contradicting yourself—they are quick to remind you, "But you said...!" Children have extraordinary powers of memory. You will be gratified to overhear them discuss with friends the many different subjects that you have discussed from time to time. They sound just like you! That is because they are responding as you have taught them, which is a reminder of the depth of your influence on them.

Finally, as mentioned in Part One, make your children aware of the dangerous influence of today's media. Explain to them how seemingly "harmless" films, TV shows and videos are, in fact, trying to justify intimate relations before/outside of marriage. Help them to see how Hollywood's portrayals of life—and their subtle and not-so-subtle eroticism—are not only far removed from reality, but also designed to "turn people on" to immodesty and rampant consumerism. Impress on your children that irresponsible individuals threaten their entire future—their health and happiness—by engaging in a few moments of illicit sexual pleasure. Explain the dangers of sexually transmitted diseases, particularly HIV. Caution your children that girls who become pregnant out of wedlock will have responsibility for the child or, if they decide to abort, will bear not only the physical trauma of killing their babies but also the deep guilt and emotional scars. Remind your children that it is just the opposite of manhood and manliness for a boy to demand sex from a girl before marriage or to abandon a girl whom he has impregnated with their child.

Of course, assure your children that, should difficulties ever occur, you would stand behind them in doing the right thing and in helping them to find forgiveness and healing—including a return to "secondary virginity." According to Focus on the Family, "Researchers Zelnik and Kantner, who interviewed teenagers who have had sex, found that only half had intercourse during the month prior to their interview. Half of the 'sexually active' girls had only one partner, and 14 percent had intercourse only once. Regarding the relative inactivity and return to abstinence among teens who had sexual intercourse, it is realistic to promote 'secondary virginity'. . . . As Dr. James Ford notes, 'These figures indicate that secondary virginity is not all that rare among teenagers. In other words, an appreciable percentage of unmarried teenagers are not currently 'sexually active.' The number of teens who are truly sexually active is relatively few.'"[5]

Love Seeks the Other

The greatest force working against genuine love and family life today is the spirit of sexual license and selfishness that has characterized the "me" generation. We must constantly emphasize to our children, through word and example, that authentic human sexuality requires maturity and generosity and that a man and woman are called to be loving collaborators in giving life to their children.

The challenges are many, but you can teach your children to swim against the current, to stand up for the values that they believe in and to remain faithful to their deepest principles. Your high expectations and

---

[5] Dinah Richard, Ph.D., *Has Sex Education Failed Our Teenagers?* (Pomona, Calif.: Focus on the Family, 1990), p. 42.

good example will challenge your children, but remember that whatever comes to them easily they will never fully appreciate.

Above all, remember that you are not alone in your day-to-day struggles as a parent. A vast number of people around the world believe in chastity, self discipline and marital fidelity—especially in developing countries that have not yet been completely polluted by massive, amoral sex education campaigns and birth control programs. You *can* protect your children and guide them to a full, healthy appreciation of love, life and family.

PART FOUR

Natural versus Unnatural Family Planning

CHAPTER TWELVE

Respecting Human Fertility and the Miracle of Life

We think of ourselves as a nation that cherishes its children, but, in fact, America treats its children like excess baggage. In all other countries, childbirth is seen as an event that is vitally important to the life and future of the nation. But . . . we treat child rearing as some kind of expensive private hobby. . . .

Sylvia Ann Hewlett
Time

The facts already covered, as well as those to come in this chapter, will equip you to teach your children basic human reproduction and a greater appreciation of the wonderful gift of human fertility.

The word "fertility," from the Latin root "ferre," to carry, refers to the ability to participate in the creation of life. The ability to bring life into the world is our most precious gift. It enables us to pass it on to a new generation. Jean Vanier comments on this miracle in his paper, "Family = Hope = The Fertility of Love":

[F]ertility is not just biological; it is also transmitting a hope transmitting a life. . . .

When human beings no longer believe in their ability to give life through a relationship, through love, they loose something very deep inside them and become productive beings; they look for leisure and try to forget; that is the case in our civilizations today, which stress productivity and leisure. We forget that each of us has sources of love that are astonishing if we let them awaken through the christian [sic] community. . . . [W]hat we have to do is to accept the risk of love, the fertility of the love God wanted for our earth. . . . The wonder of our world, when we look at the living plant or the living animal, is this ability to give life to another.[1]

One meaning of the word "sex" is "gender," which means being biologically male or female. Each of us is conceived as a sexual being; we are male or female from the moment of conception. Our fertility is directly related to our being biologically male or female.

Of course, human fertility is not limited to gender. It is part of our entire sexuality which encompasses everything that makes a person masculine or feminine throughout life, including all of our spiritual, physical, intellectual, cultural and emotional characteristics. Human fertility is usually thought of as a physical quality, but the *use* of this gift is very much a result of how people appreciate and respect themselves and others, what they value, and how they express themselves in other aspects of their lives.

Our Reproductive Systems

Many complain that parents do not educate their children about the facts of life or that parents are inept and unprepared when it comes to discussing them. The truth is that, once informed, parents are the best educators of their children. Nevertheless, many parents do not master the subject; it is often ignored or left to others who may not pass on decent morals in this important area of human life. This chapter will help enhance your knowledge as a parent and provide insights to share with your children at the appropriate time.

---

[1] Jean Vanier, "Family = Hope = The Fertility of Love," *Ninth International Congress for the Family* (Paris: Fayard, 1987), pp. 104–5.

In order to appreciate our fertility we must understand the body's reproductive system, which enables men and women to become parents. Our discussion of its anatomy and physiology will therefore include:

- a description of the male and female organs of reproduction (anatomy)

- an explanation of the function of the male and female organs of reproduction (physiology)

- an introduction of the concept of "combined fertility," the way by which the reproductive systems of men and women complement each other and work together to bring new persons into existence.

Mind over Matter: The Importance of the Human Brain

The brain is the primary sexual organ in men and women. This is true for two reasons: (1) The brain exerts control over the hormones that regulate the reproductive system; and (2) The brain is the source of sexual understanding and conscious choices.

Fertility is like a seed inside the body that begins to mature during the season of sexual development called puberty. At that time this seed, which has been buried deep within the body from the moment of conception, grows and matures. A child's body changes and begins to take on the characteristics of an adult. Our fertility blossoms as we reach maturity, when our bodies are able to bring forth the fruit of new human life.

Puberty is triggered by the action of chemical messengers called hormones. Hormones are substances that travel in the bloodstream carrying messages to different organs of the body. Different kinds of hormones cause different actions and reactions throughout the body. In addition to sexual development, they regulate functions such as growth and the conversion of food into energy.

Prior to puberty, all boys and girls have a certain amount of both male and female sex hormones in their bloodstreams. Puberty is triggered by the dramatic increase of male hormones in boys and of female hormones in girls. This increase of hormones is caused by the action of the pituitary gland in the brain. The gland acts as a "communications center," which sends hormones throughout the body. These deliver commands to different organs of the body. Each target organ answers with its own hormone. During puberty, messages from the pituitary gland are sent to young men's reproductive systems, telling them to produce sperm. Similarly, those of young girls tell the eggs in the ovaries to begin to mature. While a man's sperm count may change throughout life, a girl is born with all of the eggs she is going to have for the rest of her life.

Male Anatomy and Functions

I. EXTERNAL

   A. testicles (testes)

      1. located outside the body in a pouch called the scrotum
      2. male sex glands (usually two)
      3. produce sperm and testosterone (primary male hormone)
      4. located externally instead of internally because of the lower-than-normal body temperature required to produce sperm

   B. scrotum

      1. external pouch behind the base of the penis
      2. encloses and protects the testicles
      3. maintains testicles at a proper temperature for the production of sperm

C. penis

1. male organ of sexual intercourse—ejaculates the seminal fluid containing the sperm
2. located in front of the scrotum

II. INTERNAL

A. epididymis

1. long coiled tube inside the testicles—connects with the vas deferens
2. collects and stores sperm as they leave the testicles
3. sperm continue to mature here

B. vas deferens

1. long tube extending from the epididymis to the urethra
2. sperm expelled here to the urethra during an ejaculation
3. severed during vasectomy to terminate fertility

C. urethra

1. narrow canal which passes through the penis to the outside of the body
2. transports urine from the bladder to the outside of the body
3. transports seminal fluid to the outside of the body but not at the same time as urine

D. bladder

stores urine until it is discharged

E. prostate gland

1. surrounds the lower part of the bladder
2. secretion is part of the seminal fluid; X-chromosome sperm and Y-chromosome sperm

F. sperm

    1. male reproductive cell—the "seed of new life"

    2. smallest cell in the male body

    3. continuously produced by the testicles from puberty onward

    4. contains twenty-three chromosomes; chromosomes contain the genes, a kind of blueprint or "tape" of physical characteristics of the parents, which are passed on to offspring

    5. carries either an X or Y chromosome, whereas the female egg carries only an X chromosome; male child conceived when a Y sperm combines with the (X) egg; female conceived when an X sperm combines with the (X) egg—thus we say that the sperm is the cell that determines gender since the egg carries only the X (female) chromosome

G. ejaculation

    1. discharge of seminal fluid from the penis

    2. seminal fluid is the liquid in which the sperm are transported and nourished

    3. approximately three hundred million sperm are released at each ejaculation

Figure 9

Male Reproductive System

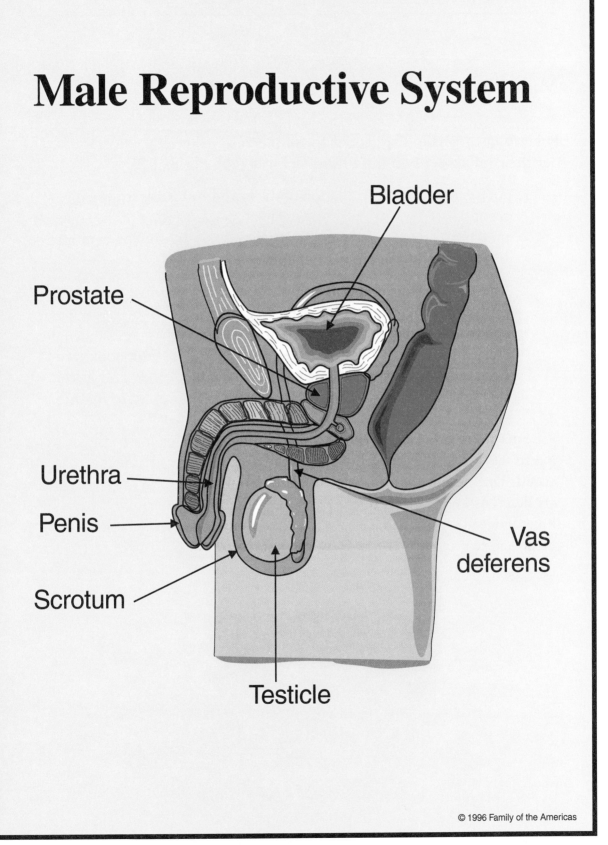

Bladder

Prostate

Urethra

Penis

Scrotum

Vas deferens

Testicle

Male Physiology

Puberty in the male is triggered by an increase of pituitary hormones. Under their influence, two important changes take place:

1. An increase in the production of the hormone **testosterone** causes secondary sex characteristics to develop—deepening of the voice, growth of facial and body hair, further growth of the genitals, broadening of the shoulders, and so on.

2. The production of **sperm** begins. Sperm are produced continuously from the onset of puberty. Occasionally, an "overflow" of sperm is ejaculated during sleep in what are known as nocturnal emissions or "wet dreams." Wet dreams and spontaneous erections of the penis are a normal part of adolescence and a sign that a young man's reproductive system is beginning to mature.

Sperm are produced from tiny cells lining the tubes inside the testicles. Sperm mature as they travel to the epididymis where they are collected and stored. During ejaculation, sperm travel from the epididymis through the vas deferens and urethra to the outside of the body. Sperm will die almost immediately unless they are in a favorable environment such as the wife's fertile cervical mucus, where they can survive as long as three to five days.

Female Anatomy and Functions

I. INTERNAL

A. ovaries

1. female sex glands
2. located on either side of the uterus
3. produce estrogen and progesterone (primary female hormones)
4. an infant girl's ovaries contain about four hundred thousand immature follicles and eggs—only about four hundred egg cells will ripen and be released by the follicles during a woman's reproductive years, usually at the rate of about one per cycle for about thirty years.

B. egg (ovum)

1. female reproductive cell—the "seed of new life"
2. largest cell in the female body
3. contains twenty-three chromosomes
4. contained in follicles inside ovary
5. usually one egg matures per cycle and is released in the process of ovulation
6. lives about twelve to twenty-four hours after leaving the ovary

D. vagina

1. muscular tube extending from the cervix to the outside of the body
2. female organ of sexual intercourse; receives the seminal fluid containing the sperm
3. birth canal—passageway for the infant during birth

E. cervix

   1. neck of the lower end of the uterus which projects into the vagina

   2. like a valve that opens and closes

   3. contains glands that produce mucus at various times during the fertility cycle

F. uterus

   1. hollow, muscular organ inside abdominal cavity; size and shape of pear

   2. can expand to many times its size

G. endometrium

   1. lining of the uterus

   2. hormones prepare endometrium to receive the fertilized egg

H. Fallopian tubes

   1. extend outward from both sides of the uterus

   2. enclosed passageways through which the eggs travel after ovulation—tubal contractions and cilia move the egg through the tube

   3. conception occurs in the outer end of the tube

II. EXTERNAL

A. vulva

   1. external sex organs

   2. includes the labia majora, labia minora and clitoris

Figure 10

Female Reproductive System

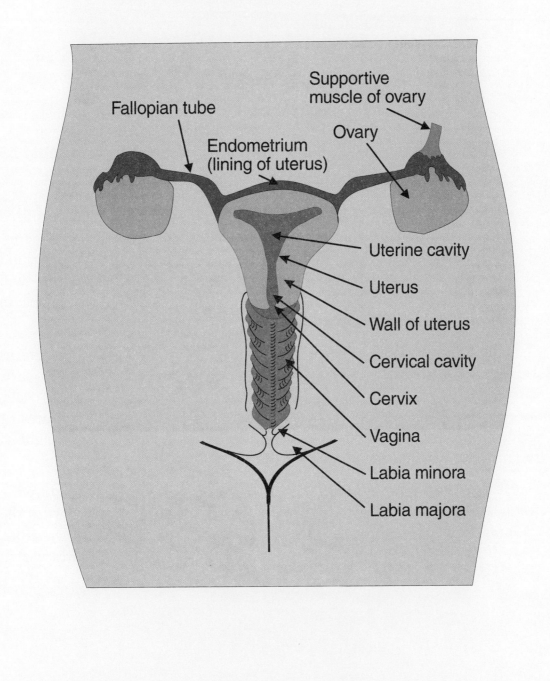

Supportive muscle of ovary

Fallopian tube

Ovary

Endometrium (lining of uterus)

Uterine cavity

Uterus

Wall of uterus

Cervical cavity

Cervix

Vagina

Labia minora

Labia majora

Female Physiology

Changes during Puberty include:

1. An increase in the hormone **estrogen** causes secondary sex characteristics to appear, such as the growth of body hair, breast enlargement, contouring of the hips, and so on.

2. **Eggs** in the ovaries begin to mature and are released during ovulation, usually at the rate of one per cycle, and menstruation occurs as a result of ovulation.

The ovaries are the organs that produce eggs, which may be fertilized by the sperm. The endometrium is the mucus membrane that lines the inside wall of the uterus. This lining is prepared each cycle to provide a kind of "nest of tissue" in which the fertilized egg—the new human life—will implant in order to develop. If the egg is not fertilized, the endometrium degenerates and is shed as menstrual bleeding at the end of the cycle.

The passageways by which eggs travel from the ovary to the uterus are the Fallopian tubes (or simply "tubes"). The egg grows in the ovary, surrounded by a group of cells called a follicle. At the start of each cycle, the brain tells the follicle to begin to mature. As the follicle matures, it sends a signal to the cervix to start producing the mucus. At the height of the process, the ripe egg bursts out of the follicle. This is ovulation.

If there has been an act of intercourse between the husband and wife, fertilization of the egg by the sperm will take place in the outer part of the Fallopian tube. The time in which the egg can be fertilized is very short. If it does not meet with the sperm during this time, it degenerates within twenty-four hours.

Fertile and Infertile Phases of a Woman's Cycle

A woman's cycle includes: menstruation, infertile phase, fertile phase, and infertile phase.

I. **First phase of the cycle—menstruation**

   uterine lining is shed

II. **Second phase of the cycle—early infertile phase**

   A. no significant activity in the ovary; ovary "at rest"

   B. cervix closed—sealed with a thick mucus plug

   C. feeling of dryness in the vaginal area

   D. infertile—not able to conceive during this phase

III. **Third phase of cycle—fertile phase**

   A. egg inside of the follicle of the ovary begins to mature

   B. uterine lining begins to build up and thicken

   C. cervix descends somewhat into the vagina and opens—mucus plug dislodges

   D. cervical mucus glands are activated

   - mucus is sticky and non-stretchy

   - mucus serves as an "outward sign" of the fertile phase of the cycle

    E. mucus becomes clear, stretchy and slippery

- peak time of fertility because the mucus favors sperm survival

    F. ovulation occurs

- mature egg is released as the follicle ruptures

- egg begins to travel along the Fallopian tube

    G. other signs of ovulation include breast tenderness, low back pain, slight pain on the right or left side in the area of the ovaries, possible weight gain because of water retention

    H. fertile—able to conceive during this phase

IV. **Fourth phase of cycle—late infertile phase**

    A. cervix closes, sealed with a mucus plug

    B. return to dryness, no mucus

    C. infertile, not able to conceive at this time

    D. followed by menstruation if no conception occurs

Figure 11

Phases of the Female Reproductive Cycle

First Phase – Menstrual Phase

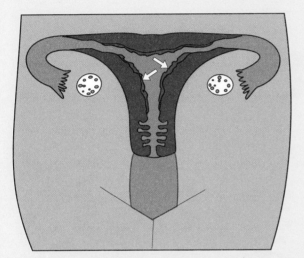

The ENDOMETRIUM is the mucus membrane that lines the inside wall of the uterus. This lining is prepared during each cycle to provide a kind of nest of tissue in which the fertilized ovum, the new life, will implant in order to develop and grow.

Fallopian Tube

Ovary

Plug

If the ovum is not fertilized, the endometrium disintegrates and is shed as menstrual bleeding at the end of the cycle.

Figure 12

Second Phase – Early Infertile Phase

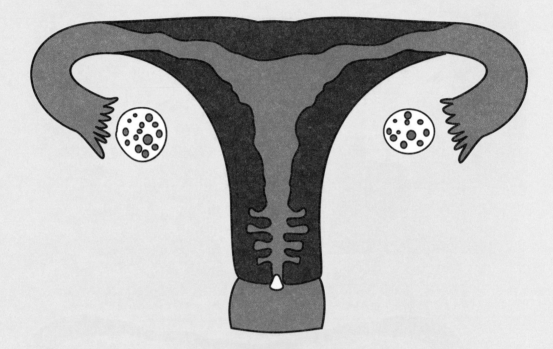

No significant activity in the ovary; ovary "at rest."

Figure 13

Third Phase –
Fertile Phase

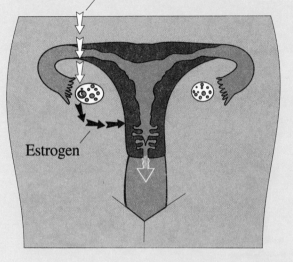

FSH

Estrogen

Follicle Stimulating Hormone (FSH) from brain signals maturation of egg in ovary. Cervical crypts, stimulated by estrogen, begin producing fertile mucus.

Luteinizing Hormone (LH) triggers the release of the egg and ovulation takes place.

Ovulation occurs and the egg begins its travel through the Fallopian tube.

Figure 14

Fourth Phase – Late Infertile Phase

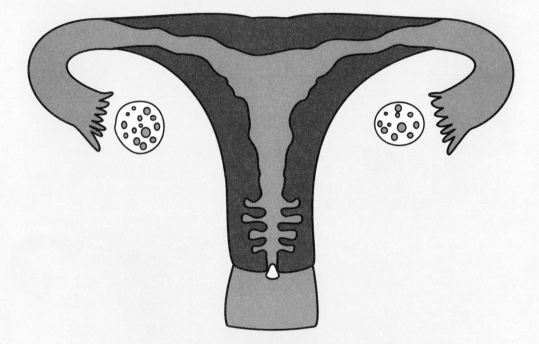

Cervix is closed – sealed with a mucus plug.

Understanding a Woman's Fertility

A woman's fertility is like the soil in which a seed can grow. For the seed to do this, it needs good soil and generous watering. Yet sometimes nothing at all grows from a seed. To find out why, we must look into the mysterious factors which, like the mechanisms of a large clock, measure out the complex timing of life, the cycles of the seasons and the rhythms of living creatures. Such mechanisms also influence the important rhythms that affect our bodies, especially those of a woman's reproductive cycle.

Every woman carries within her a kind of clock that controls the vital function of giving life to a child. A woman's body is, as we have said, the soil in which a seed is planted. Soil must be warm and moist for a seed to grow. Something similar is true in a woman's body if she is to conceive a baby. When a woman is in the fertile phase of her cycle, when she can conceive a baby, her body produces a special mucus secretion. The woman knows that her fertile phase has begun when she feels wetness and sees it. At first the mucus is cloudy and sticky. Then it gradually becomes clearer and more elastic and feels wet and slippery.

Learning to Record the Menstrual Cycle Using the Ovulation Method

In order to learn her cycle, a woman should observe and chart. When charting, the starting point of a woman's cycle is the familiar event of menstruation. Nevertheless, any woman can begin charting on any day of her cycle. On the chart, these days of the cycle are colored red. There is medical support for abstinence during menstruation.

Note this statement from Dr. Robert B. Filer, and Dr. Chung H. Wu: "Endometriosis occurred more commonly in patients who had coitus during menses than in patients who never did," the doctors wrote. "Endometriosis was associated with a higher prevalence of tubal infertility factors. . . ." Furthermore, it is noted that, "The rate of infertility among patients with endometriosis is 30–40%, twice that seen in the general population."[2]

There is medical support for abstinence during menstruation.

The incidence of endometriosis was significantly higher in women who had intercourse during their menstrual period. Once endometriosis was present, there was an increased probability of infertility as a result of the inflammatory process associated with endometriosis.

A study of 124 healthy women going through pre-menopause who had intercourse during menstruation, showed that they were 5.5 times more likely to experience heavy blood flow, with a subsequent higher rate of hysterectomy.

[Sources: Robert B. Filer, M.D. and Chung H. Wu, M.D., *Journal of Reproductive Medicine*, November 1989, pp. 887–90. Dr. Winnifred B. Cutler, as reported in *Ob-Gyn News* 26, no. 23 (December 1–14, 1991): 9.]

After menstruation, there is usually a time of dryness when the woman feels nothing at all at the vaginal opening. On the chart, these days of the cycle are colored brown, like the dry soil.

The fertile phase of the cycle begins with the appearance of the mucus secretion, which changes as the days go by. On the chart, these days of the cycle are colored white with the imprint of a baby.

After this peak time of fertility, the mucus quickly thickens and becomes sticky, cloudy and dense and forms a kind of plug at the cervix,

---

[2] Robert B. Filer, M.D., and Chung H. Wu, M.D., "Coitus During Menses: Its Effect on Endometriosis and Pelvic Inflammatory Disease," *The Journal of Reproductive Medicine* 34, no. 11 (November 1989): 887–88.

gradually sealing it off. This happens whether or not the egg has been fertilized. This plug helps to protect the uterus and the Fallopian tubes from infection. In the event of fertilization (conception), the mucus plug serves as a defense against infection, which could endanger the new life developing in the uterine cavity.

Another time of dryness follows the fertile phase. These days are also colored brown, like the soil, and will last until the next menstruation, when a new cycle begins.

The inner lining of the uterus, the endometrium, which had been prepared to receive the fertilized egg, degenerates and is shed along with the mucus plug. This is why it is correct to think of menstruation as the end of the cycle; however, just as menstruation begins, a new cycle starts. Nature begins to prepare a new nest inside the uterus, and soon the first sign of mucus will signal that the follicle with the egg inside is maturing in the ovary.

It is easy to identify the part of the cycle where the seed could grow. A seed certainly would not grow during the times that are colored brown because these are the dry, infertile days of the cycle. The seed can grow (a baby can be conceived) only when a woman is having the special mucus secretion, during the days that are charted white. The mucus is a sign to the woman that she is fertile and able to conceive. Scientific research has long affirmed the value of charting the fertile/infertile phases of a woman's cycle.

Myths and Misconceptions about Female Fertility

Now that we have an overview of the female reproductive system and how it functions, we can dispel some of the more prevalent myths and misconceptions about a woman's fertility:[3]

---

[3] Charles W. Norris, M.D., and Jeanne B. Waibel Owen, *Know Your Body* (Huntington, Ind.: Our Sunday Visitor, 1982), pp. 38–39.

Myth: Menstruation is the most important event in a woman's cycle of fertility.

Fact: The purpose of the cycle is to release an ovum from one of the ovaries; hence ovulation is the most important event in the cycle. In other words, it makes more sense to call it the "ovulatory cycle" rather than the "menstrual cycle."

Myth: Ovulation usually occurs fourteen days after the beginning of the last menstruation.

Fact: The time between menstruation and the next ovulation is what varies from woman to woman and from cycle to cycle, therefore accounting for the different lengths of women's cycles. The time between ovulation and the *next* menstruation remains fairly constant (about ten to sixteen days).

Myth: Most women have cycles of about the same number of days each month.

Fact: The reproductive cycles of most women are somewhat irregular in their overall length. In a given year, the length of the cycle may vary by as many as six days, comparing a woman's shortest cycle to her longest. However, these are still considered normal cycles.

Myth: If a woman does not ovulate and menstruate every month, something is wrong.

Fact: Some women may ovulate only two or four times per year. Such women are usually "subfertile." In the absence of disease, no treatment is needed. It is not good medical practice to treat these women with synthetic hormones in order "to bring on their periods." However, as previously noted, extreme stress can cause changes in a woman's cycle, as can factors such as nutrition and health. It is not uncommon for women who diet or exercise rigorously to experience a cessation of menses (amenorrhea). Since amenorrhea has been linked to increased risk of osteoporosis (thinning of the bones), women who experience this symptom or any other sudden or drastic changes in their normal cycles should consult a physician.

In an age when young women are pressured to look slim, many are affecting their health by failing to maintain good nutrition. Strict dieting and other habits can inhibit a woman's fertility, which will return to normal after she starts eating right. My advice to young women is that, if they wish to be slim, they should exercise regularly—not excessively—while maintaining a diet with sufficient calories and nutrients.

Myth: The beginning of pregnancy can be dated in relation to the beginning of the last previous menstruation.

Fact: This is an inaccurate method. A woman can conceive a child only when she is ovulating (about ten to sixteen days before the next menstruation, which never occurs if she does, in fact, become pregnant). An infant is likely to be born 266 days after conception, not "nine months" after the beginning of the mother's last previous menstruation.

Myth: Ovulation can occur more than once in a cycle.

Fact: *Ovulation* occurs only during the ovulatory phase of a woman's cycle. If in a given cycle more than one *ovum* is released, it happens within a twenty-four hour period, as part of the ovulatory process.

Myth: Sexual intercourse can cause or bring about ovulation.

Fact: Mating brings on ovulation in some animals (cats and rabbits, for example), but there is no evidence that intercourse causes ovulation in women.

Myth: Women can get pregnant as a result of sexual intercourse any time during their cycle.

Fact: A woman of reproductive age can conceive a child only during those intermittent periods when she is fertile (about one hundred hours per ovulatory cycle).

Myth: Contraceptives will always prevent pregnancy from occurring.

Fact: No contraceptive is completely effective. The only sure way to avoid pregnancy is to abstain from intercourse and/or genital contact. A contraceptive can "fail," per se, only when a woman is fertile.

Myth: A woman cannot become pregnant the first time that she has intercourse.

Fact: If a woman is fertile at the time of intercourse, conception can occur.

Myth: If a woman has intercourse during the time that she is fertile, she will become pregnant.

Fact: This is not necessarily true. She is most likely to conceive a child under those circumstances, but it is always possible that she might not.

Myth: In order to become pregnant, a woman must "go all the way."

Fact: During genital excitement, a man with an erection may secrete a few drops of seminal fluid without ejaculation. These droplets contain a very high concentration of sperm. If deposited on or about the vulva when fertile-type mucus is present, pregnancy can result even without penetration or ejaculation.

Understanding the way a woman's body works shows that natural regulation of conception is possible—that we can control fertility effectively without the use of pills, IUDs, sterilization, abortion or any other unnatural actions or devices. Women can determine with certainty whether they are physiologically able to procreate on a given day. Throughout the world, women at all levels of education and socioeconomic status are proving that knowing the signs of fertility is a great and liberating secret of married life —that it is now possible for couples to achieve or delay pregnancy through understanding the signs of fertility and communication about their reproductive intentions. A couple seeking a pregnancy will have sexual relations during the most fertile time. A couple seeking to avoid pregnancy will refrain from sexual contact during the fertile days.

Figure 15

The Ovulation Method

To postpone pregnancy use the infertile days

Infertile Days | Fertile Days | Infertile Days

To achieve pregnancy use the fertile days

The Ovulation Method is not the old "rhythm method" or the temperature method. It is a new, scientifically proven method, researched by Dr. John Billings, based on the simple recognition of natural signs of fertility that appear for a few days during the woman's menstrual cycle.

By keeping accurate records, a woman can now confidently identify the fertile and infertile phases of her cycle. Women with long or irregular cycles, breast-feeding mothers, and even women going through pre-menopause or who have discontinued artificial methods of family planning may use the Ovulation Method safely and effectively.

Source: Mercedes Wilson, *Love and Fertility* (Dunkirk, Md.: Family of the Americas, 1986), p. 15.

Figure 16

Keeping a Chart of an Average Cycle

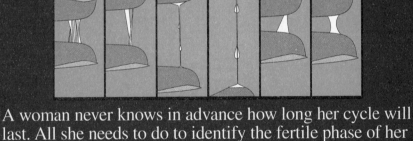

Infertile Days   Fertile Days   Infertile Days

A woman never knows in advance how long her cycle will last. All she needs to do to identify the fertile phase of her cycle is observe the presence and changing pattern of the mucus. It's as simple as that. The presence of the mucus and its changing pattern will always inform a woman of the state of her fertility, whether her cycles are regular or irregular. This is true even if she is breast-feeding, nearing the change of life or discontinuing the Pill or IUD.

This is the sign which identifies a woman's fertility. Once you recognize it, you will realize how reliable and precise it can be.

Source: Mercedes Wilson, *Love and Fertility* (Dunkirk, Md.: Family of the Americas, 1986), pp. 17-18.

Figure 17

Observing a Fertile Cycle

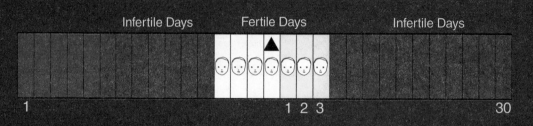

The three days following the peak are also fertile days. Scientifically, we know that ovulation usually takes place on the peak day; it can also take place 24 to 48 hours before or after the peak. Sometimes women continue having sticky, creamy, non-stretchy secretion for 3 days following the peak, as the above example shows.

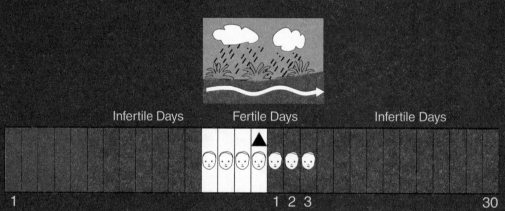

If we return to the comparison of the seed and the soil we see that although the ground appears dry, moisture underneath might still nurture the seed so that it could grow. The same is true for the woman. She may be dry after the peak. Therefore, there is still the possibility during these 3 days that sperm deposited in her body may bring about a new life. This is why abstinence must continue if pregnancy is to be postponed.

Source: Mercedes Wilson, *Love and Fertility* (Dunkirk, Md.: Family of the Americas, 1986), p. 14.

Figure 18

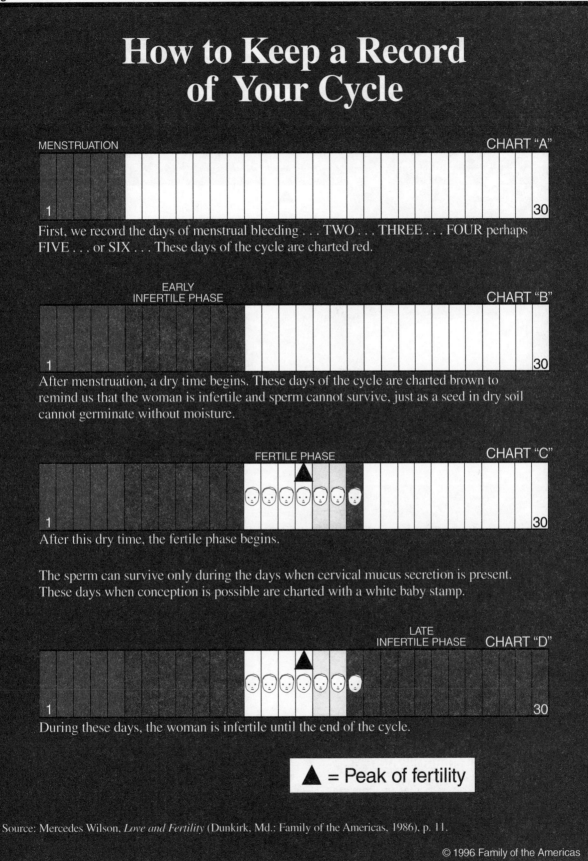

How to Keep a Record of Your Cycle

MENSTRUATION — CHART "A"

First, we record the days of menstrual bleeding . . . TWO . . . THREE . . . FOUR perhaps FIVE . . . or SIX . . . These days of the cycle are charted red.

EARLY INFERTILE PHASE — CHART "B"

After menstruation, a dry time begins. These days of the cycle are charted brown to remind us that the woman is infertile and sperm cannot survive, just as a seed in dry soil cannot germinate without moisture.

FERTILE PHASE — CHART "C"

After this dry time, the fertile phase begins.

The sperm can survive only during the days when cervical mucus secretion is present. These days when conception is possible are charted with a white baby stamp.

LATE INFERTILE PHASE — CHART "D"

During these days, the woman is infertile until the end of the cycle.

▲ = Peak of fertility

Source: Mercedes Wilson, *Love and Fertility* (Dunkirk, Md.: Family of the Americas, 1986), p. 11.

Figure 19

How to Detect the Peak of Your Fertility

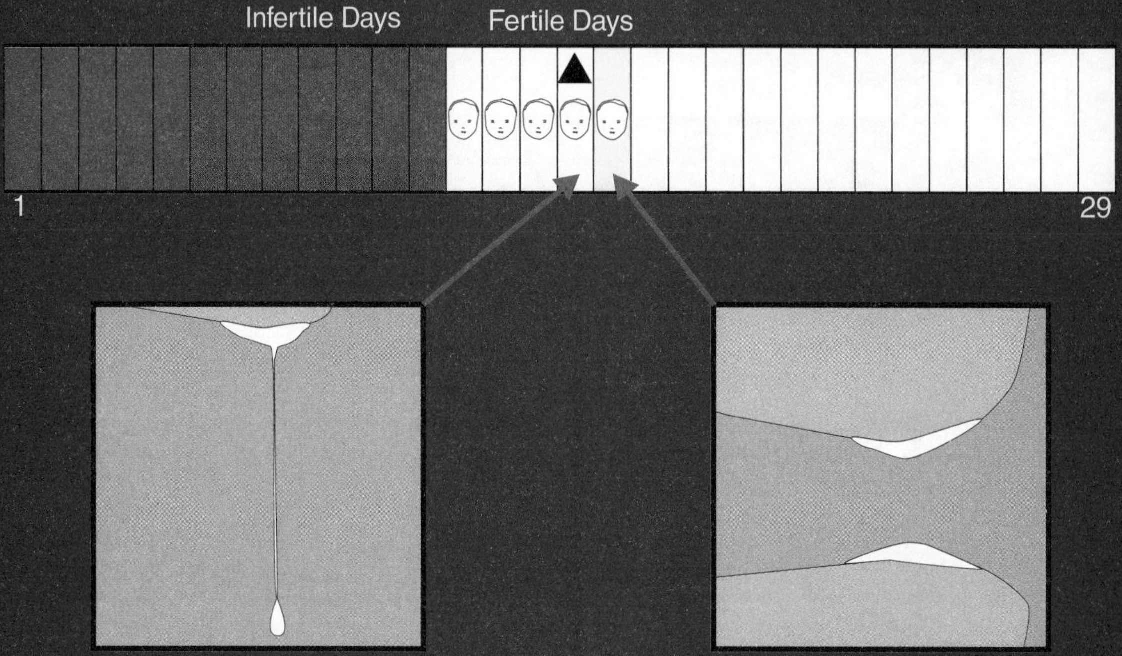

Infertile Days   Fertile Days

1   29

When the stretchy mucus becomes cloudy and sticky, and the wet, slippery feeling disappears altogether, a change has taken place.

The last day on which the woman feels wet and slippery is the "PEAK." We mark this day in a special way to distinguish it from all others because it is an important day which measures out a woman's cycle, the one day when she possesses her greatest degree of fertility and is most likely to conceive.

REMEMBER, the peak is identified the day after it takes place, when the mucus has changed and the wet, slippery sensation has disappeared altogether.

Source: Mercedes Wilson, *Love and Fertility* (Dunkirk, Md.: Family of the Americas, 1986), p. 15.

Figure 20

Hormonal Levels and Corresponding Stamp Chart during a Normal Menstrual Cycle

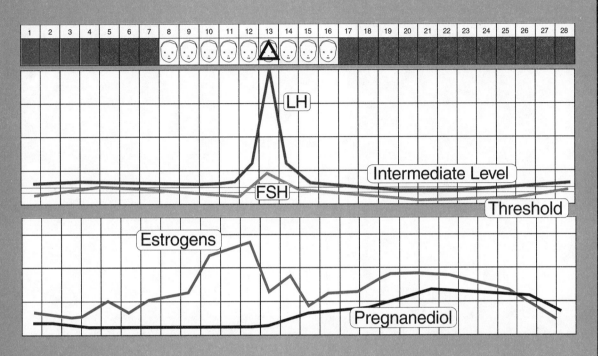

Research in 1962 by leading Australian and New Zealand scientists, Dr. John Billings and Dr. James Brown, first verified the Ovulation Method for the scientific community.

Dr. Brown (the originator of hormonal measurements in women) conducted hormonal studies to correlate the accuracy of women's observations of the cervical mucus patterns with the ovarian hormonal patterns associated with ovulation.

After thousands of women's cycles in all reproductive categories were tested, research showed that the development of the mucus symptom coordinated with the estrogen levels in the follicular phase of the cycle much better than any other symptom accompanying ovulation. The relationship between estrogen and progesterone, the cervical mucus changes and ovulation was also established.

Source: Mercedes Wilson, *Love and Fertility* (Dunkirk, Md.: Family of the Americas, 1986), p. 54.

Figure 21

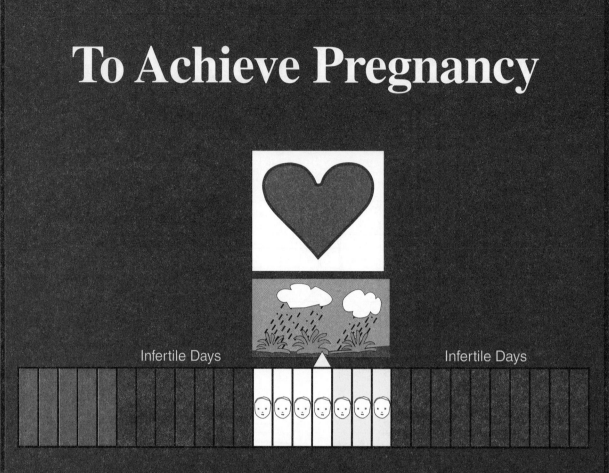

To Achieve Pregnancy

Infertile Days   Infertile Days

IF A WOMAN WANTS TO CONCEIVE, pregnancy is possible once the mucus has begun.

The most favorable time for conception is when the clear, elastic mucus feels wet and slippery.

Source: Mercedes Wilson, *Love and Fertility* (Dunkirk, Md.: Family of the Americas, 1986), p. 41.

CHAPTER THIRTEEN

Combined Fertility and Conception

You have to excuse me, I'm very, very direct. As far as your nature is concerned, I cannot see any difference between the early human being you were and the late human being you are, because in both cases, you were and you are a member of our species.

Jérôme Lejeune, M.D.
The Concentration Can

Listing the similarities and differences between male and female anatomy and physiology helps us to recall what we have learned and, at the same time, helps us appreciate the gift of combined fertility.

Similarities

1. **fertility** begins to mature at puberty

2. increase in **hormones** triggers puberty

3. **pituitary gland** controls the reproductive system through hormones

4. **sex cells** have twenty-three chromosomes

Differences

MALE	FEMALE
sperm—reproductive cell	**ovum** (egg)—reproductive cell
sperm—smallest cell in body	**ovum**—largest cell in body
testicle—sex gland	**ovary**—sex gland
continuously **fertile** after onset of puberty	**fertile** only for a few days each cycle
penis—organ of sexual intercourse	**vagina**—organ of sexual intercourse
sperm production begins at puberty	**eggs** present in ovaries at birth
testosterone—primary hormone	**estrogen** and **progesterone**—primary hormones

The similarities of male and female anatomy and physiology make the two systems compatible; differences between the two make them complementary and allow them to combine with each other in the miracle of bringing into existence a new human being. Combined fertility is the power of a man and woman to participate in the creation of a human life. Three things are needed in order for conception to take place, for a sperm to penetrate the egg at fertilization: sperm, ovum and cervical mucus.

About three hundred million sperm are ejaculated and deposited in the vagina during an act of intercourse. The fertile cervical mucus helps the sperm survive the journey to meet the egg in the Fallopian tube. It filters out abnormal sperm and enables the healthy ones to enter the cervix through channels or passageways, as if swimming up a river. The mucus also nourishes the sperm so they will be full of energy and vitality when they reach the egg in the tube. In addition, the mucus keeps some sperm alive and healthy for three to five days in the cervical crypts (tiny "niches" in the cervical wall).

The surviving sperm must travel the length of the uterus as they make their way toward the tubes. The sperm cannot know whether the egg is to the right or the left, so they enter both tubes.

Of the millions of sperm to enter the vagina, only a few hundred will actually reach the Fallopian tubes and only *one* will penetrate and fertilize the egg.

Conception occurs as the sperm and egg unite and new human life begins. The hereditary characteristics of the parents that are contained in the sperm and egg mingle and are passed on to their child. At this moment, the new person's genetic makeup—the color of his eyes and hair, and so forth—is determined. He is unique and unrepeatable. Dr. Lejeune explains:

> [L]ife has a very long history, but each of us has a unique beginning, the moment of conception. We know and all the genetics and all the zoology are there to tell us that there is a link between the parents and the children. . . . As soon as the twenty-three chromosomes carried by the sperm encounter the twenty-three chromosomes carried by the ovum, the whole information necessary and sufficient to spell out all the characteristics of the new being is gathered. . . .
>
> In the same way, when the information carried by the sperm and by the ovum have encountered each other, then a new human being is defined because its own personal and human constitution is entirely spelled out.
>
> There exist a lot of minute differences in the message given by the father and the one given by the mother, even by the same person; we do not give exactly the same minute information in each sperm or in each egg. It follows that the voting process of the fertilization produces a personal constitution, entirely typical of this very one human being, which has never occurred before and will never occur again. . . .
>
> Now, chromosomes are a long thread of DNA in which information is written. They are coiled very tightly on the chromosomes, and, in fact, a chromosome is very comparable to a mini-cassette, in which a symphony is written, the symphony of life.[1]

---

[1] Jérôme Lejeune, M.D., Ph.D. *The Concentration Can: When Does Human Life Begin? An Eminent Geneticist Testifies* (San Francisco: Ignatius Press, 1992), pp. 30–34.

Immediately after the moment of conception, when the egg and sperm unite, the cells of the new human being begin to divide and multiply at an incredibly fast rate. The new, unique life now moves down the Fallopian tube to implant in the lining of the uterus, where it is surrounded by the cells of the endometrium (which provides protection and nourishment). Meanwhile, at the cervix, the mucus plug is being formed that will help protect the developing baby until it is time for birth.

The baby will grow in the uterus for the next nine months until, at the start of labor, the mucus plug is expelled and he is born.

One last thing to consider about a woman's fertility is the mechanism that controls much of the functioning of our "clock" in the brain. The pituitary gland is at the base of the brain and regulates a woman's cycle (among other things) by sending certain signals to the ovaries. At the beginning of each cycle, the pituitary gland sends out the signal to begin the maturing of the follicle and egg. This sets off the process leading to ovulation. This process, in turn, provides the signal for the cervical mucus to be produced. When a woman is tired or affected by stress, the pituitary gland in the brain might not send the signal to the ovaries. It is as though nature recognizes that this would not be a good time for pregnancy to take place. When this happens, the woman's cycle may be long and irregular.

During breast-feeding, the brain temporarily stops the activity of the ovaries in order to protect the body's ability to provide nourishment to the baby. This helps the baby to develop better both physically and emotionally. The mother's defenses against infection are passed on to the baby through her milk. As pediatrician and author Dr. Robert L. Jackson writes:

> [E]cological breast-feeding is the natural and safe, but not well-appreciated mode of child spacing. We have gradually learned to document the hormonal changes that automatically result during breast-feeding in a period or space of about two years between births. The ovulation suppressant effect of ecological breast-feeding with consequent lactational amenorrhea . . . is now a well-recognized and proven fact.[2]

---

[2] Robert L. Jackson, M.D., *Human Ecology: A Physician's Advice for Human Life* (Petersham, Mass.: St. Bede's Publications, 1990), p. 35.

Our Life before Birth

When you teach your children about the wonderful gifts of combined fertility, that is the time to tell them the true story of how each of us comes into being in our mother's womb. Life begins at the beginning. That seems like an obvious enough statement until we remember that pro-abortion forces continue to lie about it, as if science had not already proved otherwise. *At the moment of conception, we are genetically complete human beings— unique individuals who need only time and nourishment from our mother in order to grow and to be born.* You can delight your children and instill in them respect for the miracles of life and parenthood as you explain to them how every human being has, at one time, lived and grown in the womb.

By the end of our third week of life, our backbone, spinal column and nervous system are forming and our heart begins to beat. By the end of our eighth week, we feel pain. In our third month, we can already turn our heads, open and close our mouths, move our hands and wake and sleep.

By this time, our mother knows that we are living inside of her. This discovery naturally brings great joy to most mothers, but tragically, not to all. Some expectant mothers do not have a husband who wants a baby. Some do not have a husband at all. Many of these women never realize that help *is* available to them. Even if their husband, boyfriend or family will not support them, pro-life individuals and church groups are eager and ready to help them, both before and after the baby is born. Contrary to their nature and their deepest desires, some despairing women submit to abortion. Our twelfth week of age is the time when most abortions are committed. Yet, by then, we are completely formed. We even have little hands and fingerprints.

By the end of our fourth month, we are half the height that we will be at our birth and our mother has begun to feel us moving inside her. In our fifth and sixth months of life, we can hear and know our mother's voice. By now our lungs are developed.

Many babies who are born prematurely during this time are able to survive, and science and medicine keep pushing back the age at which we can survive outside the womb. Even some of abortion's tiny victims have managed to live at this stage, although most of them are then killed, left alone to die or, worst of all, mutilated while still alive in order to obtain organs and tissue for medical experimentation.

During our last three months of life before birth (months seven, eight and nine of pregnancy) our weight triples, we use all of our senses and even sometimes perceive our mother's emotions and state of mind. We are nearly ready to be born. (Even at this time it is legal in the United States and elsewhere for us to be killed by an abortionist.)

When we are born, what joy for our mother, who has carried us inside her womb; what joy for our father, who has longed to meet us; what joy for ourselves, as we meet our family and the world!

Figure 22

Our Life before Birth: Fetal Development

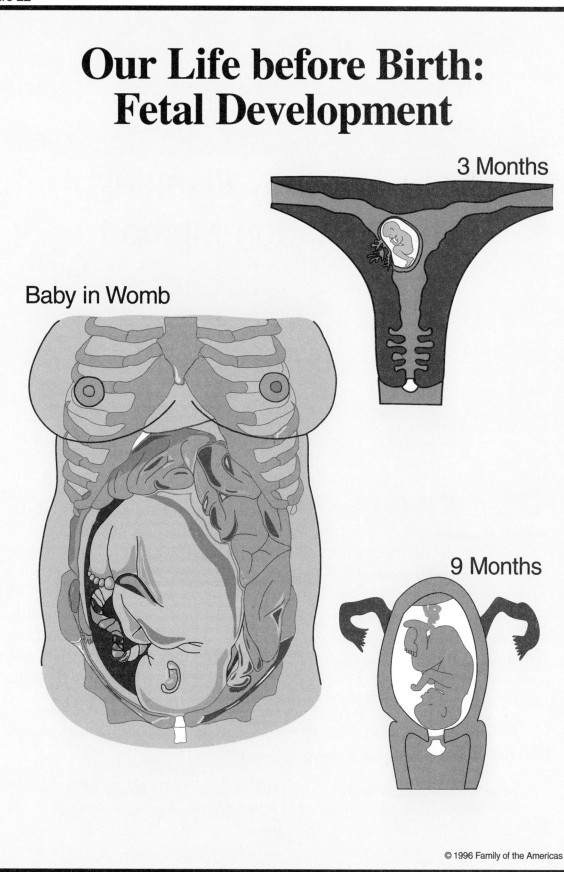

3 Months

Baby in Womb

9 Months

CHAPTER FOURTEEN

Natural Family Planning: The Ovulation Method

NFP respects nature and is regulated by it; contraception manipulates and violates nature. In one case the couple modulate their conduct by the natural rhythms of the woman's body; in the other, they interfere with nature.

Edward D. O'Connor, C.S.C.
The Catholic Vision

Natural family planning has gone through much scientific study and development since the days of the old rhythm method. The rhythm method was ineffective because it did not account for the fact that every woman's cycle is different; even for one woman, the timing of ovulation may vary from cycle to cycle. On the other hand, the Ovulation Method (OM) of natural family planning teaches each woman how to recognize her fertile days, easily and effectively. (OM was initially researched and developed by Drs. John and Evelyn Billings and has since been simplified for use around the globe by the Family of the Americas Foundation, in conjunction with missionaries and health professionals worldwide.)

Jérôme Lejeune, who was, as noted earlier, a world-renowned geneticist, had this to say about natural family planning:

Science reveals to us that the natural regulation of births, or rather of conception, is not only possible but fully effective. Any woman can recognize the signs of her fertility by learning what to look for. This awareness of fertility is the basis for the true freedom of love.[1]

It is reported that some fifty million couples in more than one hundred countries use the Ovulation (Billings) Method of natural family planning to achieve or postpone pregnancy.[2] *Worldwide studies indicate a 98–99 percent effectiveness rate in postponing pregnancy.* Tremendous results have also been achieved in Communist China, where a clinical study of 688 couples using the Ovulation Method for more than twelve months resulted in a *98.82 percent effectiveness rate in postponing pregnancy, with a continuation rate of 93.04 percent.* Chinese officials have reported that even women who, for physical reasons, were unable to use artificial methods *were* able to use the Ovulation Method. They also found that couples with higher levels of education have great misgivings about using artificial methods. Since they are eager to learn a natural method, the faculties of Beijing University and Shanghai University have requested training in the Ovulation Method.[3] It is interesting to compare the 98–99 percent effectiveness of the Ovulation Method to effectiveness rates of the various artificial (chemical and barrier) methods.[4]

Irregularity of Cycles Does Not Interfere with the Ovulation Method

The number of days between a woman's last period and the time of ovulation can vary a great deal, depending on the activity of the hormones that trigger ovulation. However, the time between ovulation and onset of

---

[1] Jérôme Lejeune, M.D., Ph.D., as cited by Mercedes Arzú Wilson, *Love and Fertility* (Dunkirk, Md.: Family of the Americas Foundation, 1986), back cover.

[2] Maria Ruiz Scaperlanda, "Natural Family Planning Pioneers Cite Worldwide Success," *Today's Catholic*, March 29, 1992, p. 6.

[3] Zhang D.-W., and Xu J.-X., "The Effectiveness of the Ovulation Method Used by 688 Couples in Shanghai," *Reproduction & Contraception* 13, no. 3 (June 13, 1996): 194–200.

[4] For more information see Wilson, *Love and Fertility.*

the next menstruation is usually about ten to sixteen days. (One of the key advantages of the Ovulation Method, which we will discuss later in this chapter, is that its effectiveness does not depend on the regularity of cycles. This method works at each stage of the woman's reproductive years, including pre-menopause and during breast-feeding.)

The cycle is not identical for all women. Even in the same woman, it can change from cycle to cycle. A woman never knows in advance how long her cycle will last. In order to identify the fertile phase of her cycle, all that the woman needs to do is observe the presence and changing pattern of the mucus. It is very simple.

To understand why the mucus is so important as an outward sign of fertility, it is necessary to find out how a woman's reproductive system works, as explained in Chapter 12.

The effectiveness of the Ovulation Method is documented in the "Scientific Support" section of *Love and Fertility*, which accompanies the program of the same name. This section presents powerful facts and the knowledge needed to understand the delicate and intricate functions of human fertility. Knowledge of female/male physiology is beneficial to everyone, especially those who are married or considering marriage.

It is important to realize that a woman is only fertile approximately one hundred hours per cycle during her reproductive years, whereas, a man is potentially fertile every day from puberty onward. After recognizing when the woman is fertile, a few days of abstinence per cycle is all that is required if the couple choose to avoid pregnancy. The couple's acceptance of the laws of nature that pertain to the wondrous gift of procreation will enhance their love and communication as they cooperate with nature for the sake of the physical and moral well-being of one another. In this way, the man and the woman accept responsibility for their combined fertility.

Figure 23

Irregularity of Cycles Does Not Interfere with the Practice of the Ovulation Method

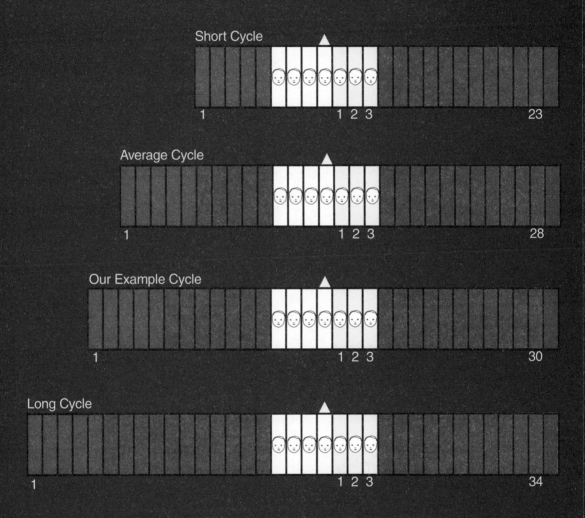

The time between the peak and the beginning of menstruation is normally about two weeks. If a cycle is to be long or short, it is the number of days between the end of menstruation and the peak that will vary. There may be no dry days before the mucus begins, or the dry days may go on for longer than usual . . . even for weeks. The number of days of menstruation and of mucus may also vary.

Source: Mercedes Wilson, *Love and Fertility* (Dunkirk, Md.: Family of the Americas, 1986), p. 16.

Effectiveness Rates of Artificial Methods and the Ovulation Method

Method	Effectiveness, theoretical (perfect use)	Effectiveness, actual (imperfect use)[5]
Norplant	99.8%	N/A
OM/Billings[6]	97.2[7] to 98.82%[8]	92.8[9] to 96.35%[10]
The Pill	94.1 to 97%[11]	91.7%[12]
IUD	96.6 to 98%[13]	86.7%[14]
Condom[15]	98%	64 to 88%
Spermicide[16]	97%	73.8 to 79%
Diaphragm[17] (+ spermicide)	94%	82 to 84.1%

---

[5] The distinction between effectiveness rates (theoretical or method-only versus rate including user error) is very important. Method-only pregnancies are those that occur despite correct application of the rules of pregnancy avoidance. Readers may note variation between these figures and those cited in the Communist China study. Whereas figures from Communist China were provided by an objective, government-run family planning program in that country, statistics such as those cited here may include biased reports from for-profit pharmaceutical companies and other entities that have a monetary interest in claiming high effectiveness rates.

[6] The Ovulation Method will provide this high effectiveness when couples abstain fully from sexual relations during the fertile phase. Couples who use barrier methods or have genital contact during the time of fertility risk an increased pregnancy rate.

[7] "A Prospective Multicentre Trial of the Ovulation Method of Natural Family Planning. II. The Effectiveness Phase," World Health Organization, as reported in *Fertility and Sterility* 36, no. 5 (November 1981): 591–98.

[8] Zhang and Xu, "The Effectiveness of the Ovulation Method Used by 688 Couples in Shanghai," pp. 194–200.

[9] *Fertility and Sterility*, November 1981.

Since there are no pills or rules to remember, there is no opportunity for "user error" with Norplant. The low pregnancy rate, however, contrasts with its high rate of discontinuation. In *Contraceptive Technology*, the authors state, "By the end of 5 years, 9 to 19 percent of women have discontinued Norplant because of bleeding irregularities."[18] According to another report, only 25 to 78 percent of women continue to use Norplant after five years.[19]

---

[10] Zhang and Xu, "The Effectiveness of the Ovulation Method Used by 688 Couples in Shanghai," pp. 194–200.

[11] Robert A. Hatcher et al., *Contraceptive Technology* (New York: Irvington Publishers, 1994), p. 229. Typical first-year failure rate for the pill is 3 percent; 4.7 percent for women less than 22 years old. Failure rate of 5.9 percent reported by Lorenzo Moreno and Noreen Goldman, "Contraceptive Failure Rates in Developing Countries: Evidence from the Demographic and Health Surveys," *International Family Planning Perspectives* 17, no. 2 (June 1991): 44–49.

[12] Alan Guttmacher Institute, as cited by Kim Painter, "The Imperfect State of Birth Control in the USA," *USA Today*, March 16, 1992, p. D4.

[13] Moreno and Goldman, "Contraceptive Failure Rates"; see also C. Tietze and S. Lewit, "Use-Effectiveness of Oral and Intrauterine Contraception," *Fertility and Sterility* no. 22 (1971): 508.

[14] J. Zipper et al., "Four Years Experience with the Cu7–200 Device-Endouterine Copper in Fertility Control," *Contraception* (January 13, 1976), pp. 7–15, as cited by Thomas W. Hilgers, M.D., "An Evaluation of Intrauterine Devices" (Department of Obstetrics/Gynecology, St. Louis University School of Medicine, undated), p. 14.

[15] Hatcher et al., *Contraceptive Technology*, p. 176. Moreover, "condoms have an annual failure rate of 18.4 percent for girls under age 18; among unmarried, minority women the annual failure rate is 36.3 percent; among unmarried Hispanic women it is as high as 44.5 percent." From "Quick Facts on 'Safe Sex,'" published by Focus on the Family. Cites Mark D. Hayward and Jonichi Yogi, "Contraceptive Failure Rate in the United States: Estimates from the 1982 National Survey of Family Growth," *Family Planning Perspectives* 18, no. 5 (September/October 1986): 204. Also Elise F. Jones and Jacqueline Darrock Forrest, "Contraceptive Failure in the United States: Revised Estimates from the 1982 National Survey of Family Growth," *Family Planning Perspectives* 21, no. 3 (May/June 1989): 103.

[16] Hatcher et al., *Contraceptive Technology*, p. 183. Also Alan Guttmacher Institute, as cited by Painter, "Imperfect State."

[17] Ibid., p. 200.

[18] Ibid., p. 309.

[19] I. Sivin, "International Experience with Norplant and Norplant II Contraceptives," *Studies*

Figure 24

Effectiveness Studies of the Ovulation Method

Study	Country	Year	Couples	Cycles Duration	* Method Related Pregnancies	References
Billings, J.	Australia	1972	165	1560	0%	*J.Irish Med. Assoc.* 70(Apr. 1977):6
Weissman	Tonga	1972	282	2503	0.5%	*Lancet* 2 (1972): 813-16
St. Cloud	U.S.A.	1974	260	1823	0.6%	Human Life Foundation Newsletter, Mar. 1974
Ball	Australia	1976	124	1635	2.9%	Europe, *J. Ob. Gyn. & Rep. Biol* 6 (1976): 2, pp. 63-66
Kyu San Cho Urban Rural	Korea	1976	465 918	11064	1.61% 1.96%	W.H.O. Meeting, Geneva, February 1976
Happy Family Movement	Korea	1977/78	3806	24414	1.4%	Annual Report, H.F.M., Korea, 1977-78, pp. 1-4
Mascarenhas	India	1978	3530	39967	0.06%	Mascarenhas M. M., "The Use-Effectiveness of the OM in India," 9:209, 1979
Dolack	U.S.A.	1978	329	3354	1.1%	Hosp. Program (Aug. 1978), p. 64 FF
Tamil Nadu F. L. Center, Bernard, C.	India	1978/79	3275	39300	0%	Annual Reports 1978-1985
Klaus, H., et al.	U.S.A.	1979	1090	12282	1.17%	*Contraception*, 19 (June 1979):6
Klaus, H.	U.S.A.	1981	72	808	0%	Presented 9th Annual Conference on Pyschosomatic Ob. Gyn. 1981
Billings, L. Premenopause	Australia	1972	98	3-4 Years	0%	"The Billings Method", ed. Anne O'Donovan, Pty., Australia
W.H.O. Study	Philippines, India, Ireland, El Salvador, New Zealand	1977/78	725	7514	2.8%	*Fert. Ster.* 36: 591, 1981
Dede, A.	Italy (Lombardia)	1985	720	2974	0%	*Medicina e Morale*, Jan. 1985 pp. 72-79
Cilacap Rural	Indonesia	1978/82	978	14541	0.27%	Pusat Metode Ovulasi, Jl. Jen. A. Yani 23, Cilacap, June, 1986
Xu J.-X. Zhang D.-W.	Peoples Republic of China	1988/90	688	11075	1.18%	*Reproduction and Contraception*, June 1993, vol. 13, no. 3 pp. 194-200.
Ryder, R.E.J.	India (Calcutta)	1993	19843	6467	0.4%	*British Medical Journal*, Sept. 18, 1993 vol. 307, pp. 723-26

* Method-related pregnancies are those which occur despite correct application of the rules for pregnancy avoidance.

This chart reports method-related pregnancies only, for purposes of this presentation.

Continuation Rates
for Artificial Methods and
the Ovulation Method

Method	Continuation Rate, One Year[20]
OM/Billings	93.04%
The Pill	72%
Norplant	85%
IUD	63%
Condoms	43%
Spermicides	58%
Diaphragm	35 to 67%

---

in Family Planning 19, no. 2 (March/April 1988): 81–94, as cited in *Population Reports*, Series K, no. 4, November 1992.

[20] Zhang and Xu, "The Effectiveness of the Ovulation Method Used by 688 Couples in Shanghai," pp. 194–200.

Figure 25

A Comparison of Artificial Methods of Birth Control and the Ovulation Method of Natural Family Planning

(U.S. Statistics 1992)

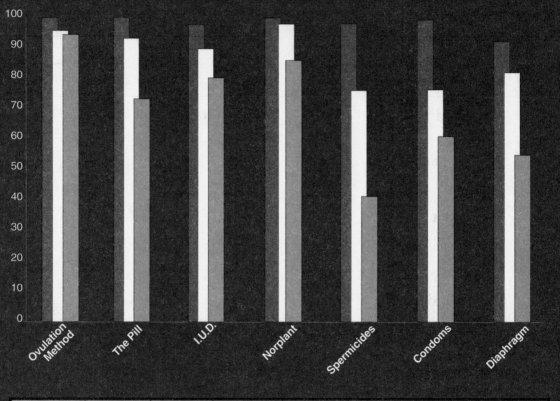

	Ovulation Method	The Pill	IUD	Norplant	Spermicides	Condoms	Diaphragm
Method Effectiveness	99 %	99 %	97 %	99 %	97 %	98 %	90 %
User Effectiveness	95 %	91.7 %	88 %	97 %	74.8 %	75 %	84 %
Continuation Rate	93 %	72 %	78-81 %	85 %*	43 %	63 %	58 %

Statistics on artificial methods are derived from several sources, including the Alan Guttmacher Institute (as cited by Kim Painter, "The Imperfect State of Birth Control in the USA," *USA Today*, 3-16-92); also Robert A. Hatcher et al., *Contraceptive Technology 1990-1992* (New York: Irvington Pub.,1990); and the Population Information Program of Johns Hopkins University. Statistical studies on OM cited by M. A.Wilson, *Love and Fertility* (Dunkirk, Md.: Family of the Americas Foundation, 1986). * By the end of 5 years, most women have discontinued using Norplant. (Source: *Population Reports*, Decisions for Norplant Programs, series K, no. 4, November 1992.)

Figure 26

A Comparison of Artificial Methods of Birth Control and the Ovulation Method of Natural Family Planning

(in Shanghai province, China, June 1988 – May 1990)

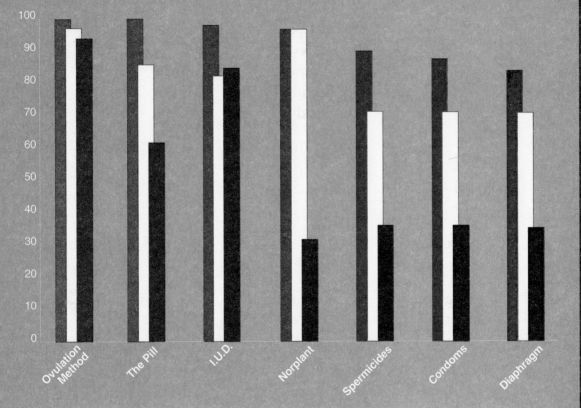

Effectiveness Rates							
	Natural	Artificial[*]					
	Ovulation Method	The Pill	IUD	Norplant	Spermicides	Condoms	Diaphragm
Method Effectiveness	98.82 %	99 %	97 %	95 %	90 %	85 %	82.5 %
User Effectiveness	95 %	85 %	81 %	95 %	70 %	70 %	70 %
Continuation Rate	93.04 %	60 %	81.4 %	30 %	35 %	35 %	35 %

Source: Dr. Zhang D.-W. and Xu J.-X.: "The Effectiveness of the Ovulation Method used by 688 Couples in Shanghai". *Reproduction and Contraception*, June 1993, vol. 13, no. 3 pp. 194-200.
* Personal Communication: Dr. Zhang De-Wei.

Related Costs of Artificial Methods and the Ovulation Method

Method	Per Item Cost as Subsidized* by U.S. Taxpayers to Developing World (commodity alone)	Total Costs & Fees, U.S. user
Norplant	$23–$29	$600–$800[21]
The Pill	$6–$24	$248+ per year[22]
IUD	$.70–$1	$350+ per year
Depo-Provera		$140+ per year[23]
Spermicide	$30–$43	
Diaphragm (+ spermicide)	$6.50 diaphragm $32–$66 spermicide	$51–$70+ per year
Condoms	$9–$28	$63.52+ per year
OM/Billings	$0	$15–$30 *lifetime*[24]

[21] Painter, "Imperfect State."

[22] Ibid. Year average (1993 dollars) provided by Dr. John Bruchalski, an obstetrician-gynecologist in private practice in the eastern United States. Dr. Bruchalski also points out that all artificial methods require check-ups with pap smears once a year—in the United States this means an additional $90-$140 each year. See also a report by the Associated Press, "Depo-Provera Birth Control's Cost Defended by Upjohn Co.," *The Times-Picayne* (New Orleans), January 13, 1993.

[23] Hatcher et al., *Contraceptive Technology*, p. 291.

[24] This small, one-time cost is incurred only by couples who use an initial teaching and charting kit (such as the Love and Fertility kit offered by Family of the Americas). However, the Ovulation Method of Natural Family Planning is simple enough that even couples in poor nations are able to learn the method from qualified teachers without actually purchasing an instructional video (using only the book or charts).

*Approximate individual commodity costs for 3 to 5 years (U.S. dollars). Prices to the United States Agency for International Development and the United Nations Population Fund reflect commodity cost. In addition, prices from International Planned Parenthood Federation to its affiliates include commodity, shipping and shipping insurance.[25] For an idea of what such costs imply on a global scale (at least in the developing world), consider the following statement from the Alan Guttmacher Institute:

> If the population of the world is not to exceed the United Nations Medium Population projection for the year 2000, no more than 969 million people can be added during the 1990s. This will require an increase in the contraceptive prevalence rate from 51 percent in 1990 to 59 percent in the year 2000. To meet these prevalence levels, service providers will have to perform more than 150 million sterilizations and distribute almost 8.8 billion cycles of oral contraceptives, 663 million contraceptive injections, 310 million IUDs, and 44 billion condoms over the 10-year period. Furnishing these commodities is likely to cost in excess of $5 billion.[26]

Clearly, the American taxpayer is being asked to pay a tremendous price for the anti-family/pro-abortion/pro-sterilization activities of the population controllers.

In concluding her speech at the National Prayer Breakfast in February 1994, Mother Teresa urged Americans to take the lead in the fight against abortion:

> If we remember that God loves us, and that we can love others as He loves us, then America can become a sign of peace for the world. From here, a sign of care for the weakest of the weak—the unborn child—must go out to the world. If you become a burning light of justice and peace in the world, then really you will be true to what the founders of this country stood for. God bless you![27]

---

[25] *Population Reports*, p. 4.

[26] W. Parker Mauldin and John A. Ross, "Contraceptive Use and Commodity Costs in Developing Countries, 1990–2000," *International Family Planning Perspectives* 18, no. 1 (March 1992): 4, introductory paragraph.

[27] Mother Teresa of Calcutta, "Whatever You Did unto One of the Least, You Did unto Me," speech at the National Prayer Breakfast, Washington, D.C., February 3, 1994.

"Contraception" vs. Natural Regulation

Even in the United States there is growing dissatisfaction with current artificial methods of contraception. In fact, the December 1991 issue of the *American Journal of Obstetrics and Gynecology* states, "NFP [natural family planning] is an important topic. . . . It is generally accepted that new hormonal or surgical methods of contraception will not be available in the next decade and that the need for nonhormonal, noninvasive methods is well documented."[28]

Scientists and couples alike are eager to find an ideal method. What would be ideal? According to an article in one major American newspaper: "All the experts agree it should be reliable, safe, affordable, easily reversible, easy to use, have no side effects, prevent disease as well as pregnancy and be acceptable to all couples at all stages of life."[29]

For the reasons that have been outlined in this book, the Ovulation Method is *the* ideal method. Research in 1962 by Dr. John Billings and Dr. James Brown first verified the Ovulation Method for the scientific community. Dr. Brown, the originator of hormonal measurements in women, conducted studies in order to correlate the accuracy of women's observations of the cervical mucus patterns with the ovarian hormonal patterns associated with ovulation. After thousands of women's cycles in all reproductive categories were tested, research showed that the development of the cervical secretion coordinated with the estrogen levels in the follicular phase of the cycle much better than any other symptom accompanying ovulation. The relationship between estrogen and progesterone, cervical mucus changes, and ovulation was also established. (See figure 20, p. 237.)

This is, of course, good news to millions of men and women. Yet we never hear about it because it flies in the face of the contraceptive mentality,

---

[28] John T. Queenan, M.D. et al., introduction to supplement to *American Journal of Obstetrics and Gynecology* 165, no. 6, pt. 2 (December 1991): 1977.

[29] Painter, "Imperfect State," p. D4.

the "accepted wisdom" pushed by the sex education and population control lobbies and their allies since the 1960s, when birth control pills were introduced. The promoters of the pill would have us believe that women who want to delay having babies must take powerful drugs—*not* to treat any defect or illness, but to interfere with the natural result of a sexual act. The promoters of sex education and school-based "clinics" even want young high school girls to start using their wares—despite current risks of HIV infection and the known side effects of birth control pills and devices such as Norplant. (See additional details later in this chapter.)

What can you do to keep your daughter safely away from the promoters of harmful artificial birth control? Come to understand the truths that are related here about the wonderful gift of fertility and the genuine power that this knowledge gives women and couples. You can use this good news in your own life and teach your daughter to do the same when she is preparing for marriage. You can also point out the diametrically opposed aspects of contraception and natural regulation of fertility.

Dr. Josef Seifert has done exactly that. First, he observes that there is a natural connection between the sexual act and procreation. Unless there is deliberate intervention, a child will result if sexual relations take place during the fertile phase of the woman's cycle. The same sexual act that is the cause of conception also expresses love between spouses and establishes an inseparable bond between them.

Spousal love is the source of new generations of human beings. When allowed to bear fruit, it brings forth new life and promise for the future. Yet husband and wife alone cannot give life. They can try to achieve conception, but we are soul as well as body, and only our Heavenly Father can decide when to create a new soul. The wonder of human fertility is that Almighty God uses this gift to bring new human beings—each unique, unrepeatable and immortal—into the world. Natural regulation of fertility uses a couple's understanding of the fertile times to space childbearing and so does not thwart God's design. By contrast, contraception actively intervenes, manipulating the sexual act (and obstructing or destroying fertility) to frustrate God's plan.

Separating sex from procreation is not in harmony with the nature of the sexual act and excludes God from an act that He has destined to be a part of the creation of new life. Natural methods of regulating fertility, however, preserve the immense dignity of the sexual act in its unitive and procreative nature and, as Seifert says, do not betray wedded love's generosity—the gift of self to other, or due reverence for spouse, marriage and the sovereignty of our Creator. Expressed another way, the difference between contraceptive sex and non-contraceptive sex is one which in the final analysis involves two irreconcilable concepts of the human person and human sexuality.

Pope John Paul II has often addressed the issue of artificial methods of birth control:

> Artificial contraception often expresses a utilitarian approach to human sexuality that easily leads to dissociating its physical aspects from the full context of married love as commitment, mutual fidelity, responsibility and openness to the mystery of life. On the other hand, the way of living which follows from the exercise of periodic continence leads the couple to deepen their knowledge of each other and to achieve a harmony of body, mind and spirit which strengthens them and encourages them on their journey together through life. It is marked by a constant dialogue and enriched by the tenderness and affection which constitute the heart of human sexuality.[30]

It is not surprising, therefore, that couples who practice natural family planning enjoy happier, stronger marriages. In fact, University of Dallas professor Janet E. Smith notes, "There is evidence that it is very rare for couples using NFP to divorce, whereas over 50 percent of all marriages end in divorce. Indeed, one researcher attributes 50 percent of the rise in the divorce rate from the early [nineteen] sixties to the midseventies to the increased use of contraception."[31] Staying in harmony with God and nature is moral, healthful and sensible. Yes, there are times when difficulties

---

[30] His Holiness John Paul II, address at the Rome Summit meeting on the Natural Regulation of Fertility, December 9–11, 1992.

[31] Janet E. Smith, Ph.D., *Humanae Vitae: A Generation Later* (Washington, D.C.: Catholic University of America Press, 1991), p. 127.

arise because the husband and wife disagree about the regulation of fertility and about demands for intercourse. However, resorting to the unnatural, unhealthy "solution" of artificial contraception is not the answer. Spouses should seek the help of trusted friends and/or a pro-life pastor, counselor or volunteer who can help them to recognize the blessings of natural regulation of fertility.

While more than 50% of all marriages end in divorce, it is very rare for couples using Natural Family Planning to divorce (2–5%)

[Sources: Janet E. Smith, Ph.D., in *Humanae Vitae: A Generation Later* (Washington, D.C.: Catholic University of America Press, 1991), p. 127. Nona Aguilar, *The New No-Pill, No Risk Birth Control* (New York: Rawson Associates, 1986), pp. 186–91. Jeff Brand, *Marital Duration and Natural Family Planning* (Cincinnati, Ohio: Couple to Couple League, 1995).]

The dignity of the spousal act and its connections with God in the creation of new human lives are strong reasons—along with the inherent personhood and worth of every human being from the moment of conception—to oppose not only abortion but also *in vitro* fertilization and other "test-tube baby" technologies. Although such technologies are sought by many well-intentioned couples who are desperate to become parents, such perversions of science treat newly conceived human beings as products—and as disposable experiments. Indeed, dubbed with the euphemism "pre-embryo," many artificially conceived human beings are destroyed as laboratory "extras." University Professor Donald DeMarco adds:

With IVF [in vitro fertilization] the natural process of begetting a child is shifted toward an artificial process of manufacturing a product. This shift inevitably introduces factors that depersonalize and mechanize human procreation, on the one hand, and sunder and violate the two-in-one-flesh intimacy of the married couple, on the other. . . . IVF exteriorizes a process that is meant to be an intimate and inseparable part of a profoundly personal expression of love. "Is there possibly some wisdom in the mystery of nature," asks Leon Kass, "which joins the pleasure of sex, the communication of love and the desire for children in the very activity by which we continue the chain of human existence? . . . People do not have a right to have a child, since no one has a right to another person. . . . The attempt to define human activity solely in terms of rational activity is one of the curiosities of our time, a case of science usurping the place of a broader, more inclusive philosophy of man. . . . Rational control does not make man moral.[32]

Research indicates that 50% of the rise in divorce rates from the early 1960s to the mid-1970s is attributable to the increased use of contraception.

[Source: Robert T. Michael, "Why Did the U.S. Divorce Rate Double within a Decade?" Research in Population 6 (Greenwich, Conn.: JAI Press, 1988), pp. 361–99, as cited by Janet E. Smith, Ph.D., in *Humanae Vitae: A Generation Later* (Washington, D.C.: Catholic University of America Press, 1991), p. 127.]

---

[32] Donald DeMarco, Ph.D., "Infertility and In Vitro Fertilization: Its Meaning and Morality" (Edmonton, Alberta, Can.: Life Ethics Centre, St. Joseph's University College, University of Alberta, 1985).

A Comparison between NFP and Artificial Methods: Values and Nonvalues

Natural Family Planning

1. With the natural method, the woman is able to know herself— to learn and appreciate the processes of her own body.

2. Using natural means the woman accepts, controls and respects her fertility from the beginning to the end of her reproductive years.

3. The natural method fosters communication between husband and wife because the two cooperate in planning their family, taking into account each phase of the woman's cycle. This fosters a mutual respect between the spouses.

4. When the couple must postpone a pregnancy, the very abstinence that the natural method requires can help strengthen the marriage. The sacrifice involved is proof of the respect that the husband has for his companion as a person with dignity and not exclusively as the instrument of his own selfish pleasure. She, in turn, appreciates his willingness to sacrifice for her good and the good of the marriage, and her love for him increases.

5. The love of the couple is renewed after a period of abstinence with the natural method. Interest is kept high, as well as the appreciation for the other.

6. The attitude of the spouses with the natural method is: "Our fertility is a gift from God." This helps to bring about a relationship of peace and closeness.

7. The natural means are completely safe, with no harmful medical side effects.

8. The natural method is simple to learn and to use. It neither deforms the sexual act nor involves distasteful procedures. The spouses do nothing to their bodies. They merely plan their sexual relations according to their fertile and infertile days.

9. The natural method is as effective (98–99 percent) as any contraceptive when used to avoid pregnancy, but it does not carry the medical dangers.

10. The natural method costs nothing more than the initial price of some simple learning materials.

11. Natural family planning can be used to achieve as well as avoid pregnancy. It is immediately reversible when the couple changes their decision to achieve or postpone pregnancy.

12. Natural family planning is acceptable to people of all cultures, social and educational levels, and religious beliefs. The couple can use it with a clear conscience. This method, when used generously and not for selfish or materialistic reasons, respects life and the privilege of transmitting life. With regard to postponing pregnancy, some ask what the moral difference is between natural and artificial means if the purpose is the same. The answer is that there is an important difference between abstaining ("not using" the gift of fertility) and attacking or suppressing this gift through contraceptives.

Artificial Methods

1. Contraceptives are often used blindly, without the woman knowing how they are affecting her body.

2. With contraception, the spouses suppress their own fertility. They treat the normal, healthy functioning of their bodies as an adversary that has to be overcome.

3. Often with contraception, spouses never communicate with one another about something so basic as the woman's fertility cycle. The husband often leaves everything to her and wants to hear no more about it. Physically, some contraceptives are literally a barrier between the spouses. All involve dishonesty because at the most intimate possible moment, when the spouses should be expressing their love to its fullest, they reject their own fertility, which is part of their very personhood, and thus do not give themselves to one another completely.

4. The wife can feel exploited and used when the husband insists that she use contraceptives because "he wants what he wants when he wants it," even during her fertile days when they have decided to postpone sexual intercourse.

5. When the couple is never required to make the sacrifice of abstaining, sexual relations can lose their deeper meaning. What is always available can never be truly special.

6. The attitude of the couple using contraception is: "Our fertility is a problem." This can cause a tension between them, especially when contraceptives cause medical problems.

7. Every contraceptive method involves some medical risk, some of which are very serious.

8. Contraception involves ingesting dangerous drugs or using distasteful devices.

9. The more effective the artificial method, the more dangerous it is (the Pill and IUD).

10. Contraceptives involve a continual expense.

11. Contraception is not a method of "planning a family" but of "avoiding a child." When the spouses change their minds, they have to stop using it. Even then, some contraceptives can have a lasting effect and the woman does not always return so easily to her cycle of fertility.

12. The level of discontent and the discontinuance rate of many contraceptives is extremely high in several countries, especially in the Third World. Contraceptive use goes against many religious and cultural traditions because it involves a direct attack on the capacity to transmit life. In addition, certain "contraceptives" such as the IUD, and at times the Pill, do not prevent the fertilization of the ovum, but instead produce a very early abortion a few days after conception by preventing the newly conceived human being from implanting in the womb.

Speaking on this subject, Mother Teresa of Calcutta has remarked:

I know that couples have to plan their family and for that there is natural family planning. The way to plan the family is natural family planning, not contraception. In destroying the power of giving life, through contraception, a husband or wife is doing something to self. This turns the attention to self and so it destroys the gift of love in him or her. In loving, the husband and wife must turn the attention to each other as happens in natural family planning, and not to self, as happens in contraception.

Once that living love is destroyed by contraception, abortion follows very easily.

I also know that there are great problems in the world—that many spouses do not love each other enough to practice natural family planning. We cannot solve all the problems in the world, but let us never bring in the worst problem of all, and that is to destroy love.

The poor are very great people. They can teach us so many beautiful things. Once one of them came to thank us for teaching her natural family planning and said, "You people who have practiced chastity, you are the best people to teach us natural family planning because it is nothing more than self-control out of love for each other." And what this poor person said is very true. These poor people maybe have nothing to eat, maybe they have not a home to live in, but they can still be great people when they are spiritually rich.[33]

---

[33] Mother Teresa of Calcutta, "Whatever You Did."

CHAPTER FIFTEEN

The Facts on Contraception, Sterilization and Abortion

Even more fundamental is the contradiction between the truly pro-life concern voiced by pro-control organizations about nuclear war and pollution, and their advocacy of population control which is purely anti-life.

Julian L. Simon
Population Matters:
People, Resources and Immigration

As we learned in Chapter 14, the difference between contraceptive and non-contraceptive sex is one that involves two diametrically opposed views of humanity. Whereas contraception often expresses a utilitarian approach to sex (in which the gift of fertility is treated as an obstacle or annoyance and the other person is treated merely as an object of satisfaction and pleasure), the way of life that follows from the exercise of periodic abstinence enhances communication in marriage and enriches a couple's love for each other through a deeper appreciation of heart, mind, body and soul.

Following is Mother Teresa's plea at the National Prayer Breakfast in Washington, D.C., on February 3, 1994, where she spoke so strongly on the abortion issue:

I feel that the greatest destroyer of peace today is abortion. . . . It is a war against the child, a direct killing of the innocent child, murder by the mother herself. And if we accept that a mother can kill even her own child, how can we tell other people not to kill one another? How do we persuade a woman not to have an abortion? As always, we must persuade her with love and we remind ourselves that love means to be willing to give until it hurts. . . .

By abortion, the mother does not learn to love, but kills even her own child to solve her problems. And, by abortion, the father is told that he does not have to take any responsibility at all for the child he has brought into the world. That father is likely to put other women into the same trouble. So abortion just leads to more abortion. Any country that accepts abortion is not teaching its people to love, but to use any violence to get what they want. This is why the greatest destroyer of love and peace is abortion. . . .

I will tell you something beautiful. We are fighting abortion by adoption—by care of the mother and adoption for her baby. We have saved thousands of lives. We have sent word to the clinics, to the hospitals and police stations: "Please don't destroy the child; we will take the child." So we always have someone tell the mothers in trouble: "Come, we will take care of you, we will get a home for your child." And we have a tremendous demand from couples who cannot have a child—but I never give a child to a couple who have done something not to have a child. Jesus said, "Anyone who receives a child in my name, receives me." By adopting a child, these couples receive Jesus but, by aborting a child, a couple refuses to receive Jesus.

Please don't kill the child. I want the child. Please give me the child. I am willing to accept any child who would be aborted and to give that child to a married couple who will love the child and be loved by the child.[1]

In the United States alone, the estimated number of couples seeking to adopt a child is 1,500,000, while the number of infants available for adoption is only twenty-five thousand.[2]

---

[1] Mother Teresa of Calcutta, "Whatever You Did unto One of the Least, You Did unto Me," speech at the National Prayer Breakfast, Washington, D.C., February 3, 1994.

[2] "Vital Signs," *Health*, January/February 1994, p. 14.

There are, of course, additional reasons for avoiding contraception. At the aesthetic level alone, artificial methods of birth control mock the unitive nature of human intercourse. An act that is meant to express the total love and complete self-giving between two persons should not require that men and women arm themselves like modern-day gladiators with rubber, foams, creams, pills and devices. Moreover, artificial methods of birth control treat the wonderful gift of fertility as if it were a disability or disease, not a sign of health and promise for the future. Indeed, such methods often put an individual's health and fertility at risk. In one of its publications, even the International Planned Parenthood Federation has reported extremely high discontinuation rates for contraceptives in many developing countries.

For example, in Niger and Gambia, a discontinuation rate of almost 30 percent within the first seven months was noted. Among IUD users in India, the discontinuation rate after less than four months was 35 percent. In parts of Indonesia, "as many as 72 percent of women who did not receive the method they requested stopped using contraception." Among the reasons cited for these high rates were dissatisfaction with the current method, unplanned pregnancy due to incorrect use of the method and lack of contraceptive supplies at clinics.[3] The risks are especially high among women (who are the primary targets of the purveyors of artificial contraception).

The Clinton Administration in the United States is proposing an increase in American contributions to such ineffective population control programs—more than doubling the current expenditure for international family planning efforts from about five hundred million dollars a year to between 1.2 and 1.4 billion dollars a year.[4] The U.S. State Department's stated goal is to "provide family-planning services, a comprehensive family-planning package, to every woman in the world who wants them." At the same time, they acknowledge that one of the problems in limiting global

---

[3] The Family Planning Manager 2, no. 3 (May/June 1993), as reported in *IPPF Open File*, October 1993.

[4] Joyce Price, "White House Aims to Finance Family Planning around the World," *The Washington Times*, January 12, 1994.

population growth is that many of the countries receiving family planning program assistance have cultural barriers to be overcome. Large families are desired and the population has resisted government efforts to decrease family size.[5]

The population control policy of the Clinton Administration is openly disinterested in considering or respecting the will or desire of other countries in regard to family planning. This policy will have tragic consequences, not only in the United States, but throughout the world. Their programs are clearly ineffective and wasteful from the point of view of the taxpayers and the foreign governments who are "persuaded" to accept such physically and morally harmful programs. In addition, developing countries find it difficult to afford the medical care needed as a result of adverse physical side effects. We will begin our discussion here with the Pill, which acts upon the primary organ of human sexuality—the brain.

"The Pill"

I. Facts

A. two kinds: "combined pill," which contains two female hormones, estrogen and progestin, and is taken twenty-one days out of each month, and "mini-pill," which contains progestin only and is taken continuously

B. cost of use averages $15 per month—$248–$300 per year[6]

---

[5] Thomas Lippman, "Population Control Is Called a 'Top Priority' in Foreign Policy," *The Washington Post*, January 12, 1994, p. A4.

[6] Kim Painter, "The Imperfect State of Birth Control in the U.S.A.," *USA Today*, March 16, 1992; also Associated Press report, "Depo-Provera Birth Control's Cost Defended by Upjohn Co.," *The Times-Picayune* (New Orleans), January 13, 1993. Similar figures on contraceptive costs (including medical fees) provided by Dr. John Bruchalski, an obstetrician-gynecologist practicing in the eastern United States.

C. typical first-year failure rate is 3 percent; 4.7 percent for women less than twenty-two years old[7] (failure rate even higher for imperfect use; i.e., user forgets or "skips" a pill now and then)

D. no protection against HIV

II. Mode of Action

A. through chemical signals to the brain, suppresses ovulation (essential action of estrogens)

B. thickens cervical mucus, making it impenetrable to sperm (essential action of progestins)

C. alters endometrium so uterus is not receptive to implantation of fertilized egg (newly conceived human life); therefore, sometimes acts as abortifacient

III. Potential Side Effects

A. nausea, vomiting, headache and weight gain or loss[8]

B. increased blood pressure (hypertension) and impaired vision

C. increased risk of stroke or heart attack, even with new "low" dose pill[9]

---

[7] Robert A. Hatcher et al., *Contraceptive Technology* (New York: Irvington Publishers, 1994), p. 229.

[8] Schering Chemicals advertisement for Eugynon 30 Microgynon 30.

[9] Dr. Ojvind Lidegaard et al., study reported in *British Medical Journal*, April 1993, and cited in *Europe Today*, no. 23 (May 3, 1993). Study of 2,400 women aged 15 to 44 revealed that 800 suffered some degree of cerebral thrombosis (although not all of these blood clots led to a cerebral infarction). According to Dr. J. H. L. Evers, professor of gynecology at the University Clinic in Maastricht, The Netherlands, "This study demonstrates clearly and for the first time the risk of cerebral thrombosis that women take when they use pills that contain even light doses of hormones."

D. possible link to cancer of reproductive organs

E. possible link to breast cancer

F. increased risk of gall bladder disease

G. increased danger of developing liver tumors

H. difficulty in conceiving after discontinuing use

I. residual risk of heart attack, even after discontinuation of long-term use

J. reduced blood levels of essential vitamins

K. development of depressive personality changes

These are among the possible complications listed on "detailed patient labeling" for common, brand-name birth control pills such as Brevicon, Norinyl, and Nor-QD. More than thirty known side effects have been documented in medical journals and advisories provided by government health organizations.[10] Those listed represent only the most serious and most frequently occurring complications.

It must also be noted that a study among prostitutes in Nairobi found that those who took birth control pills were infected with AIDS at a rate nearly *one-third* higher than those who did not. Addressing the Third International Conference on AIDS, Dr. Francis A. Plummer suggested that oral contraceptives may alter the female genital tract, making it more susceptible to HIV infection. He also suggested that birth control pills could increase the risk of chlamydia—a venereal disease that could in turn increase chances of HIV infection.[11]

---

[10] See also the 1993 *Physicians' Desk Reference.*

[11] Michael Specter, "AIDS Infection and Birth Control Pills," *The Washington Post,* June 2, 1987.

According to a study by Dr. Margorie Profet, a specialist in evolutionary biology at the University of California at Berkeley, menstrual periods naturally protect the uterus and the Fallopian tubes from sterility and infections transmitted by sperm. Dr. Profet urges women to avoid taking the pill because it stops menstrual periods, thus blocking this regular cleaning of the uterus. Her conclusions are published in the *Quarterly Review of Biology*. The menstrual period acts to clean and protect the uterus by abrading the internal surface of the uterus, thereby dislodging germs. In addition, says Dr. Profet, the loss of blood during menstruation cleans out the germs in a bath of immunizing cells. Dr. Profet also asserts that when a woman experiences unexplained bleeding, it could be a defense mechanism against infection.[12]

Norplant

I. Facts

A. There are two forms: Norplant and Norplant 2.

B. A series of six rubber "rods" or capsules are surgically implanted under the skin in the inside portion of a woman's upper arm.

C. Contraceptive effects can last for five years (however, continuation rates drop to 76 percent after one year and to as low as 33 percent by year five).[13]

D. Norplant 2 differs in the number and size of the rods; its contraceptive effects last for seven years.

---

[12] Dr. Margorie Profet, *Quarterly Review of Biology*, as cited in *Europe Today*, no. 44 (October 18, 1993).

[13] Population Information Program of the Johns Hopkins University, supplement to *Population Reports*, "Decisions for Norplant Programs," vol. 20, series K, no. 4 (November 1992).

E. Cost averages $600–$800 for a five-year supply, insertion and removal.[14]

II. Mode of Action

A. It suppresses ovulation in only about 50 percent of cycles. Progestins cause thickening of the cervical mucus, making sperm migration difficult.

B. Just as often, Norplant induces early abortion. The lining of the uterus (endometrium) is altered, making it inhospitable to implantation of a fertilized egg (newly conceived human being); hence, it sometimes acts as an abortifacient.[15]

III. Potential Side Effects[16]

A. severe lower abdominal pain

B. prolonged or heavy vaginal bleeding; or amenorrhea (absence of periods)[17] experienced by more than two-thirds of all users

---

[14] Painter, "Imperfect State." It is also worthwhile to note here the serious ethical questions that have been raised by attempts to use Norplant as a tool of government social policy. As reported in *Newsweek*, February 15, 1993, lawmakers in more than a dozen states have proposed legislation that aims to use Norplant to control reproduction among welfare recipients, criminal offenders and so forth—all in the name of reducing public costs. *Newsweek* cites the concerns of Arthur Caplan, a bioethicist at the University of Minnesota, who, among many others, foresees the significant potential for abuse of government power in this area.

[15] *Fertility and Sterility*, May 1993.

[16] Except when otherwise noted, this information is derived from patient labeling for the Norplant system, Wyeth Laboratories, Inc., issued December 1990. See also "Consent for Norplant Implant System," form distributed by the North Carolina Department of Environment, Health and Natural Resources, Division of Maternal and Child Health.

[17] Hatcher et al., *Contraceptive Technology*. Note that some studies show that, "by the end of 5 years, 9 to 19 percent of women have discontinued Norplant because of bleeding irregularities." Also, according to the "Decisions for Norplant Programs" by the Population Information Program of Johns Hopkins University, "Some 70 percent of users experience irregular menstrual bleeding or amenorrhea."

C. arm pain and infection

D. expulsion of an implant

E. migraine headaches, repeated painful headaches, or blurred vision

F. changes in lipid metabolism (digestion of fats)[18]

G. ovarian cysts (experienced by one in ten users)

H. high blood pressure, increased risk of heart attack or stroke

I. hair loss

J. nervousness

K. liver tumors

L. gall bladder disease

One hundred serious complications of the hormonal implant Norplant —including bleeding, stroke and other complications requiring hospitalization—were reported to the U.S. Food and Drug Administration between February 1991 and December 1993.[19] Well over four hundred women have joined a class-action lawsuit against Wyeth-Ayerst, the manufacturer of Norplant, alleging serious removal problems ranging from scarring and pain to nerve and muscle damage.[20]

---

[18] Hatcher et al., *Contraceptive Technology*, p. 312. "In some studies, decreases in high density lipoproteins on the order of 10 to 15 percent were observed among Norplant users. In another study, increases rather than decreases were found."

[19] D. K. Wysowski and L. Green, "Serious Adverse Events in Norplant Users Reported to the Food and Drug Administration's Medwatch Spontaneous Reporting System," *Obstetrics and Gynecology* 85 (1995): 538–42.

[20] J. Roberts, "Women in U.S. Sue Makers of Norplant," *British Medical Journal* 309, no. 145 (1994).

Contraceptive Injections

I. Facts

A. Depo-Provera (medroxy-progesterone acetate) is injected every three to six months

B. cost of the drug is $29.50 per injection, or up to about $120 per year, plus another $80 per year in medical fees for administering the drug (total: up to about $200 per year)[21]

II. Mode of Action

A. prevents pregnancy by inhibiting ovulation

B. abortifacient: alters normal growth of endometrium and prevents implantation of newly conceived baby

III. Potential Side Effects

A. major disturbances of menstrual pattern

B. prolonged and unpredictable delay in return to fertility

C. mild deterioration of carbohydrate tolerance

D. severe and prolonged bleeding

E. decrease in breast milk production

F. depression and reduction in libido

---

[21] Jack Jackson, senior vice president of the Upjohn pharmaceutical company, as quoted by the Associated Press, "Depo-Provera Birth Control's Costs."

G. danger to fetus in event of pregnancy: some women, especially those who are breast-feeding, are already pregnant when they receive first injection and may receive second injection before they know that they are pregnant; drugs of this type known to be associated with fetal abnormalities, mainly some masculinizing effects in females

Many developing countries have long permitted use of Depo-Provera for population control, yet the drug has only recently been approved for use as a contraceptive in the United States because some studies caused public concern when they indicated that the drug creates a tendency to develop benign and malignant breast lumps.[22] There is also a suspicion that Depo-Provera may cause cervical cancer. Use of Depo-Provera in developing countries has been encouraged by international organizations whose funds are often supplied (usually indirectly) by USAID, which offers aid to those developing nations that accept population control.

---

[22] Paul, Skegg and Spears, "Depot Medroxyprogesterone (Depo-Provera) and Risk of Breast Cancer," *British Medical Journal* 299 (1989): 759–62. (Depo-Provera was approved by the United States Food and Drug Administration in October 1992.)

Figure 27

Abortifacient Effect of the Pill, Norplant and Injectables

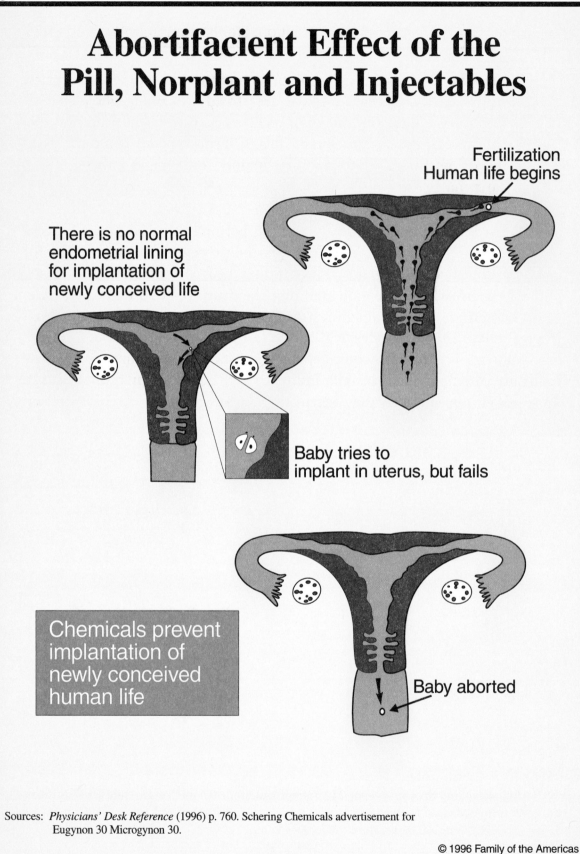

Fertilization
Human life begins

There is no normal endometrial lining for implantation of newly conceived life

Baby tries to implant in uterus, but fails

Chemicals prevent implantation of newly conceived human life

Baby aborted

Sources: *Physicians' Desk Reference* (1996) p. 760. Schering Chemicals advertisement for Eugynon 30 Microgynon 30.

Figure 28

Hormonal Contraceptives Can Cause Early Abortion

Note: Baby may be depicted at a more advanced stage of development in these diagrams to express the reality of its unique humanity.

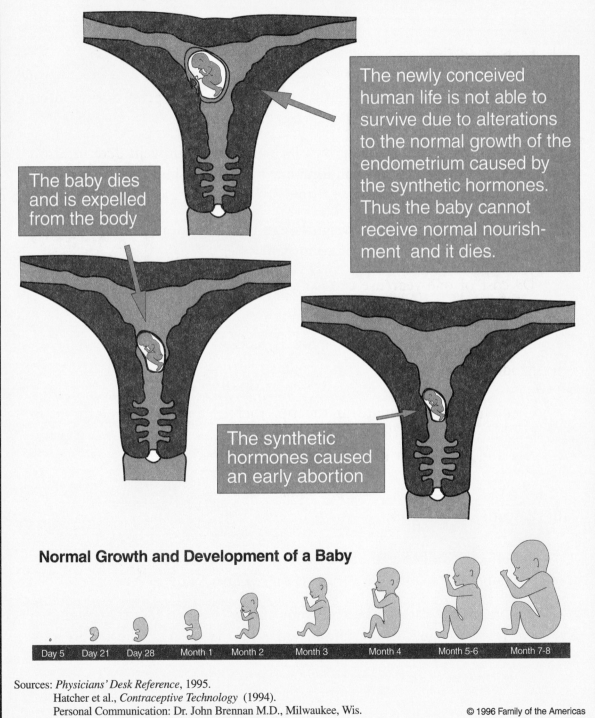

The newly conceived human life is not able to survive due to alterations to the normal growth of the endometrium caused by the synthetic hormones. Thus the baby cannot receive normal nourishment and it dies.

The baby dies and is expelled from the body

The synthetic hormones caused an early abortion

Normal Growth and Development of a Baby

| Day 5 | Day 21 | Day 28 | Month 1 | Month 2 | Month 3 | Month 4 | Month 5-6 | Month 7-8 |

Sources: *Physicians' Desk Reference*, 1995.
　　　Hatcher et al., *Contraceptive Technology* (1994).
　　　Personal Communication: Dr. John Brennan M.D., Milwaukee, Wis.

Condoms

I. Facts

A. thin rubber or latex sheath worn over the erect penis during intercourse

B. must be stored in cool, dry place in order to prevent deterioration of rubber; likewise, condoms have limited "shelf life" as condom materials deteriorate over time

C. lubricants and/or spermicides can cause condom failure by accelerating deterioration of condom rubber

D. cost of one-year use can be more than $63 per year (intercourse four times weekly)

II. Mode of Action

Condoms trap ejaculate in the tip, thereby preventing sperm from reaching the ovum (hence it is essential that a condom be worn properly and not tear or slip off during intercourse).

III. Potential Side Effects

A. effective only 84 to 88 percent of the time, at best (chance of pregnancy over one year of use is one in six)

B. pregnancy rate of 18.4 percent among women less than eighteen years of age; among unmarried minority women the failure rate of condoms is even higher, some 36 percent; among unmarried Hispanic women the failure rate is as high as 44.5 percent[23]

C. Contrary to claims that condoms can be an effective means of preventing the spread of HIV, the fact is that the human immunodeficiency virus is 500 times smaller than a human sperm. Obviously, since condoms fail anywhere from 12 to 44 percent of the time in preventing pregnancy, they are even less effective in preventing the transmission of this tiny virus.[24]

Intrauterine Device (IUD)

I. Facts

A. plastic device placed in uterus through the cervical canal; may contain trace metals or hormones to increase contraceptive efficacy

B. only about 84 percent effective

C. cost of IUD and insertion range from $200–$300 per year[25]

---

[23] "Quick Facts on 'Safe Sex,'" Focus on the Family. Cites Mark D. Hayward and Jonichi Yogi, "Contraceptive Failure Rate in the United States: Estimates from the 1982 National Survey of Family Growth," *Family Planning Perspectives* 18, no. 5 (September/October 1986): 204. Also Elise F. Jones and Jacqueline Darrock Forrest, "Contraceptive Failure in the United States: Revised Estimates from the 1982 Survey of Family Growth," *Family Planning Perspectives* 21, no.3, (May/June 1989): 103.

[24] Moreover, there exists direct evidence of voids in condom rubber. Electron micrographs reveal voids five microns in size (fifty times larger than the virus [HIV]), while fracture mechanics analyses, sensitive to the largest flaws present, suggest inherent flaws as large as fifty microns (five hundred times the size of the virus). C. M. Roland, editor of *Rubber Chemistry and Technology* for the National Research Laboratory, "Letters," *The Washington Post*, July 3, 1992.

[25] Hatcher et al., *Contraceptive Technology*, p. 350.

II. Mode of Action

The mechanisms by which an IUD works are not well understood. It seems to create chronic inflammation of the endometrium, which prevents implantation of newly conceived human life (an abortifacient effect).

III. Potential Side Effects

A. occasional perforation of uterus or cervix requiring surgery

B. increased risk of miscarriage (spontaneous abortion)

C. ectopic (extrauterine) pregnancies ten times above usual incidence in women

D. pelvic inflammations that can cause sterility[26]

E. anemia due to excessive menstrual bleeding[27]

F. embedding, migration or fragmentation of IUD

G. spotting or prolongation of menstrual flow

H. presence of actinomyces in pap smears of 90 percent of users; infection of reproductive organs by actinomyces rare, but is typically found in long-term IUD users

I. increased risk of HIV infection[28]

---

[26] Ibid., p. 383: "Infections from IUDs can be serious and, if untreated, can lead to hysterectomy (removal of the uterus) or even death."

[27] Ibid., p. 370: "Approximately 15 percent of IUD users will have their IUD removed because of symptoms and/or signs associated with bleeding or spotting."

[28] Ibid., p. 360: "The effect of the IUD on the uterine lining may create an environment favorable to HIV transmission . . . studies to address the question are planned. The increased bleeding associated with IUD use may increase the spread of the virus (if the woman were HIV positive), and the IUD's possible effect on the inside of the uterus may increase [her] infection rate." Authors cite K. Treiman and L. Liskin, "IUDs: A New Look," *Population Reports*, 1988, series B, vol. 5 (1988): 1–31.

Figure 29

Abortifacient Effect of the IUD

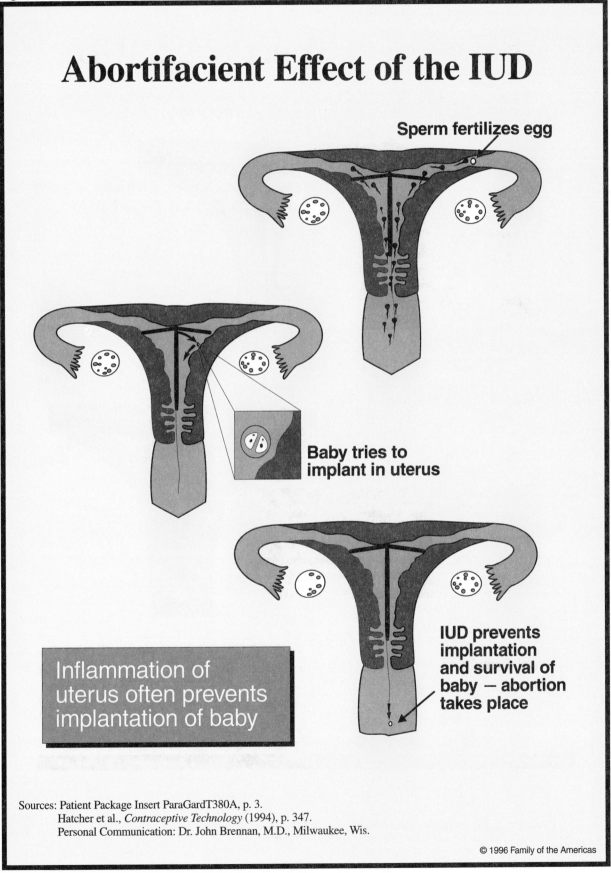

Sperm fertilizes egg

Baby tries to
implant in uterus

Inflammation of
uterus often prevents
implantation of baby

IUD prevents
implantation
and survival of
baby — abortion
takes place

Sources: Patient Package Insert ParaGardT380A, p. 3.
Hatcher et al., *Contraceptive Technology* (1994), p. 347.
Personal Communication: Dr. John Brennan, M.D., Milwaukee, Wis.

© 1996 Family of the Americas

Figure 30

Abortifacient Effect of the IUD

Note: Baby is depicted at a more advanced stage of development in these diagrams to express the reality of its unique humanity.

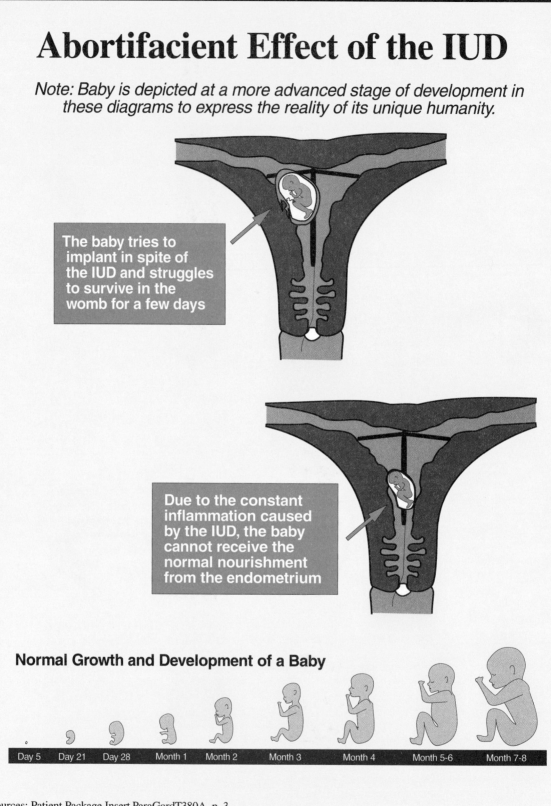

The baby tries to implant in spite of the IUD and struggles to survive in the womb for a few days

Due to the constant inflammation caused by the IUD, the baby cannot receive the normal nourishment from the endometrium

Normal Growth and Development of a Baby

| Day 5 | Day 21 | Day 28 | Month 1 | Month 2 | Month 3 | Month 4 | Month 5-6 | Month 7-8 |

Sources: Patient Package Insert ParaGardT380A, p. 3.
     Hatcher, et al., *Contraceptive Technology* (1994) p. 347.
     Personal Communication: Dr. John Brennan, M.D., Milwaukee, Wis.

Figure 31

Abortifacient Effect
of the IUD

Note: Baby is depicted at a more advanced stage of development in these diagrams to express the reality of its unique humanity.

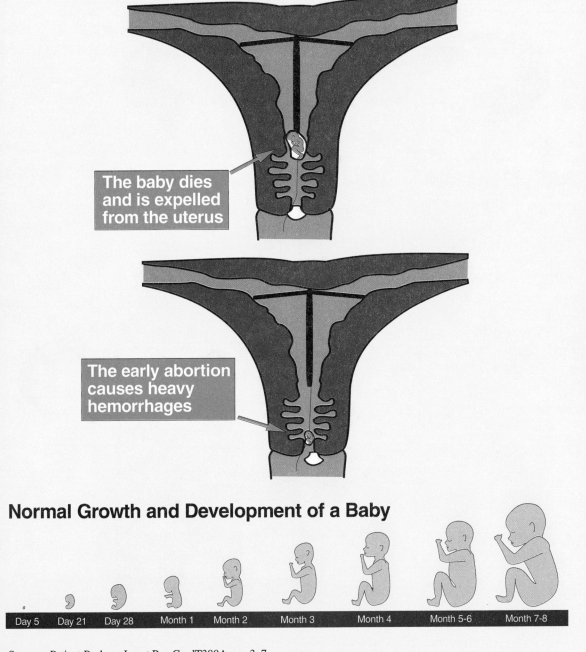

The baby dies and is expelled from the uterus

The early abortion causes heavy hemorrhages

Normal Growth and Development of a Baby

| Day 5 | Day 21 | Day 28 | Month 1 | Month 2 | Month 3 | Month 4 | Month 5-6 | Month 7-8 |

Sources: Patient Package Insert ParaGardT380A, pp. 3, 7.
　　　Hatcher et al., *Contraceptive Technology* (1994), pp. 347, 365-75.
　　　Personal Communication: Dr. John Brennan, M.D., Milwaukee, Wis.

© 1996 Family of the Americas

Figure 32

Complications of the Intrauterine Device (IUD)

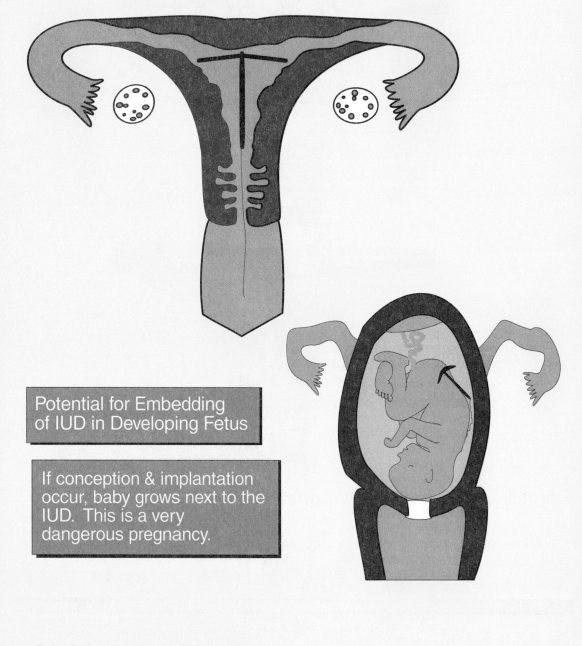

Potential for Embedding of IUD in Developing Fetus

If conception & implantation occur, baby grows next to the IUD. This is a very dangerous pregnancy.

Sources: Patient Package Insert ParaGardT380A, p. 10.
Hatcher et al., *Contraceptive Technology* (1994), pp. 370-73.
Personal Communication: Dr. John Brennan, M.D., Milwaukee, Wis.

© 1996 Family of the Americas

Figure 33

Fetal Growth with IUD in Place

Note: Baby may be depicted at a more advanced stage of development in these diagrams to express the reality of its unique humanity.

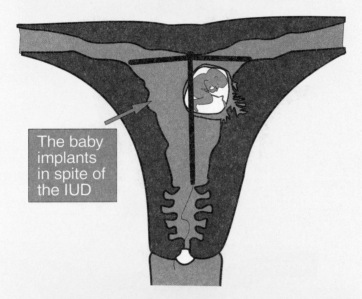

The baby implants in spite of the IUD

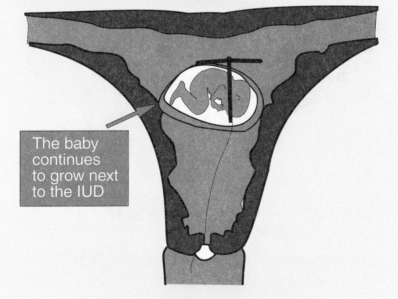

The baby continues to grow next to the IUD

Source: Personal Communication: Dr. John Brennan, M.D., Milwaukee, Wis.

Figure 34

IUD Endangers Growing Baby

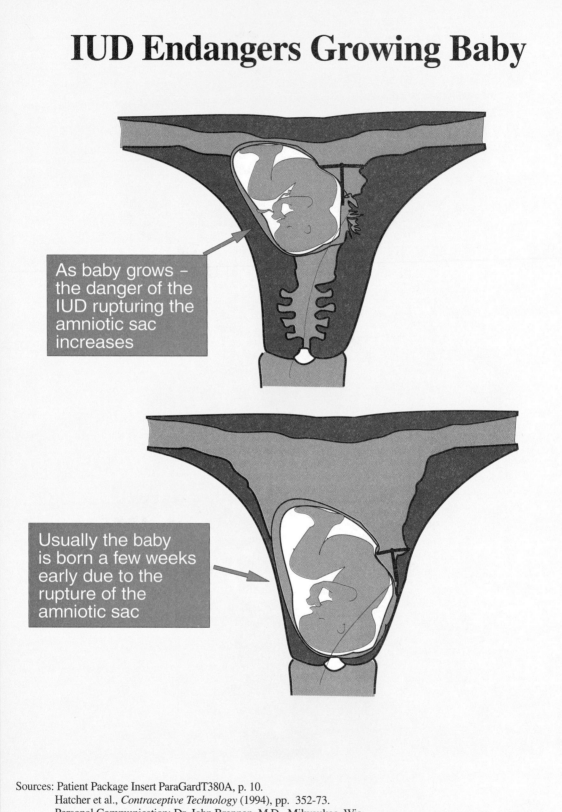

As baby grows – the danger of the IUD rupturing the amniotic sac increases

Usually the baby is born a few weeks early due to the rupture of the amniotic sac

Sources: Patient Package Insert ParaGardT380A, p. 10.
Hatcher et al., *Contraceptive Technology* (1994), pp. 352-73.
Personal Communication: Dr. John Brennan, M.D., Milwaukee, Wis.

Spermicides

I. Facts

A. available in many forms, including creams, jellies, suppositories, aerosol foam and foam tablets

B. only 74.8 percent effective

II. Mode of Action

Spermicides form a chemical barrier at the opening to the uterus that prevents sperm from reaching the egg in the uterus. Spermicides may also destroy or damage sperm.

III. Potential Side Effects

A. greater incidence of these congenital disorders in innocent children who are conceived during use of spermicides: Down's Syndrome, limb reduction malformations, malignant neoplasms (cancerous tissue growths) and severe hypospadias

B. increased chance of vaginal infections because absorption of spermicide alters vagina's normal chemical environment

C. possible link to increased risk of HIV[29]

---

[29] *1991 Progress Report*, Center for Population Research, National Institute of Child Health and Human Development (USA), p. 123: "[A] presentation at the Fifth International Conference on AIDS in 1989 reported that African prostitutes using a contraceptive sponge containing Nonoxynol-9 had an increased incidence of HIV infection. . . . [W]hether the increase was due to N-9, to the effect of the sponge as a foreign object or to some other factor is unknown. . . . It is possible that women who have high levels of sexual activity could develop abrasions from sponges and other vaginal inserts. If data from the sponge use [with spermicides] are correct, vaginal douching and diaphragm insertion might also offer some risk of increased HIV susceptibility."

Diaphragm

I. Facts

    A. flexible metal ring covered with rubber in shape of shallow dome

    B. only 84.1 percent effective

    C. risk of failure is increased when the user is less than thirty years old or has intercourse three times or more weekly[30]

II. Mode of Action

    A. placed in vagina to encircle the cervix completely and to prevent sperm from entering the uterus

    B. usually used with spermicidal jelly or cream applied to side of dome facing cervix

III. Potential Side Effects

    A. *New England Journal of Medicine* reports evidence of link between diaphragm use and toxic shock syndrome[31]

    B. local skin irritation caused by sensitivity or allergy

---

[30] Hatcher et al., *Contraceptive Technology*, p. 200.

[31] See also G. Faich, K. Pearson et al., "Toxic Shock Syndrome and the Vaginal Contraceptive Sponge," *Journal of the American Medical Association* 255 (1988): 216–18.

Sterilization (Female)

I. Facts

A. more or less irreversible technique for preventing conception

B. two types:

    1. tubal ligation or electrocoagulation, which seals off Fallopian tubes and prevents passage of eggs between ovaries and uterus (overall failure rate of .15 percent)

    2. hysterectomy, which removes uterus

II. Potential Side Effects

A. severe bleeding

B. pelvic infection

C. ectopic pregnancy (risk as much as three times higher)[32]

D. subsequent hysterectomy because of severe menstrual problems

E. death due to anesthesia, perforation of aorta, and bowel burns

F. post-operative depression

G. sexual dysfunction

H. risk of later desire for sterilization reversal

---

[32] Fleet et al., *British Journal of Obstetrics and Gynecology* 95 (August 1988): 740–46, as cited by Denis St. Marie in "Sterilization, Pervasive and Insidious." Also: "A three-fold increase in ectopic pregnancies was noted since 1970 with a rate of 6.4 per 1000 pregnancies."

I. women who have had tubal ligations report more cramping than they were accustomed to previously, and chances of pregnancy after tubal ligation are two to five percent

Sterilization (Male)

I. Facts

A. called vasectomy—virtually irreversible operation that removes a piece of both the left and the right vas deferens (tubes through which sperm travel from the testes to the prostate) and ties off ends

B. may not be effective for up to three months because of residual sperm cells

C. failure rate of .15 percent; recannulation (re-establishment of vas deferens by internal healing process) occurs in one case per one thousand

II. Potential Side Effects

A. Sperm production is same as before the procedure (about fifty thousand spermatozoa are produced every minute). However, sperm are not ejaculated, so they enter the bloodstream where antibodies are produced to remove the sperm from the bodily system. This can lead to thyroid and joint disorders, heart and circulatory diseases, and diabetes. When the body activates defenses to ward off cells of its own making, as after a vasectomy, the body becomes "auto-immune" (allergic to itself). Several studies have found such antibodies generated in response to sperm antigens in

55 to 75 percent of patients within two years after their vasectomies.[33]

B. Two studies in the United States have found that men with vasectomies have an 85–90 percent higher risk of being diagnosed later with prostate cancer than men who elect not to have the surgery.[34]

C. Psychological difficulties may develop, including anxiety and feelings of low self-worth and decreased sexual desire. A standard personality disorder test found that over 40 percent of one vasectomy study group experienced personality disturbances between their first testing and testing a year later, after the operation.[35]

D. There is an increased risk of kidney problems, including kidney stones.[36]

The only surgery that is done deliberately to destroy the natural functioning of sound, healthy organs, sterilization for birth control is an extreme act of self-mutilation that often has a profound negative effect on the personal relationship between husband and wife. Having made their love lifeless, sterilized couples deprive each other of the miraculous gift of combined fertility, a truly wonderful gift that would otherwise enable them to be co-creators with God in the conception of new life. That's certainly one way to take the "magic" out of one's marriage.

---

[33] "Sexual Sterilization: Some Questions and Answers," Couple to Couple League brochure, 1981.

[34] Giovannucci et al., *Journal of the American Medical Association*, February 16, 1993.

[35] St. Marie, "Sterilization."

[36] Kromal et al., *The Lancet* 1, no. 2 (1988), as cited by St. Marie, "Sterilization." A collaborative study of 11,205 men enrolled in a U.S. Coronary Artery Surgery Study found that the risk of kidney stones increased 2.6 times for men age 30–55 years; 1.3 times for those age 55–65. "There was a highly significant relation between vasectomy and renal disease."

Figure 35

The Most Widely Used Method of Birth Control in the U.S. Is Sterilization!

30% of women of fertile age who practice some form of birth control have been sterilized!

15% of men who practice some form of birth control have been sterilized!

Sources: U.S. National Center for Health Statistics, *New York Times*, Feb. 17, 1993.

Figure 36

Male and Female Sterilization

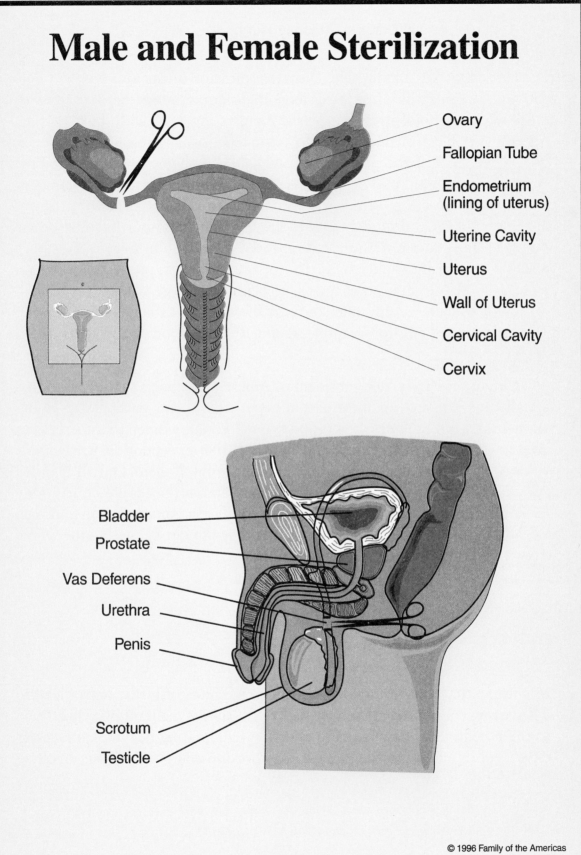

Ovary

Fallopian Tube

Endometrium
(lining of uterus)

Uterine Cavity

Uterus

Wall of Uterus

Cervical Cavity

Cervix

Bladder

Prostate

Vas Deferens

Urethra

Penis

Scrotum

Testicle

Patricia Pitkus Bainbridge, executive director of the anti-Planned Parenthood organization Life Decisions International, has been critical of those who withhold or downplay the dangers involved with the use of artificial methods of birth control. "A basic tenet of feminism is that women should have all of the information available to them to make decisions. Planned Parenthood and other like-minded organizations tend to limit information in an effort to sell women on the so-called benefits of artificial birth control." Bainbridge points to studies that link abortion and breast cancer as an example. "Planned Parenthood's reaction to numerous studies which demonstrate an increased risk for breast cancer, particularly when a woman aborts her first pregnancy, is to claim that more studies are needed. If, however, there is only one study to show a health benefit from taking the birth control pill, for example, Planned Parenthood accepts that as the definitive truth."[37]

Christopher P. Tyrrell, president of American Collegians for Life, is also appalled by the lack of information given to women, particularly young women: "Asking Planned Parenthood to tell young women that its services are dangerous to their minds and bodies is like expecting R. J. Reynolds voluntarily to tell its customers that smoking will kill them. Only if Planned Parenthood is forced to act will it take any action that could conceivably decrease its customer base." However, Tyrrell says young women and men are becoming increasingly suspicious that they are not being told the whole story by "family planning" organizations.[38]

Induced Abortion

It is fitting that our discussion of artificial methods of birth control lead to a discussion of abortion, because the contraceptive mentality (saying "No" to the potential for new life) and abortion (eliminating new life) are clearly entwined. In fact, according to the pro-abortion Alan Guttmacher Institute

---

[37] Patricia Pitkus Bainbridge, personal interview, May 8, 1996.

[38] Christopher P. Tyrrell, personal interview, May 8, 1996.

of the United States, 75 percent of all women who have abortions do so for reasons of "convenience," not health (only 7 percent).[39] Obviously, for many women, abortion is simply a "back up" to artificial birth control, which often fails.

I. Facts

A. all forms of induced abortion involve the premeditated killing of the unborn baby in the mother's womb

B. more than 1.5 million annually in the United States alone

C. estimated 36 million to 53 million abortions around the world annually[40]

II. Abortion Methods and Their Complications

A. Early Abortion

SUCTION or DILATION AND CURETTAGE (D&C)

Most abortions are done using these methods at around eleven to twelve weeks gestation. It is important to note that, as early as nine weeks, the unborn baby responds to touch and can feel pain. The fetal heart is beating, and eyes, fingers and toes are distinguishable.

In a suction abortion, the abortionist inserts a long hollow tube through the cervix and then, with powerful vacuum force, tears the placenta away from the uterine wall, dismembering the baby (fetus) and drawing his remains into an attached jar.

---

[39] Alan Guttmacher Institute, January 1993, as cited by Carolyn Hax, "No Birth, No Pangs," *The Washington Post*, March 21, 1993, p. C1.

[40] World Health Organization, "Reproductive Health, A Key to a Brighter Future," June 1992.

In a D&C, the abortionist inserts a loop-shaped knife into the mother's dilated cervix and by scraping the uterine wall, dismembers the baby (fetus). To ensure that the procedure is complete and no body parts remain in the womb (where they may cause infection), the abortionist or nurse must "reassemble" the fetal body to ensure that head, torso, and limbs are present. (A similar procedure, dilation and evacuation [D&E], "extends both the traditional D and C and the vacuum curettage into the second trimester. D and E is especially appropriate for procedures done in the range of 13–16 weeks gestation, although many proponents use this method up through 20+ weeks.")[41]

Complications include:

- laceration of cervix by suction apparatus or knife

- hemorrhage

- perforated uterus

- laceration of urinary bladder and ureters

- pulmonary embolism (air bubble in bloodstream)

- laceration of bowel and subsequent infection

- shock

- reactions to anesthesia, including bronchial obstruction, anaphylactic shock, and cardiac arrest

- reaction to blood transfusion

- laparotomy (surgical section of abdominal wall)

- hysterectomy

- retained tissue

---

[41] Hatcher et al., *Contraceptive Technology*, p. 451.

- death of mother
- much higher risk of developing breast cancer[42]

Susanne Logan, a Maryland woman who won a $2.6 million lawsuit against her local clinic for a botched abortion, died in December 1992.[43] About the same time, nineteen-year-old DaNette Ferguson died during an elective abortion in Arizona. These women are but two of the many who have been victimized by supporters of so-called "safe, legal abortion."

B. Late Abortion

SALINE

After sixteen weeks, the baby (fetus) is too large to be killed by the procedures mentioned above, so abortionists resort to saline injection (salt poisoning). It is important to note that, since eleven weeks gestation, all of the baby's organs have been complete and functioning. At sixteen weeks, medical photographers and ultra-sonographers have pictured unborn babies kicking and swimming —even sucking their thumbs. Shockingly, according to the U.S. Centers for Disease Control and Prevention, more than 77,000 American babies are aborted each year at this age or older.

In a saline abortion, the abortionist inserts a long needle through the mother's abdomen, siphons off some of the amniotic fluid that protects the baby and replaces that amount with a saline (salt) solution that both poisons the baby as he swallows and burns away his skin. The mother goes into labor and delivers a dead infant.

---

[42] Women who abort their first pregnancy almost double their chance of developing breast cancer. *The Deadly After-Effect of Abortion—Breast Cancer*, pamphlet published by Hayes Publishing Co., Cincinnati, Ohio.

[43] "Botched-Abortion Victim Dies in Baltimore," *The Washington Times*, December 2, 1992, p. B2.

Complications include:

- transplacental hemorrhage
- reactions to anesthesia
- hypernatremia
- edema (swelling) of brain
- convulsions
- coma
- kidney failure
- heart failure
- failure to abort after death of baby
- baby born alive and badly burned

(In 1990, seventeen-year-old Tralisha Nicole Gillespie sued a Nashville abortion clinic after the procedure failed, and she gave birth prematurely to an infant girl of twenty-six weeks gestation.)[44]

Similar to saline abortions are those by the injection of prostaglandins (powerful hormones that induce violent labor and premature birth). Abortionists may inject toxin to kill the baby first. "Clinicians are performing an increasing percentage of second trimester instillation abortions by combinations of the just described methods."[45]

---

[44] "Abortion Clinic Sued after Teen Has Baby," *The Washington Times*, January 12, 1990.

[45] Hatcher et al., *Contraceptive Technology*, p. 453.

C. Late Abortion

HYSTEROTOMY

Similar to a cesarean section, this late-term form of abortion involves removal of the baby from the uterus. The child is killed or left to die.

Complications include:

- hemorrhage
- reaction to blood transfusion
- reaction to anesthesia
- hysterectomy
- high mortality rate for mothers

D. RU-486

Also known as the "abortion pill," RU-486 actually involves a cumbersome and expensive four-step regimen that includes the taking of several powerful drugs and at least four visits to the abortionist.

Janice Raymond, self-proclaimed "feminist" and associate director of the Institute on Women and Technology at MIT, says, "Claims that RU 486 abortion is private and demedicalized are belied by the number of medical visits and the whole drug cocktail a woman may be exposed to."[46]

---

[46] Susan Ince, "The Trouble with RU 486," *Vogue*, July 1991, p. 88.

By preventing the action of progesterone in the womb, RU-486 works as an abortifacient for the first eight to ten weeks after conception. RU-486 is used with prostaglandins (misoprostol) to increase lethality.

Complications include:

- nausea

- vomiting

- diarrhea

- severe and sometimes prolonged bleeding (in some women, even two months after discontinuance)[47]

- failure to expel baby (this happens in one out of every twenty cases,[48] so another method of abortion is sought)

- cardiovascular shock

- maternal death[49]

---

[47] "In a recent clinical study in Britain, five hundred eighty-eight women were given abortions with RU-486 combined with the prostaglandin gemeprost. Five of the women bled so much that they required transfusions. One hundred sixty-six of them needed narcotics to ease the pain. . . . Thirty five failed to abort and had to undergo a follow-up surgical procedure. And together they averaged more than twenty days of heavy bleeding afterwards." George Grant, *The Quick and the Dead: RU-486 and the New Chemical Warfare against Your Family* (Wheaton, Ill.: Good News Publishers, 1991), p. 50. Cites August 1991 issue of the *American Druggist*.

[48] Grant, *Quick and the Dead*, p. 53.

[49] Ibid., p. 51. When the first maternal deaths were reported in 1991, the French Ministry of Health devised stringent new regulations for the use of RU-486.

E. PROSTAGLANDIN-INDUCED ABORTION

As mentioned under entry for saline abortion and RU-486, prostaglandins are powerful hormones that induce violent contractions of the womb and expulsion of the baby.

Complications include:

- retained fetal tissue
- readmission for surgery
- septicemia (massive infection)
- pelvic inflammatory disease
- peritonitis
- blood dyscrasias—afibrinogenanemia (failure of blood to clot)
- bleeding
- lung abscess (aspiration of vomitus during anesthesia)
- deep vein thrombosis
- death of mother
- Post-Abortion Syndrome

F. DILATION AND EXTRACTION (D&X)

Developed by an abortionist who notes that "most surgeons find [fetal] dismemberment at 20 weeks and beyond to be difficult due to the toughness of fetal tissues at this stage," D&X requires the mother's cervix to be dilated and the placenta (bag of waters) to be broken. The abortionist's assistant then uses ultrasound to scan the mother's abdomen and to locate the lower extremities of the unborn baby. Using forceps, the abortionist pulls the baby, by its legs, down into the vagina. The abortionist uses his hands to pull the fetal arms and shoulders from the womb and to turn the baby on his or her stomach. The baby's head, which is too large to pass through, remains lodged at the cervix. Holding sharp, curved scissors, the abortionist follows the curve of the fetal spine to find the base of the skull. "He then forces the scissors into the base of the skull. Having entered the skull he then spreads the scissors to enlarge the opening. He then removes the scissors and introduces a suction catheter into the hole and evacuates the skull contents." Once the skull is empty, it is more readily crushed, enabling the baby's body to be removed entirely from his or her mother. This is the D&X procedure as described by Ohio abortionist Martin Haskell, who claims to have performed more than seven hundred such procedures in his two offices.[50] Some two hundred of these procedures are done each year in the state of Ohio alone.

In September, 1993 Brenda Pratt Shafer, a registered nurse with thirteen years of experience, was assigned by her nursing agency to an abortion clinic. Since Nurse Shafer considered herself "very pro-choice," she didn't think this assignment would be a problem. She was wrong.

This is what Nurse Shafer saw:

> I stood at the doctor's side and watched him perform a partial-birth abortion on a woman who was six months pregnant. The baby's heartbeat was clearly visible on the ultrasound screen. The doctor delivered the baby's body and arms, everything but his little head. The baby's body was moving. His little fingers were clasping together. He was kicking his feet. The doctor took a pair

---

[50] Dr. Martin Haskell, paper presented at the National Abortion Federation Risk Management Seminar, Dallas, Texas, September 13, 1992. Several states, including Ohio, and at least one U.S. Congressional Representative have drafted legislation that, if enacted and enforced, would prohibit these partial-birth killings.

of scissors and inserted them into the back of the baby's head, and the baby's arms jerked out in a flinch, a startle reaction, like a baby does when he thinks that he might fall. Then the doctor opened the scissors up. Then he stuck the high-powered suction tube into the hole and sucked the baby's brains out. Now the baby was completely limp.

I never went back to the clinic. But I am still haunted by the face of that little boy. It was the most perfect, angelic face I have ever seen.

The "Partial Birth Abortion" Bill, which would have made this technique illegal, was vetoed by President Clinton on April 10, 1996.

III. Effects of Abortion on Subsequent Childbearing

- potential sterility
- 50 percent increase in spontaneous miscarriage
- 200 percent increase in ectopic pregnancy

All forms of abortion may include a reaction to or admission of participation in death of one's own infant. This may manifest itself as severe and prolonged depression, mourning, sense of loss (sometimes delayed for years), plus:

- 40 percent increase in mental retardation among children
- prolonged labor
- rupture of uterine scar (post-hysterectomy)
- development of Rh antibodies in Rh-negative mother
- cervical incompetence (after early abortions) resulting in miscarriages

Figure 37

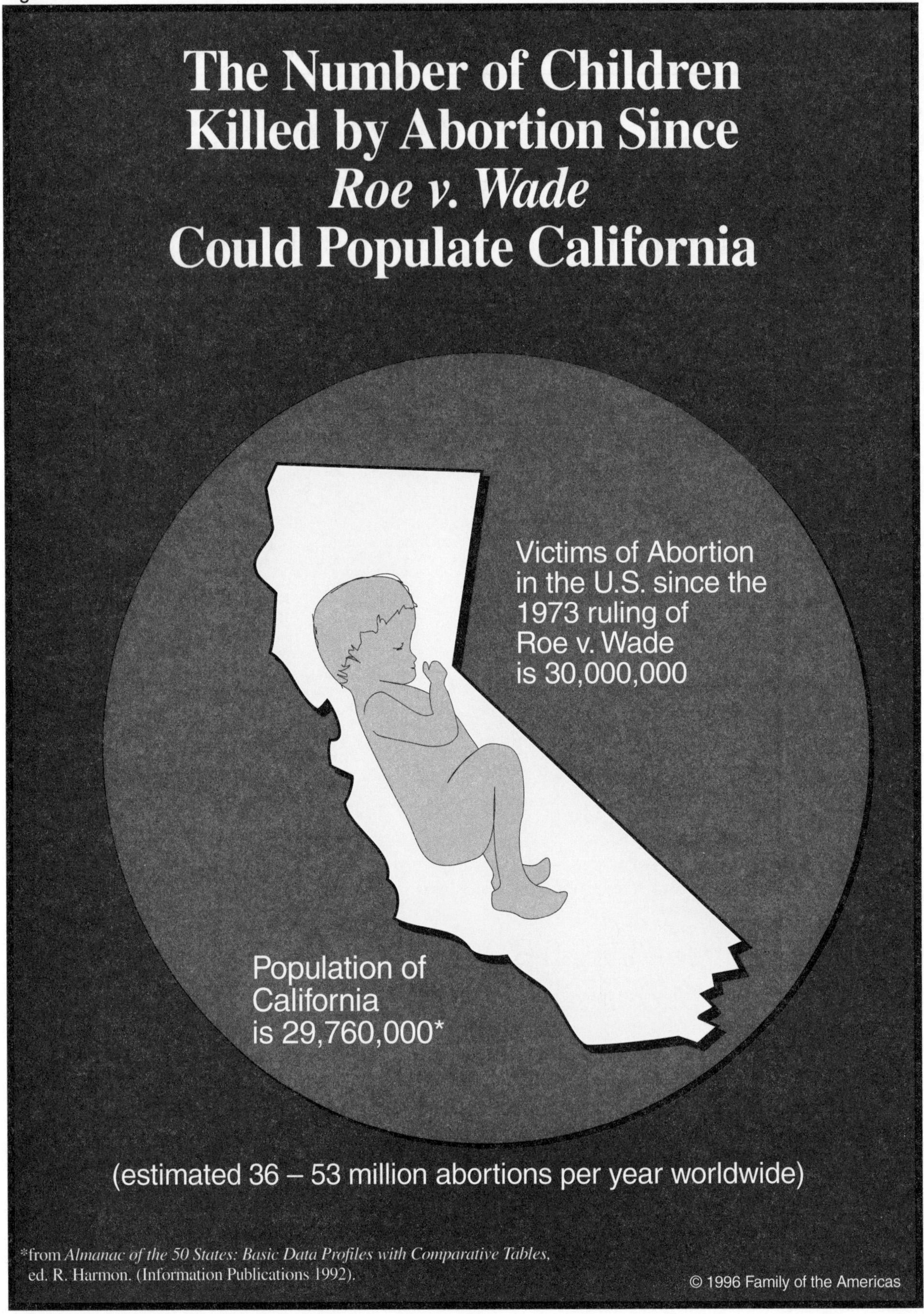
The Number of Children
Killed by Abortion Since
Roe v. Wade
Could Populate California
Victims of Abortion
in the U.S. since the
1973 ruling of
Roe v. Wade
is 30,000,000
Population of
California
is 29,760,000*
(estimated 36 – 53 million abortions per year worldwide)
*from *Almanac of the 50 States: Basic Data Profiles with Comparative Tables*, ed. R. Harmon. (Information Publications 1992).
© 1996 Family of the Americas

Figure 38

36-53 Million Babies Aborted Every Year throughout the World

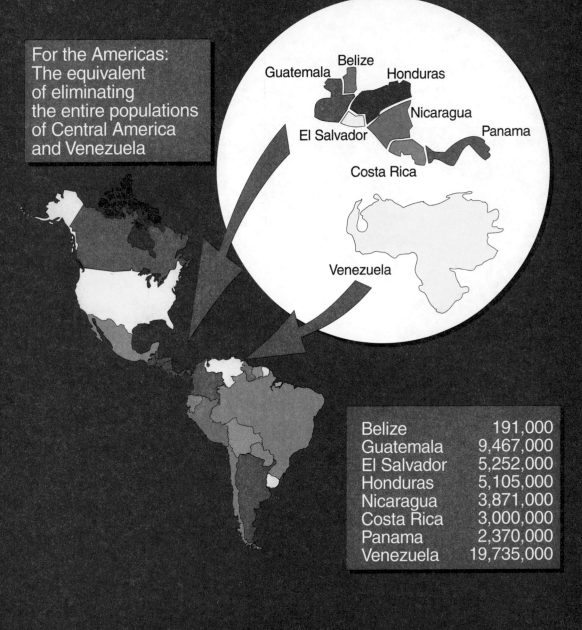

For the Americas:
The equivalent
of eliminating
the entire populations
of Central America
and Venezuela

Belize	191,000
Guatemala	9,467,000
El Salvador	5,252,000
Honduras	5,105,000
Nicaragua	3,871,000
Costa Rica	3,000,000
Panama	2,370,000
Venezuela	19,735,000

Sources: 1993 *Whitaker's Almanac* (London: J. Whitaker & Sons). 1991 *U.N. Demographic Year Book.*

Figure 39

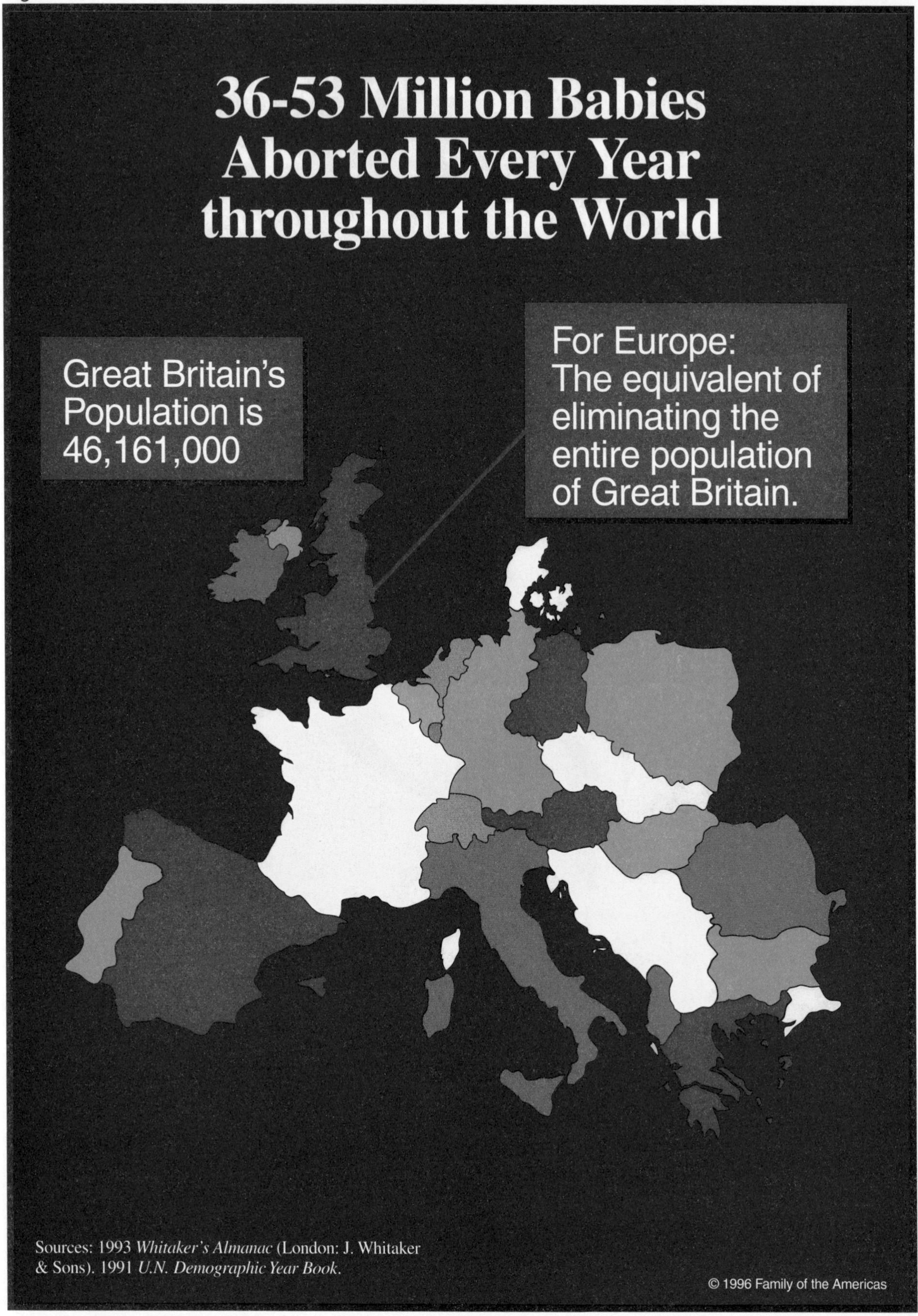

36-53 Million Babies Aborted Every Year throughout the World

Great Britain's Population is 46,161,000

For Europe: The equivalent of eliminating the entire population of Great Britain.

Sources: 1993 *Whitaker's Almanac* (London: J. Whitaker & Sons). 1991 *U.N. Demographic Year Book*.

© 1996 Family of the Americas

Figure 40

36-53 Million Babies Aborted Every Year throughout the World

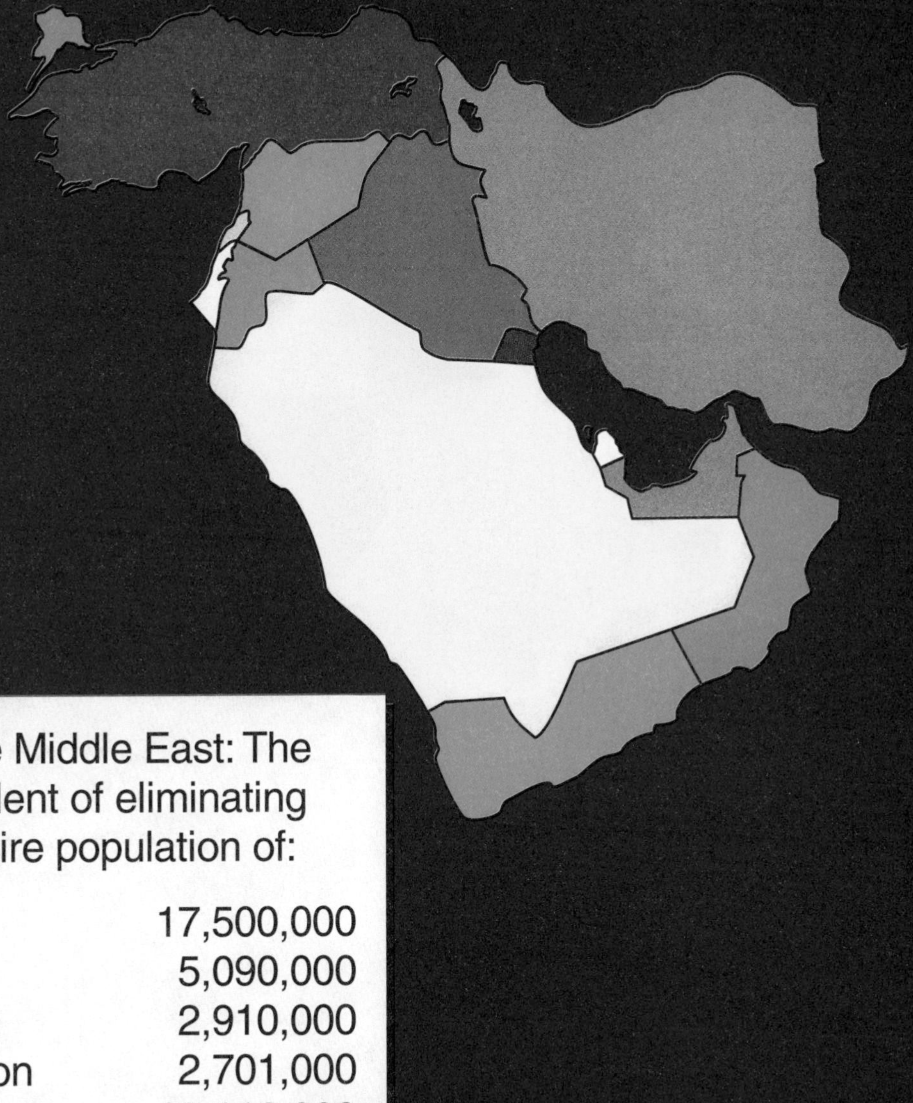

For the Middle East: The equivalent of eliminating the entire population of:

Iraq	17,500,000
Israel	5,090,000
Jordan	2,910,000
Lebanon	2,701,000
Syria	12,116,000
Saudi Arabia	14,870,000

Sources: 1993 *Whitaker's Almanac* (London: J. Whitaker & Sons). 1991 *U.N. Demographic Year Book*.

Figure 41

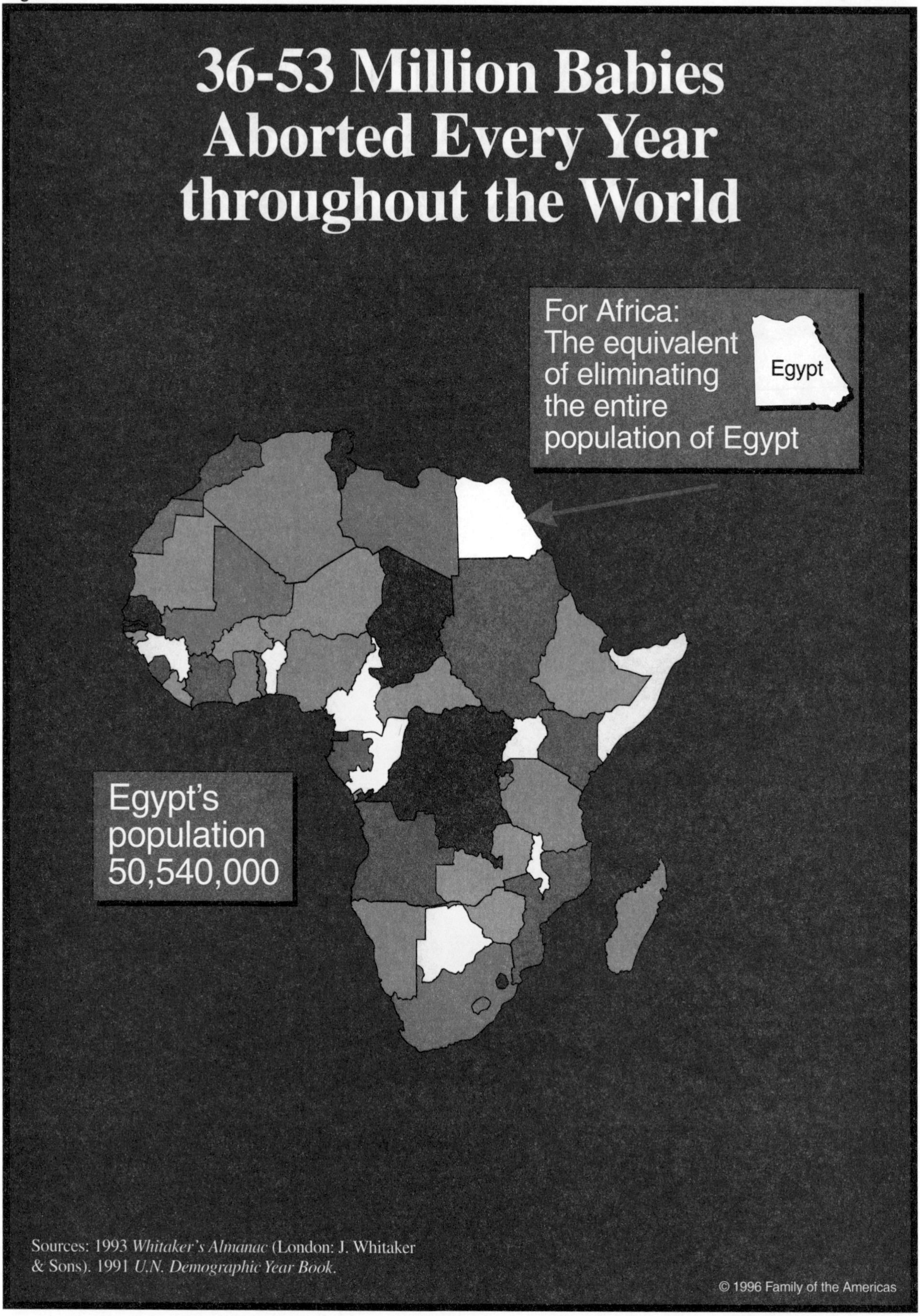
36-53 Million Babies Aborted Every Year throughout the World
For Africa:
The equivalent of eliminating the entire population of Egypt
Egypt
Egypt's population 50,540,000
Sources: 1993 Whitaker's Almanac (London: J. Whitaker & Sons). 1991 U.N. Demographic Year Book.
© 1996 Family of the Americas

Figure 42

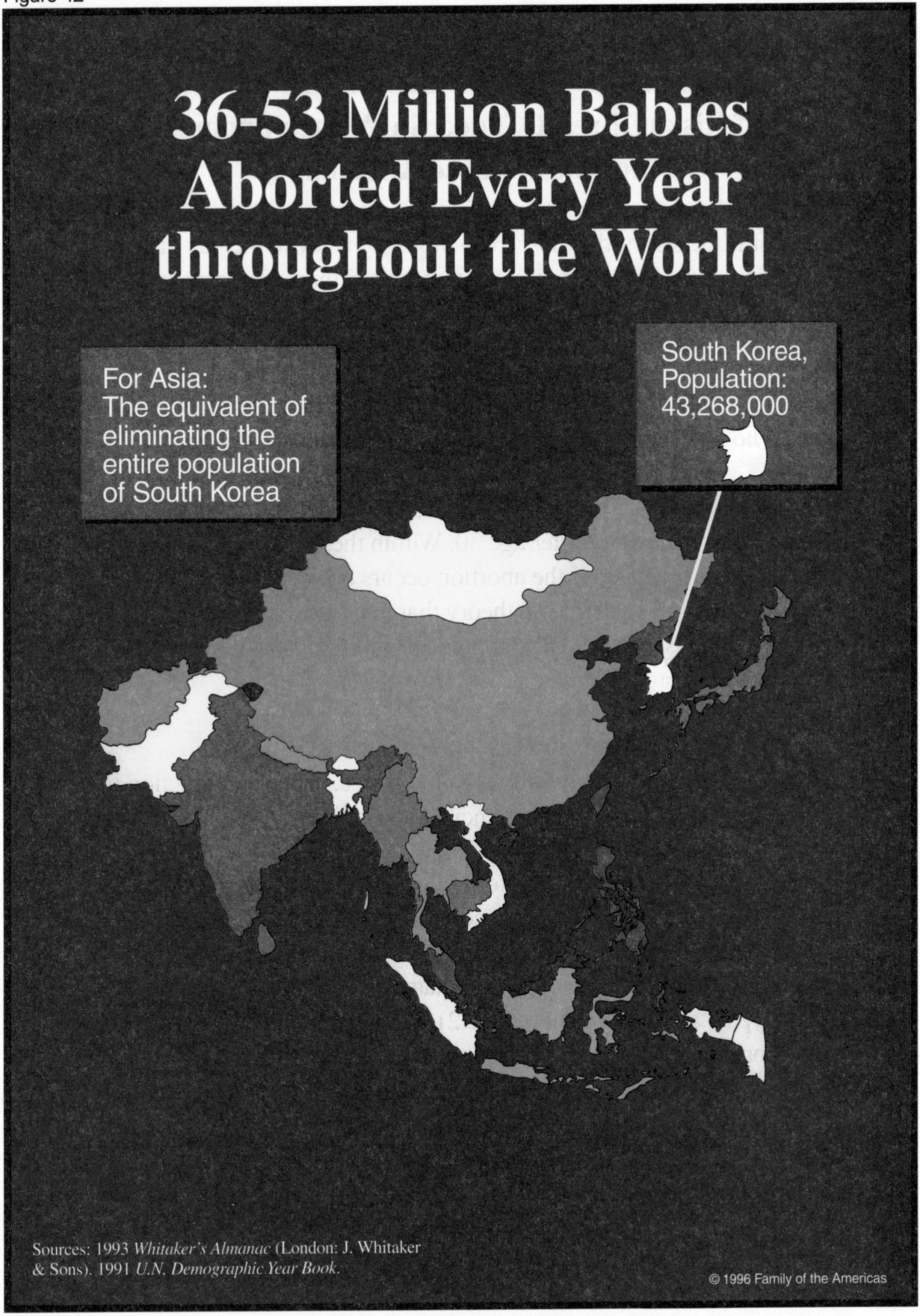
36-53 Million Babies Aborted Every Year throughout the World
For Asia: The equivalent of eliminating the entire population of South Korea
South Korea, Population: 43,268,000
Sources: 1993 *Whitaker's Almanac* (London: J. Whitaker & Sons). 1991 *U.N. Demographic Year Book.*
© 1996 Family of the Americas

Figure 43

Introduction to the National Cancer Institute Funded Study of Risk of Breast Cancer in Women under Age 45 Who Had Induced Abortion(s)

The breast is the site of the most frequent malignancy in the human female population. Breast cancer is the second in mortality (cancer deaths in women). A woman's risk of breast cancer is influenced by her reproductive history.

Researchers at the Fred Hutchinson Cancer Center in Seattle found that women who had been pregnant at least once and who had had an abortion face a 50% greater risk of developing breast cancer than those who had never had an abortion. The risk was highest among those who had abortions before age 18 or after age 30. Within these two groups, the risk of breast cancer increases if the abortion occurs between the eighth and twelfth weeks of pregnancy. The theory that this study supports is that the link between breast cancer risk and induced abortion is due to differentiation in breast lobular structures.

The mammary gland seems to be the only organ that is not fully developed at birth. It changes dramatically in size, shape and function in response to growth, puberty, pregnancy and lactation.

It is known that women with a history of early, full-term pregnancy are at lower risk for developing breast cancer than those who have never had a child. Differentiation of breast structures has been credited with this protective effect since carcinomas originate in undifferentiated cells (Lobule type 1 and, on occasion, type 2). When pregnancy is terminated by abortion, cell differentiation does not occur, thus increasing the number of cells susceptible to cancer-causing agents. When abortion takes place prior to the second trimester, cells have not yet progressed to Lobule 3 stage. Undifferentiated Lobule types 1 and 2 predominate, increasing the possibility of tumors.

Source: *Journal of the National Cancer Institute*, 86, no. 21 (November 2, 1994).
The Houston Chronicle, October 26, 1994, p.10A, by Tom Paulson, *Seattle Post-Intelligence.*

Figure 44

Risk of Breast Cancer among Young Women: Relationship to Induced Abortion

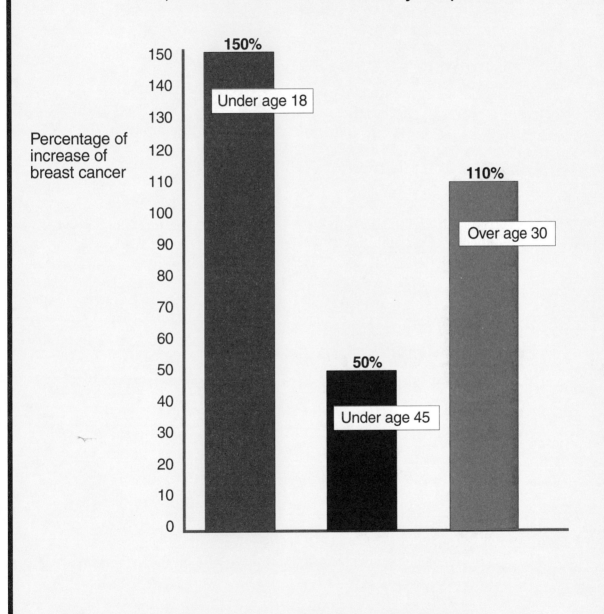

According to a National Cancer Institute Study
of 1,800 women over a seven-year period.

Source: *Journal of the National Cancer Institute*, 86, no. 21 (November 2, 1994).
The Houston Chronicle, October 26, 1994, p.10A, by Tom Paulson, *Seattle Post-Intelligence.*

Figure 45

Female Breast
Developmental Stages (Lobules)

 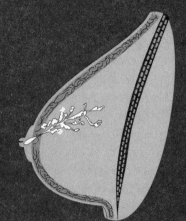

Lobule Type 1
The most undifferentiated.
Predominates in immature
female breast before menarche
and in women who have never
been pregnant.

Lobule Type 2
Evolves from type 1 and is
more structurally complex.

Lobule Type 3
Frequently seen in breasts of
pregnant women and is much
more specialized.

Lobule Type 4
The most differentiated.
Present in breasts of
lactating women.

Sources: "Review: Human Papillomaviruses and Cervical Neoplasia," *Cancer Epidemiology,
Biomarkers & Prevention* 3 (June 1994): 353; *Clinical Symposia* 37, no. 1 (1985).

Figure 46

Anatomy of the Adult Female Breast

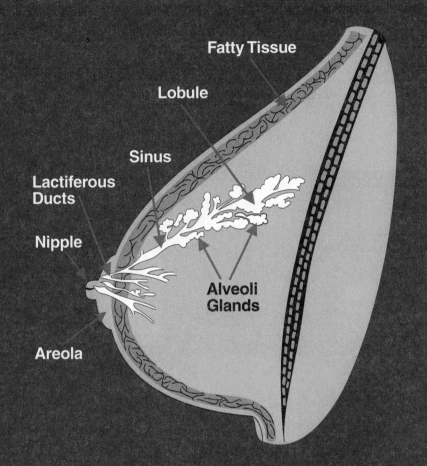

Fatty Tissue

Lobule

Sinus

Lactiferous Ducts

Nipple

Alveoli Glands

Areola

The physiology of the human breast has been a major biological puzzle. This is mainly due to the fact that the composition or make-up of the mammary gland changes many times during the development of a woman from child to adult. No other organ presents such dramatic changes in size, shape and function as does the breast during growth, puberty, menstrual cycles, pregnancy, and lactation.

Sources: "Review: Human Papillomaviruses and Cervical Neoplasia," *Cancer Epidemiology, Biomarkers & Prevention* 3 (June 1994): 358; *Clinical Symposia* 37, no. 1 (1985).

Figure 47

Life Cycle of the Breast of the Parous Woman

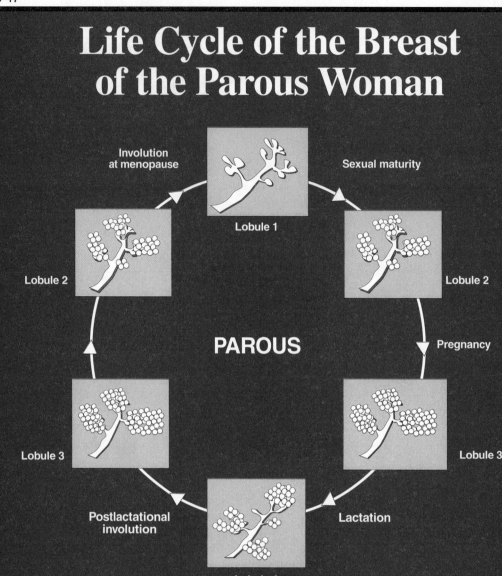

Involution at menopause

Sexual maturity

Lobule 1

Lobule 2

Lobule 2

PAROUS

Pregnancy

Lobule 3

Lobule 3

Postlactational involution

Lactation

Lobule 4

The breast undergoes a complete cycle of development through the formation of lobules types 1 to 4 (with pregnancy and lactation) which later regress, or involute, to lobules types 2 and 1. Steps in development are:

Lobule 1 to 2 - growth of immature cells

Pregnancy to Lobule 4 - differentiation

Lobule 4 to 2 (regressing) - milk-producing cells die

Note: Cells that the body produces for lactation during pregnancy die when no longer needed. Some pre-cancerous cells are naturally killed during involution.

Sources: "Review: Human Papillomaviruses and Cervical Neoplasia," *Cancer Epidemiology, Biomarkers & Prevention* 3 (June 1994): 359.

Figure 48

Life Cycle of the Breast of the Nulliparous Woman

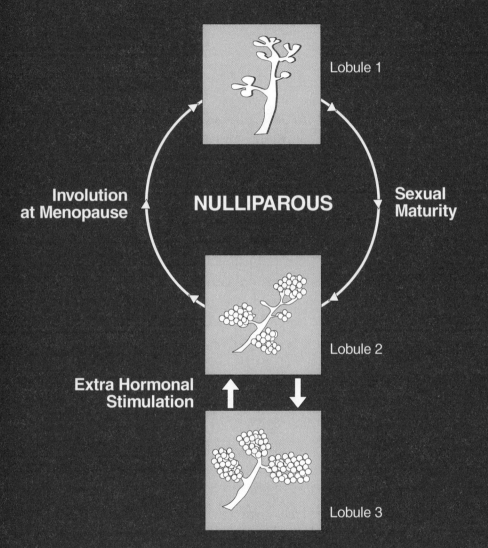

The breast is primarily composed of lobules type 1 with some progression to type 2. Lobule type 2 is where the breast undergoes the most development and cancer risk is highest. There is only minimal formation of lobules type 3 during sexual maturity, which involute (regress) to lobule type 1 at menopause.

Sources: "Review: Human Papillomaviruses and Cervical Neoplasia," *Cancer Epidemiology, Biomarkers & Prevention* 3 (June 1994): 357

IV. Abortion on Demand = Supply of Human Flesh for Fetal Tissue Research

As gruesome as that may sound, some members of the scientific community are eager to profit by the deaths of unborn babies.

In one of his first official actions, President Bill Clinton of the United States lifted the Federal Government's existing ban against scientific research using tissues obtained from babies killed by induced abortion. Such research has been fueled by claims that injecting fetal cells into the brains of persons suffering from Parkinson's disease has helped to alleviate patients' symptoms. According to a letter written by Professor Linda Gourash:

> The 1989 *Archives of Neurology* published the most detailed description of this procedure, outlining that an unborn baby's brain must be selectively sucked out by a tube inserted in the mother's womb to ensure that the living fetal brain cells are harvested in fresh transplantable condition. This process kills the fetus, who is then aborted.[51]

Now we hear news from Edinburgh, Scotland, that researchers are working to perfect a process whereby eggs from aborted baby girls could be implanted in living women in order help them achieve a pregnancy.

In an editorial for *The Catholic World Report*, Philip F. Lawler writes:

> Having severed the link between the process of reproduction and the act of marital love, the researchers are now laboriously trying to patch together their own artificial sequence of causes and effects. And like simple children with a complicated jigsaw puzzle, they can't fit the pieces together properly.
>
> During the past decade, scientists have made enormous strides in understanding the process of human reproduction; yet the incidence of sterility has reached unprecedented levels. From their earliest days of school, youngsters are taught how to avoid sexually transmitted dis-

---

[51] Linda Gourash, M.D., "Letters," *The Washington Post*, May 31, 1991, p. A18.

eases; yet epidemics of those diseases are ripping through our society. Pharmacists offer a bewildering array of devices to thwart the process of conception; yet "unplanned" pregnancies are soaring out of control. And now the good doctors of Edinburgh offer the ghoulish promise that while we butcher unborn children in the womb, we might yet raise up healthy lives from their dismembered corpses![52]

Presumably, as with other fetal tissue uses, these egg cells would have to be harvested while the soon-to-be aborted baby is still alive.

Lawler continues:

For millennia, the process of pregnancy was expected to flow naturally out of an act of love. And lo and behold, that natural system usually worked without a flaw, without any wizard's intervention. Oh, there have always been those who sought to thwart that process; the "magicians" were at work even in the days of ancient Israel. But until this brave new century, their enterprises were generally recognized as perversions.

Through all those millennia, a young woman knew that she could bear a child if she made one loving act of self-giving. For fashionable women today pregnancy involves two more careful calculations: the decision to eschew contraceptives, then the decision to forego an abortion. And for increasing numbers of women—thanks to modern science—pregnancy can occur without that self-surrender. A child born today has no guarantee that his life began with an act of love.

If life is a gift, how can we snatch it away from the baby girl who was aborted to start this whole process? If every birth in effect justifies itself, should we churn out as many children as possible, by every means at our disposal, fair or foul? And if an act can be justified simply because it brings happiness to someone, are any moral restraints intact?[53]

As another observer puts it, "Common sense tells us that dead tissue is not useful for human transplantation. Have you ever heard of someone

---

[52] Philip F. Lawler, "Poverty of Love, Poverty of Logic: The Moral Bankruptcy of Bioengineering Is Matched by the Ethical Reasoning that Supports It," *The Catholic World Report*, February 1994, p. 1.

[53] Ibid.

getting a kidney or other organ that was transplanted from a cadaver? No, tissue for transplantation must be *living*. . . . Doctors must extract living tissue, which, consequently, tortures and kills the [unborn] child."[54]

How could any scientist rationalize such macabre acts? Incredibly, some try. "Abortion is a tragedy," says one transplant researcher, "but as long as it occurs, I believe it is immoral to let tissues and materials go to waste."[55] Surprisingly, a self-proclaimed "pro-choice," "feminist" university professor, Janice Raymond of the University of Massachusetts and Massachusetts Institute of Technology (MIT), was among those who echoed the Bopp and Burtchaell warning that fetal transplants would increase abortions and, she added, make women mere factories for medical experiments: "Women become the resources whose bodies are mined for scientific gold."[56]

---

[54] Kate Wolf, "Fetal Tissue Research," February 1993 newsletter of A-A-A Women for Choice (Manassas, Va.).

[55] Dr. Eugene Redmond, Jr., director of Yale Medical School's neurobehavioral laboratory, in *The New York Times*, March 15, 1988, as cited by James Bopp, Jr., and James T. Burtchaell in "Fetal Tissue Transplantation: The Fetus as Medical Commodity," statement of dissent to the Report of the Human Fetal Tissue Transplantation Research Panel of the National Institutes of Health, December 1988.

[56] Professor Janice Raymond of MIT, testimony before a Congressional subcommittee hearing on fetal tissue transplantation research, 1991, as reported in *The Washington Times*, January 6, 1992. For additional reading on human fetal tissue transplantation, see "Cures from the Womb," *Newsweek*, February 22, 1993.

CHAPTER SIXTEEN

Venereal Diseases, Infections and AIDS: The "Safe Sex" Lie

No culture endures forever: Of those that have vanished . . . most have expired in consequence of internal decay.

Russell Kirk
America's British Culture

In addition to knowing the truth about the devastating consequences of abortion and artificial contraception, your children *must* be aware of the dangerous infectious diseases that can be transmitted through sexual contact. Many of these diseases have reached epidemic levels. Sexually transmitted diseases (also known as venereal infections/diseases) include those that have been known for many years, such as gonorrhea and syphilis. Yet insidious diseases such as acquired immunodeficiency syndrome and genital herpes are now common as well. "[T]hirty years ago, there were five clinically apparent venereal diseases. At present there are more than fifty disease entities caused by at least twenty microorganisms or viruses that are transmitted to sexual associates during intercourse and to babies during pregnancy or childbirth."[1]

Obviously, the more sexual partners, the more promiscuously a person behaves, the greater the risk of contracting one or more forms of vene-

---

[1] Robert G. Marshall and Charles A. Donovan, *Blessed Are the Barren* (San Francisco: Ignatius Press, 1991), p. 313.

real disease. The toll among young people is particularly tragic. Sexually transmitted diseases affect some eight million young Americans annually. In fact, as we noted earlier in this book, some 66 percent of all STD cases occur among persons who are less than twenty-five years of age. According to the United States Centers for Disease Control and Prevention, in 1992 more than fifty thousand young Americans between the ages of thirteen and twenty-nine were reported to have AIDS.[2]

The consequences of sexually transmitted diseases are disastrous, particularly for women. Many STDs can cause irreparable damage to the reproductive system.[3] *Moreover, there is no cure for AIDS, and the disease is always fatal.*

Beware: STDs are contagious even when no outward symptoms are noted, and many new strains of STDs are resistant to treatment. Moreover, teens are much more susceptible to STD damage because they have on average a lower level of antibodies than do adults.

In addition to threatening the physical well-being of men and women, sexually transmitted diseases also inflict great emotional and psychological harm, including loss of self-respect and withdrawal from others. The cost to entire nations in terms of lost productivity and health care expenses is staggering—in the billions of dollars each year.

Obviously, money for research on AIDS and and other sexually transmitted diseases is needed. (The amount of money needed is, of course, open to debate, but the fact is that in 1991 more than $4.3 billion was spent on AIDS research in the United States alone—ten times more per patient than

---

[2] U.S. Centers for Disease Control and Prevention, "HIV/AIDS Surveillance Report" 5, no. 1 (May 1993): 11. The current epidemics of AIDS and sexually transmitted diseases might well be considered the "dual dangers" of early/promiscuous sexual behavior: "According to the World Health Organization, diseases such as gonorrhea, genital herpes, syphilis and other sexually transmitted diseases, which weaken immune defenses, as well as ulcerative lesions of the genitals, increase the likelihood of infection with the AIDS virus by 300 percent." Mariano Yee Melgar, M.D., "AIDS-Reality and Prevention," *Siglo Veintiuno* (Guatemala), December 9, 1992.

[3] According to the World Health Organization, there are more than 60 million infertile couples around the globe. It is not surprising that world fertility rates have dropped dramatically in recent years, considering the devastating toll that abortion, sexually transmitted diseases, and artificial methods of birth control have taken on the reproductive health of women.

was spent on cancer.)[4] However, the epidemic of AIDS and other sexually transmitted diseases will never be conquered by research alone. There *must* be a return to high standards of sexual morality in society as a whole. Natural laws not only account for the breathtaking order and beauty in our universe but also protect us from harm—physical, emotional and spiritual. Early sexual activity, sex with multiple partners, the practice of sodomy and so forth—these and other violations of Natural Law (what America's Founders reverently called "the laws of Nature and of Nature's God")— threaten individuals, families, nations and generations to come. As noted early in Chapter 2, it is not true that people are free to do whatever they want in the privacy of their own homes, as though "unseen" behavior did not affect others. Be it illicit sexual activity or drug use, such behavior undermines the dignity and self-control of the individuals involved and, when such behavior leads to the transmission of HIV or some other sexually transmitted disease, taxpayers often end up sharing the bill through increased health care costs. Dr. Siegfried Ernst adds:

> One thing should be clear to even the simplest person: it is senseless to proclaim an absence of [absolute] standards governing the most intimate and closest human relations—between man and woman, and also between parents and children—and yet at the same time to demand fixed behavioral norms for the bigger social organisms or, in fact, absolute "justice" among peoples, classes and races. Despite peace marches and peace councils, peace will remain a total illusion until we end the war between man and woman and against children, the war resulting from the sexual revolution.[5]

---

[4] White House press release, August 19, 1992, text of address by President George Bush to the Republican National Committee, Houston, Texas.

[5] Dr. Siegfried Ernst, *Is Humanae Vitae Outdated?* (Gaithersburg, Md.: Human Life International, 1990), p. 7.

AIDS (Acquired Immunodeficiency Syndrome)

I. Facts

A. AIDS is caused by the human immunodeficiency virus, present in bodily fluids including blood, semen and vaginal discharge.

B. High-risk groups are male homosexuals (originally, some 73 percent of all cases appeared among gay men; HIV transmitted essentially by sodomy); now, an increasing percentage of cases result from intravenous injections (drug addicts sharing needles). Also contracted via heterosexual intercourse with an infected individual; and more rarely, from transfusions of infected blood or being born to an infected mother.

C. HIV is transmitted primarily by persons who show no outward symptoms (*before* AIDS fully develops). Infected individuals may be asymptomatic for as long as ten years, during which time they may feel well and exhibit little presence of the virus in the bloodstream—thereby posing a risk of spreading the disease, unknowingly, to others.[6]

D. AIDS is incurable and *always* fatal.

E. The U.S. Centers for Disease Control and Prevention estimates there are now at least 1 to 1.5 million cases of HIV infection in the United States (one in 250 Americans); World Health Organization estimates some ten million cases worldwide.

F. HIV is 500 times smaller than the human sperm.

---

[6] William A. Haseltine, Ph.D., "The Future of AIDS," speech delivered at the French Academy of Sciences, Paris, November 16, 1992. Studies by Dr. Anthony Fauci of the United States National Institutes of Health and by Dr. Ashley T. Haase of the University of Minnesota. Investigators found "massive covert infection" in the lymphatic systems of patients. That is, HIV remains hidden in the lymph nodes and similar tissues long before an individual develops full-blown AIDS.

II. Symptoms

A. Symptoms of AIDS include night sweats, fever, anorexia, extreme fatigue and development of Kaposi's sarcoma (cancer involving the lymphatic system, often marked by purplish blotches on skin and mumps-like symptoms at lymph nodes).

B. Many persons carry HIV without displaying symptoms. There can also be a delay of several months between date of infection and a positive HIV test. (Hence, a negative HIV test is *not* a guarantee of safety to persons who engage in high-risk behavior.)

C. Opportunistic infections (which the body can normally resist) are also a result of AIDS. As noted earlier in this book, a "sinister combine" of AIDS, substance abuse and new drug resistant strains of tuberculosis has led to its resurgence in American cities and less-developed nations. The number of cases has climbed "relentlessly" since 1985.[7]

III. Effects

A. breakdown of the body's immune system (ability to fight off infection and disease)

B. individual subjected to repeated infections and malignancies

C. brain damage as the body's nervous system is attacked

D. imminent death (While some therapies have "postponed" death, there is no cure for AIDS.)

The fact is that all stages of AIDS are infectious. It is a retrovirus (a person can be in the "carrier" stage or have the "full-blown" stage and still pass the virus). *All stages are infectious.*

---

[7] Joseph A. Califano, Jr., "Three-Headed Dog from Hell," *The Washington Post*, December 21, 1992, p. A24.

Cancer of the Cervix and Pre-Cancerous Changes

I. Facts

    A. Dysplasia refers to early cancerous or pre-cancerous changes in cervical cells.

    B. It begins in the transformation zone (T-zone) of the cervix of young women with immature reproductive systems.

    C. There is strong evidence that human papilloma virus (HPV) is the sexually transmitted agent that causes dysplasia, which may develop into cancer of the cervix. In the June 1995 *Journal of the National Cancer Institute*, scientists from the Johns Hopkins School of Hygiene and Public Health argued that cervical cancer should be fought as an infectious sexually transmitted disease. The multinational team of researchers found HPV to be the leading cause of cervical cancers worldwide.

    D. Women at high risk include: those who are sexually active before age twenty; have intercourse with three or more sexual partners before age thirty-five; or have intercourse with someone who has had three or more partners.

    E. Women at increased risk include: long-term users of the pill and other oral contraceptives. Three recent studies—one in Los Angeles, another in Quebec and an international study by the World Health Organization—each indicate that use of oral contraceptives increases a woman's risk of developing adenocarcinoma of the cervix by 30–40 percent, with the risk for long-term users *doubling*, as compared to women who never used it.[8]

    F. Diagnosis is by pap smear.

---

[8] G. Ursin et al., "Oral Contraceptive Users May Be at Some Increased Risk of Cervical Carcinoma," *Family Planning Perspectives* 27, no. 3 (May/June 1995): 134.

II. Symptoms

A. often no visible symptoms

B. abnormal vaginal spotting or bleeding

III. Effects

A. If untreated, it can develop into pre-invasive cancer (carcinoma-in-situ), invasive cancer of ovaries and/or uterus and cancer that spreads to other parts of the body.

B. It requires surgical excision, cauterization, cryosurgery or laser surgery to remove abnormal cells.

Chlamydia

I. Facts

A. affects genital tracts of both sexes and Fallopian tubes in women

B. caused by bacteria of its own order; treatable with antibiotics

C. most common venereal disease in the United States

D. four million cases of genital chlamydia occur in the United States each year, causing an estimated $2.2 billion in direct and indirect costs.[9] (Please note that health care providers are *not* required to report chlamydia. The actual number of cases is likely much higher.)

---

[9] "Is Sex Safe?" (Boise, Idaho: Grapevine Publications, 1992), p. 3.

II. Symptoms

    A. painful urination in men; itching and burning discharge in women

    B. in many cases, no symptoms[10] (some 70 percent not aware they are infected)

III. Effects

    A. pelvic inflammatory disease (PID) in women (see below for more details about PID); possible infertility

    B. miscarriage, stillbirth

    C. conjunctivitis in newborn

Gonorrhea

I. Facts

    A. bacterial infection of the genital and urinary tracts of both men and women

    B. some 1.4 million cases annually

    C. most commonly *reported* STD

    D. may resemble other diseases—should be confirmed by medical test

    E. curable if treated with penicillin (however, some strains of the disease have developed that are resistant to penicillin)

---

[10] Ibid.

II. Symptoms

    A. may be transmitted by asymptomatic carriers (Many men and women who carry the organism that causes gonorrhea have no obvious symptoms.)

    B. burning sensation during urination

    C. pus from penis or vaginal discharge

III. Effects

    A. can cause permanent sterility in both men and women

    B. scarring of urethra and urinary tract infections[11]

    C. 40 percent of untreated women develop pelvic inflammatory disease

    D. possible blindness in newborn

    E. possible damage to joints, heart, liver, brain and spinal cord

Herpes Genitalis

I. Facts

    A. caused by herpes simplex virus (HSV), Types I and II; these viruses cannot be distinguished clinically

    B. epidemic in the United States (some thirty million people infected)[12]

---

[11] Ibid.

[12] Medical Institute for Sexual Health, "Safe Sex" slide and lecture program, 1992 (P.O. Box 4919, Austin, TX, 78765).

    C. some five hundred thousand new cases annually; 70 percent of sexually active persons have this disease[13]

    D. can be treated but cannot be cured

    E. highly contagious even if there are no visible, blister-like sores

II. Symptoms

    A. first symptom—a sore on or near the genitals; initial infection will lapse into a latent state

    B. recurring painful blisters on genitals, thighs, buttocks and anal areas

    C. accompanied by flu-like symptoms (fever, sore throat, swollen glands)

    D. itching and pain in genital area, burning sensation with urination, vaginal discharge

    E. recurring infections brought on by stress and other unidentified causes

III. Effects

    A. increased risk of cervical cancer

    B. newborn can be infected in birth canal, with possibility of developing mental retardation; death

---

[13] "Is Sex Safe?"

Pelvic Inflammatory Disease (PID)

I. Facts

    A. inflammation of pelvic organs in women

    B. caused by variety of microbial agents, including gonorrhea and chlamydia

    C. one million new cases annually

    D. some 420,000 sufferers seek treatment every year, at a cost of $2 billion[14]

II. Symptoms

    A. pain and tenderness involving lower abdomen, cervix and uterus

    B. fever and chills

    C. elevated white blood count

III. Effects

    A. inflammation makes Fallopian tubes susceptible to invasion by other organisms

    B. possible infertility, premature hysterectomy and depression

    C. possible life-threatening complications, including ectopic (tubal) pregnancy and pelvic abscesses

---

[14] "Safer Sex," *Newsweek*, December 9, 1991, p. 52.

Syphilis

I. Facts

A. curable if treated with penicillin and antibiotics; however, damage cannot be reversed

B. may resemble other diseases—should be confirmed by medical test

C. 130,000 or more new infections annually

II. Symptoms

A. primary sign: a very contagious but usually painless chancre or sore on the penis or in/around the vagina (This sore may not necessarily appear or may go undetected.)

B. secondary signs: flu-like symptoms, rash on hands and feet, loss of hair

C. latent or quiet stage: outward symptoms disappear, but disease still active and doing damage to the body

III. Effects

A. damage to the brain, heart, blood vessels, bones, insanity, blindness

B. sometimes fatal

C. unborn child can be seriously affected and die (congenital transmission)

Venereal Warts
(Condyloma)

I. Facts

A. caused by human papilloma virus (HPV)

B. very contagious

C. treated by freezing or burning

D. an estimated three million HPV cases are diagnosed yearly (including cervical HPV infections)[15]

II. Symptoms

A. warts on or near genital and anal areas

B. sub-clinical warts (flat condyloma) on the cervix

III. Effects

strong evidence that certain types of HPV are causally related to cancer of the cervix (also indications of increased risk of cancer of the penis)[16]

---

[15] See Robert A. Hatcher et al., *Contraceptive Technology* (New York: Irvington Publishers, 1994), p. 108.

[16] "The Facts about the Sexually Transmitted Disease Epidemic," Medical Institute for Sexual Health, undated brochure (circa 1993).

Hepatitis B

I. Facts

   A. three hundred thousand new cases annually

   B. most common sexually transmitted disease in the world

II. Symptoms

   A. often none

   B. some experience jaundice (yellowing of skin, eyes), fatigue, dark urine, grayish stool

III. Effects

   severe liver damage (including cirrhosis, cancer of the liver)

A Point To Ponder:

Next to the common cold and flu, the most common infections in the United States are those which are sexually transmitted.

[Source: American College of Obstetricians and Gynecologists, as cited in "Resource Director" for the "Is Sex Safe?" pamphlet, Grapevine Publications, November 1992.]

CHAPTER SEVENTEEN

What to Remember about Sexual Activity among Adolescents

[S]omething is missing from our national portrait when "safe sex" is considered an antidote to AIDS. . . .

Kathleen Parker
Buffalo News

In addition to the rampant spread of venereal disease, one of the consequences of early genital activity among adolescents is teenage pregnancy and its effects on the child, the young parents, and their families, as well as their communities and society as a whole. While between 1970 and 1990 the United States spent more than two billion dollars on programs designed to promote contraceptive use to reduce pregnancy, the number of nonmarital teen births increased by an overwhelming 61 percent. Teenage abortions have likewise sky-rocketed during the past two decades.

We have, of course, learned about the insidious act of abortion and the moral imperative to choose life. Yet in cases of teenage pregnancy, planning for the future requires difficult decisions about possible marriage, raising the child or placement for adoption.

Ideally, a family should be supportive of a daughter, even though learning of her situation may have caused much grief and distress. It is not wise to pressure teenage parents into a marriage that will likely fail. It would be better for the grandparents of the baby to welcome that child into their home to live with his mother (their daughter). As the daughter matures, she may have another opportunity for a stable marriage.

In addition to family support, there are countless agencies and volunteer organizations that are committed to assisting teenage parents and their families. These groups offer assistance such as counseling, transportation and referrals for prenatal care, material support (housing, clothing, financial aid, and so forth)—whatever is necessary to help a young woman carry her child to term.

One of the most common myths about teenage pregnancy is that an adolescent mother is at greater risk of maternal mortality. That is not true. A girl of fifteen is at no greater risk than a woman in her thirties.

Teenagers who are faced with difficult decisions regarding their future and that of their child should be encouraged to consider—realistically—the physical, emotional and financial demands of caring for a child. These considerations become more crucial for the young woman who must care for a child without the support of a husband or her family.

In the absence of familial support, adoption constitutes a positive option for allowing one's child to enjoy the gift of life. In virtually all cases, responsible adoption agencies are able to place babies with loving couples who have longed for children—some of these couples wait for years to adopt. Sadly, however, the younger the teen parents, the more pressure there is from society to "take the easy way out"—to abort the unborn baby.

Like any mother, a teen will experience a deep sense of loss when she must relinquish her baby for adoption. She may understand that it is best for the child, but it is only natural that she *feel* grief and anguish. Friends and family members can help a young woman to overcome these feelings by reminding her that, through her unselfish decision, she has given her baby the precious gift of life and the chance at a wonderful future with loving parents.

Conclusion

The Culture of Death

We are living in a world where a minority of powerful groups and individuals are imposing a secular humanist doctrine on the rest of the world. The clever way in which these powerful adversaries disguise their programs as benevolent protection for the family is repugnant. The majority of the citizens of the West are not aware that this culture of death, funded by their taxes, is contributing to their own destruction by depleting their population below replacement level. According to the United Nations, the population of the world begins its decline at the beginning of the next century, at which time, retirement systems will tumble. There already are not enough tax-paying young people to finance the retirement of each retiree. Hence, the next step will be to eliminate the elderly and handicapped by officially legalizing euthanasia, as well as using the subtle arguments of "death with dignity" and "living wills." Already we are witnessing the brainwashing of the population to prepare the minds of citizens to accept less health care and to be considerate by not becoming a financial burden to future generations. The linguistic "warfare" against the powerless is already taking place. Just as the killing of the unborn child was legalized, now there is a rush to accept the legalization of the elimination of the disabled and infirmed.

A few decades ago, an abortionist would have been put in jail for his crime—today those who protest the massive murder of innocent life are being punished.

The inborn modesty and natural innocence of the young are being destroyed under the disguise of "sex education" without morals and by values that totally exclude the rights of parents.

Sodomic practices once considered an abomination are now being protected by law. The epidemic of deadly venereal diseases keeps expanding all over the world while special interest groups continue to profit from the consequences of promiscuous behavior.

The Culture of Life

The future of humanity is in our hands. We must rescue the family from the claws of darkness. As we enter the third millenium, we must unite with those who are sincerely concerned about the future of mankind. As John Paul II said in his Sunday Angelus message February 13, 1994,

> Authentic love is not a vague sentiment or a blind passion. It is an inner attitude that involves the whole human being. It is looking at others, not to use them but to serve them. It is the ability to rejoice with those who are rejoicing and to suffer with those who are suffering. It is sharing what one possesses so that no one may continue to be deprived of what he needs. Love, in a word, is *the gift of self. . . .* The family, the great *workshop of love*, is the *first school*, indeed, a lasting school where people are not taught to love with barren ideas, but with the incisive power of experience. May every family truly rediscover *its own vocation to love!* Love that absolutely respects *God's plan*, love that *is the choice and reciprocal gift of self* within the family unit.[1]

Our influence as parents and educators can defeat the forces of darkness. We must not underestimate the power of self-control that young people possess and should be challenged to put into practice. "True love waits for marriage" is the answer to their future happiness.

Married couples do not have to remain slaves to the lucrative market of artificial birth control, sterilization or abortion that continues to exploit them. Natural family planning unites the couple, increases communication and contributes to the disappearance of divorce.

---

[1] John Paul II, "The Family Is a Great Workshop of Love," *L'Osservatore Romano*, English ed., 27, no. 7 (February 16, 1994): 1.

In the preceding chapters we have learned about the miraculous way that we come into the world, about God's magnificent design for human fertility, and about the integral role of love, lifelong commitment, family and morality in creating and protecting the children with whom we are blessed. By sharing with your children this profound sense of wonder, awe and reverence for human life, you will help them to develop values and virtues that will always guide them into the future.

Glossary

abortifacient: Anything used to cause or induce an abortion.

abortion: The termination of pregnancy—usually before the stage of viability (sometime between the twentieth and twenty-eighth week of gestation).

spontaneous: loss of a pregnancy without any manipulation or administration of medication to cause the loss of the fetus; also called "miscarriage."

induced: the purposeful termination of a pregnancy by the use of instruments or medication.

acini: The milk-secreting glands of the breast.

alveoli: Sac-like units in the breast lobules where acini are located.

amenorrhea: Absence or suppression of menstruation; normal before puberty, after menopause, during pregnancy and lactation.

amniocentesis: The removal of a sample of amniotic fluid by abdominal puncture.

amnion: A membranous sac which surrounds the developing infant. Fluid occupies the amniotic cavity and increases steadily in amount until the sixth or seventh month of pregnancy. The fluid protects the fetus from injury and allows it to move freely within the uterus. Rupture of the amnion and escape of the amniotic fluid during labor is referred to as "the waters breaking."

amniotic fluid: Liquid surrounding the fetus.

ampulla (of Fallopian tube): distal third of Fallopian tube, where fertilization normally takes place.

androgens: Male sex hormones that stimulate the activity of the accessory sex organs and encourage the development of the male sex characteristics (*see* "testosterone").

anovulation: Suspension or cessation of ovulation.

anovulatory menstrual cycle: A menstrual cycle in which ovulation does not occur.

areola: Erectile tissue surrounding nipple.

arousal fluid: A lubricative secretion produced by the Bartholin's glands that results during sexual stimulation. It lubricates the vagina in preparation for intercourse.

bafting: The use of barrier methods of contraception at a fertile time.

barrier methods: Methods of contraception, including condoms, caps, diaphragms, etc., used to prevent sperm from meeting the ovum.

Bartholin's glands: Glands situated on each side of the vaginal opening that produce a watery secretion which acts as a lubricant prior to and during sexual intercourse. This secretion is sometimes called "arousal fluid."

Basal Body Temperature (BBT): Refers to a rise in body temperature of 0.4 to 1.0 degree F following ovulation; the temperature shift is caused by progesterone, drops again before menses, or continues elevated if pregnancy occurs.

Basal Body Temperature Method: A method of family planning in which the postovulatory infertile phase of the menstrual cycle is identified by a temperature shift in the BBT curve.

Basic Infertile Pattern (BIP): The term used in the Billings Ovulation Method to mean the physiological manifestation of relative ovarian inactivity before the beginning of follicular maturation. The BIP can be either dryness or a constant, unchanging discharge that remains the same day after day, or a combination of the two; the assistance of an instructor is recommended in identifying a BIP.

birth canal: Channel through which fetus passes during birth; cervix and vagina.

bladder: The muscular sac which stores the urine before it is periodically discharged.

blastocyst: The stage of development of the human zygote at the time of implantation in the endometrium.

Calendar Method: A method of family planning in which the time of the fertile phase is predicted by calculations based on calendar records of past menstrual cycles (also referred to as the Rhythm Method).

capacitation: A process whereby spermatozoa acquire the ability to fertilize ova. This process occurs in the female genital tract. This process occurs in some animal species and is thought to occur in humans.

carcinoma in situ: Cancer which has not invaded tissue beneath the epithelium.

cervical os, external: Vaginal opening (orifice) of the uterine cervix.

cervical os, internal: Cervical opening (orifice) into intrauterine cavity.

cervicitis/endocervicitis: Inflammation of ecto- or endocervix; may be due to the same causes as vaginitis.

cervix: The neck of the uterus or womb, the cervix consists of the:

endocervix: Inner part, and

ectocervix: Outer part which protrudes into the vagina.

endocervical canal: An inch-long canal that transverses the cervix, this canal connects the vagina with the uterine cavity.

endocervical crypts: Indentations along the endocervical canal which are lined by mucus-secreting epithelial cells (approximately four hundred gland-like units).

chorion: The fetal component of the placenta. Its complex functions include the secretion of a hormone (human chorionic gonadotropin [HCG]) which stimulates the development of the corpus luteum of the maternal ovary until about five-months' gestation. After that the placenta takes over the function of the corpus luteum, secreting both estrogen and progesterone.

chromosomes: Microscopic bodies formed from chromatin in the nucleus; especially conspicuous during mitosis. Chromosomes contain genes which are responsible for the transmission of hereditary characteristics to the offspring. Human cells contain forty-six chromosomes (the diploid number) arranged in pairs. Forty-four (twenty-two pairs) are termed *autosomal chromosomes*; two (one pair) are *sex chromosomes*. All cells in the body contain forty-six chromosomes except the sperm and ova which contain twenty-three each (the haploid number). The sperm contains either an X or a Y chromosome, and fertilization of an ovum by an X-containing sperm (female sperm) produces a girl, whereas fertilization by a Y-containing sperm (male sperm) produces a boy.

climacteric: The phase of a woman's life during which reproductive function ceases. It is sometimes called "the change of life" or peri-meno-pause.

clitoris: Erectile structure located below apex of the inner labia. Homologous to the penis.

Clomid: Clomiphene citrate, a fertility drug used to induce ovulation. Clomid works by stopping up the estrogen receptor sites in the hypothalamus and tricking the brain into thinking that there is no estrogen in the blood. When Clomid is stopped, usually after five days, the receptor sites on the hypothalamus detect the high level of estrogen. Directed by the hypothalamus, the pituitary then releases LH and ovulation results.

colostrum: The fluid secreted by the mother's breast the first day or two post-partum. Colostrum is rich in protein and antibodies.

combined fertility: A term used in NFP to emphasize the joint contribution of husband and wife in conception. Although a man is continuously able to father a child, the couple can conceive only during the fertile phase of the woman's cycle.

conception: The union of the sperm cell and ovum (fertilization).

contact conception: Conception resulting from intimate contact between the sexual organs, without penetration of the penis into the vagina and even without ejaculation.

Corpora albicans: Residual of corpus luteum.

corpus luteum: The yellow structure resulting from the rupture of an ovarian follicle at ovulation which produces progesterone until the end of the cycle, when it degenerates if pregnancy does not occur. If the ovum is fertilized, the corpus luteum grows and produces hormones that support the pregnancy for several months.

Cowper's glands: Two small pea-shaped glands located on either side of urethra. During ejaculation, they release their mucous secretion into the penile urethra, where it serves as a lubricant (also known as bulbourethral glands).

cystocele: Hernia of the bladder caused by weakening of vaginal muscles.

cysts: Bladder-like or closed sac structure containing fluid.

differentiation: The modification of cells for performance of particular function. The result of the processes whereby apparently indifferent (immature and simple) cells, tissues and structures attain their adult/complete form and function. (In the human breast, irreversible commitment of immature breast cells capable of producing milk occurs during lactation.)

douche: Lavage of the vagina with water or medicinal fluid.

duct: Tubular structure giving exit to the secretion of a gland.

dysmenorrhea: Difficult and painful menstruation.

dyspareunia: The occurrence of pain during sexual intercourse.

dysplasia: Abnormal tissue development.

    cervical: Premalignant changes in the squamous epithelial cells of cervix.

ectocervix: *see* cervix

ectopic pregnancy: Implantation of the human zygote outside of uterine cavity, usually in Fallopian tube.

ectopy (cervical): Presence of endocervical columnar epithelium (cells) on ectocervix (from the Greek EK = out of + TOPOS = place).

ejaculation: The discharge of semen from the penis.

E-mucus (estrogen mucus): Secretion produced in the cervical glands in response to estrogen; provides proper pH, nutrition and transport system for sperm; appears at the opening of the vagina at and near the time of ovulation, providing an external sign of fertility, as used in the Ovulation Method of Natural Family Planning; pH of 7.8 to 8.5.

embryo: The stage in prenatal development between the ovum and fetus; from the second through the eighth week inclusive.

endocervical canal: *see* cervix

endocervical crypts: *see* cervix

endocervix: *see* cervix

endocrine: Pertaining to internal secretion; ductless glands that secrete into the bloodstream.

endogenous: Originating or produced within the organism.

endometrial cavity: Space inside the uterus.

endometrial cycle: Changes of the endometrium during the menstrual cycle, consisting of menses, proliferative phase and secretory phase.

> *proliferative phase:* The phase of the endometrial cycle from menses to ovulation during which the basal cells of the endometrium are stimulated by estrogen to multiply.

> *secretory phase:* The phase of the endometrial cycle from ovulation to the start of menstruation, during which the endometrial cells reorganize to form mucus-producing glands and distinct layers. Small blood vessels grow into the lining to nourish it and to be available in case a fertilized egg implants. This occurs as a result of the estrogen and progesterone secreted by the corpus luteum.

endometrial fluid: Produced by the endometrial glands; provides nutrition necessary for the survival of the new human being between the time of fertilization and implantation.

endometrial glands: Develop during proliferative phase of endometrial cycle and secrete endometrial fluid during the secretory phase.

endometriosis: The presence of endometrial tissue in abnormal locations such as Fallopian tubes, ovary, cervix, vagina, etc.

endometritis: Inflammation of endometrium; may be due to the same causes as vaginitis.

endometrium: The mucous membrane which lines the uterine cavity. The embryo normally implants in the endometrium. If fertilization does not occur, the thick superficial layer of the endometrium is sloughed off during menstruation.

epididymis: The elongated organ connected to the testis, consisting of several yards of tubules along which the sperm cells move and mature. The epididymis becomes continuous with the vas deferens.

erosion (cervical): The destruction of squamous epithelium of ectocervix by inflammatory or physical processes.

estrogen: Hormone produced in the ovarian follicle theca interna cells, in response to LH; causes regeneration of the endometrium (proliferative phase of the endometrial cycle); stimulates cervical glands to produce E-mucus; triggers the LH surge; in pregnancy, is secreted by the placenta and stimulates development of breast lactiferous ducts.

exogenous: Originating or produced outside of the organism.

Fallopian tubes: The two tubes which extend from the upper part of the uterus toward the ovaries and through which: (a) ova pass from the ovaries to the uterus, and (b) spermatozoa progress from the uterus toward the ovaries. Fertilization normally takes place in a Fallopian tube.

fern pattern: The fern and palm leaf patterns which E-L and E-S cervical mucus assume under a microscope during certain stages of the menstrual cycle. The pattern, caused by crystallization of the mucus as it dries, is dependent upon the concentration of electrolytes present, especially sodium chloride.

fertile: Capable of reproducing.

fertile days: Those days of the menstrual cycle during which intercourse or genital contact can result in a pregnancy.

fertile phase: That phase of the menstrual cycle during which sexual intercourse or genital contact can result in pregnancy.

fertility: A term that may signify either: (a) the ability of a man to father a child or of a woman to establish and successfully maintain a pregnancy and give birth; or (b) the ability of a couple to achieve pregnancy.

fertilization: The union of the sperm cell and ovum; conception.

fetus: The child in utero from the third month to birth. The term fetus (the young one) is applied when the infant is recognizably human, even to the unscientific gaze.

fimbria: The finger-like projections of tissue on ends of the Fallopian tubes.

follicle: A structure within the ovary, consisting of a layer of cells surrounding a fluid-containing cavity, in which the ovum is located.

follicle stimulating hormone (FSH): A gonadotropin produced by the anterior pituitary. In the female, FSH acts on the ovary to stimulate maturation of the ovarian follicle; in the male, it acts on the testis to stimulate spermatogenesis.

follicular phase: *see* ovarian cycle

fornix, fornices: Recess(es) in upper portion of vagina produced by protrusion of the cervix into vagina.

fraternal twins: Result from ovulation of two ova, fertilized by two sperm; nonidentical twins.

galactorrhea: A spontaneous flow of milk from the nipple; a continuous discharge of milk from the breasts in the intervals of nursing or after the child has been weaned.

gamete: A mature sperm or egg capable of participating in fertilization.

genital contact: Contact of the penis with the vulva without ejaculation.

genitalia: The reproductive organs.

germ cell: A cell having reproduction as its principal function, especially an egg or a sperm.

gestagen: That which produces progestational effects. This general term is usually applied to natural or synthetic steroids used to alter reproductive physiology.

gonad: A generic term referring to both the female sex glands, or ovaries, and the male sex glands, or testes. Each form the cells necessary for human reproduction, spermatozoa from the testes, ova from the ovaries.

Gonadotropic Releasing Hormone (GnRH): A hormone secreted by the hypothalamus which activates the pituitary gland to secrete stimulating hormones.

gonadotropin: A hormone secreted by the pituitary gland or the placenta which stimulates the growth or secretory activity of the gonads.

Graafian follicle: Mature follicle, just before ovulation.

granulosa cells: The cells in the corpus luteum which produce progesterone in the post-ovulatory phase of the menstrual cycle; stimulated by LH from the pituitary, and if pregnancy occurs, by HCG from the placenta.

gravid: Pregnant.

Human Chorionic Gonadotropins (HCG): Hormones secreted by chorionic cells of the placenta. Their presence in the blood and urine is the basis for pregnancy tests. Stimulates production of progesterone by the granulosa cells of the corpus luteum in early pregnancy.

Human Menopausal Gonadotropin (HMG): A potent fertility drug also called Pergonal. HMG is a hormone collected from the urine of menopausal/post-menopausal women, used to stimulate ovulation in infertile women. HMG is an equal combination of LH and FSH. When used as a fertility drug, it bypasses the hypothalamus and directly stimulates the ovaries. HMG can overstimulate the ovaries and cause them to rupture, if not carefully monitored.

hormone: A chemical substance, formed in one organ or part of the body and carried in the blood to another organ or part. Depending on the specificity of their effects, hormones can alter the functional activity, and sometimes the structure, of just one organ or of various numbers of them.

hymen: A fold of mucous membrane which normally partially covers the entrance to the vagina in the virgin.

hymenal ring: Residual ridge of tissue around entrance of vagina, just inside the labia minora.

hyper-: Prefix to words of Greek derivation, denoting excessive or above the normal: corresponds to the Latin prefix *super-*.

hyperprolactinemia: An elevated level of prolactin, which is a normal physiological reaction during lactation but pathological with nonphysiological lactation; prolactin may also be elevated in cases of certain pituitary tumors and in other conditions. Amenorrhea is often present.

hypo-: Prefix used with words of Greek derivation, denoting: (1) a location beneath something else; (2) a diminution or deficiency; (3) the lowest, or least rich in oxygen, of a series of chemical compounds, it corresponds to the Latin *sub-*.

hypothalamus: A collection of nerve cells arranged in groups at about the third ventricle at the base of the brain; a major control center of the body; interacts with the pituitary gland which lies just below it.

implantation: Embedding of the blastocyst in the endometrium.

infertility: Relative sterility, diminished or absent fertility; does not imply the existence of as positive or irreversible a condition as sterility. Infertility may be present in either or both sexual partners and is usually reversible. Diagnostic investigation includes special tests of both partners, as well as complete physical examination. Some factors responsible for infertility are immature or abnormal reproductive systems, anomalies of other organs in that vicinity, infections, endocrine dysfunction and emotional problems.

in situ: In position.

intercourse, sexual, complete: Sexual activity during which the penis is inserted into the vagina where ejaculation takes place.

intercourse, sexual, incomplete: A term that includes the following forms of sexual activity:

coitus interruptus: Sexual activity during which the penis is withdrawn from the vagina before ejaculation so that ejaculation occurs outside the vagina (also commonly called "withdrawal").

coitus reservatus: Sexual activity during which the penis is inserted into the vagina, but ejaculation is deliberately avoided.

interlabial intercourse: Sexual activity during which the penis is inserted between the labia, where ejaculation takes place.

intermenstrual bleeding: Marginal bleeding occurring between menses—should always be evaluated by a physician.

introitus: External opening of the vagina.

in vitro fertilization (IVF): Literally, fertilization "in glass." A technique whereby ova, which are harvested by laparoscopy from a woman's ovary, are fertilized in a glass dish by semen collected from a donor (usually the woman's husband). The fertilized ova are then placed in the uterus of the woman at a later stage of development.

involute/involution: The return of cells or lobules to a former condition.

LH surge: Rapid rise of luteinizing hormone (LH) in the blood stream, caused by rise of estrogen, which causes ovulation to occur (*see* luteinizing hormone).

labia (inner and outer): The skin folds surrounding the entrance to the vagina.

lactation: The secretion or production of milk after pregnancy which allows for breast-feeding.

lactiferous ducts: Ducts of the mammary glands. There are twenty to twenty-four lactiferous ducts which carry milk from lobules and open into the nipples.

lactogen: An agent that stimulates milk production or secretion; human placental lactogen (HPL) is a protein hormone of placental origin; its biological activity weakly mimics that of human pituitary growth hormone and prolactin.

laparoscopy: The direct visual examination of the interior of the abdomen by means of an optical instrument (laparoscope) inserted through an opening below the umbilicus.

ligaments, uterine: Broad, uterosacral (posterior) cardinal (lateral) and round (anterior). Tissue structures which hold the uterus in place in pelvis.

lobes: Milk-producing parts of the breast; each breast contains fifteen to twenty-four lobes.

lobule: Group of cells within the breast formed by the growth of cells that structure or form ducts (for milk) as the breast matures.

lochia: The discharge of blood, mucus and tissue from the uterus during the first few weeks after childbirth.

luteal: Pertaining to the corpus luteum, its cells, or its hormone.

luteal phase: The portion of the ovarian cycle, occurring after ovulation, in which the corpus luteum is producing progesterone; corresponds to the post-ovulatory phase of the menstrual cycle and secretory phase of the endometrial cycle (*see* ovarian cycle).

luteinizing hormone (LH): A gonadotropin produced by the anterior pituitary; in the female, it stimulates progesterone production from the corpus luteum granulosa cells, causes ovulation.

luteolysis: The degeneration or destruction of ovarian luteinized tissue.

maternal twins: Twins who arise from splitting of the zygote, morula or blastocyst, after fertilization (also called "identical twins").

mature follicle: Graafian follicle, just before ovulation.

menarche: The first menstruation. The establishment of the menstrual function.

menometrorrhagia: Irregular or excessive bleeding during menstruation and between menstrual periods: this is a symptom but not an acceptable diagnosis.

menopause: That period of natural cessation or termination of menstruation occurring usually between the ages of forty-five and fifty-five (also called "change of life").

menorrhagia: Hypermenorrhea.

menses: The periodic discharge of blood, mucus and cellular debris from the uterus, also commonly called menstruation or period, occurring at more or less regular intervals during the life of a woman, from age of puberty to menopause.

menstrual cycle: The female reproductive cycle beginning with the first day of menstrual flow and ending with the last day before the following menses.

menstruation: *see* menses

metaplasia: The abnormal transformation of an adult, fully differentiated tissue of one kind into a differentiated tissue of another kind.

mittelschmerz: Abdominal pain, specifically from the ovulation site, midway between menstrual periods, occurring at time of ovulation.

morula: Stage of human development in which there are at least four cells but less than fifty cells.

mucosa: Mucous membrane; a lining membrane that consists of a layer of mucus-secreting epithelium supported by a layer of connective tissue.

mucus: A secretion containing water, inorganic salts, epithelial cells, leukocytes and a mixture of glycoproteins (mucin).

myoma (fibroids): Nonmalignant solid tumors arising in muscle tissue of uterus (myometrium).

myometrium: The muscular portion of the uterus.

Nabothian cysts: Cysts formed by outpouching through the T-zone by cervical crypts whose mouths have been closed by squamous metaplastic process.

Natural Family Planning (NFP): Methods for achieving or avoiding pregnancy which are based on the observation of the naturally occurring signs and symptoms of the fertile and infertile phases of the menstrual cycle. It is considered implicit in the definition of natural family planning that when used to avoid pregnancy: (a) drugs, devices and surgical procedures are not used; and (b) there is abstinence from all genital contact during the fertile phase of the cycle; and (c) the act of sexual intercourse, when occurring, is complete.

nipple: Protruberance from the front of each breast, through which the lactiferous ducts discharge milk; each nipple has fifteen to twenty-four duct openings (one for each lobe).

nulliparous: A woman who has not given birth.

oligomenorrhea: Scanty menstruation.

oogenesis: The process of ovum production in the ovary, under the influence of FSH.

oophoritis: Inflammation of the ovaries.

ovarian cycle: A cyclic series of events occurring in the ovary during which the follicle matures, ovulates and is converted into the corpus luteum.

follicular phase: phase of the ovarian cycle during which the follicle matures, generally from menstruation to ovulation.

luteal phase: phase of the ovarian cycle during which the ruptured follicle becomes the corpus luteum, generally from ovulation to menstruation.

ovarian cysts:

follicular: Cysts arising from follicles which may fail to rupture and continue to secrete estrogen or may luteinize and secrete both progesterone and estrogen without eruption of ovum.

luteal: Cysts arising from corpus luteum which may persist in secreting progesterone and estrogen beyond normal luteal phase.

ovarian ligament: The support structure of the ovary.

ovary: One of the glands in the female reproductive system; produces the ovum, the reproductive cell, and two hormones, estradiol (estrogen) and progesterone.

ovulation: The release of the ovum from a mature ovarian follicle.

ovulatory mucus pattern: A sequence of changes in the physical characteristics of the cervical mucus around the time of ovulation, produced by changes in levels of estrogen and progesterone.

ovum (plural: ova): The mature female germ cell.

oxytocin: A hormone obtained from the posterior lobe of the pituitary gland, which causes uterine contraction and the "letting down" of the milk.

parous: A woman who has given birth.

penis: The male organ of copulation and urination.

Pergonal: *see* Human Menopausal Gonadotropin (HMG)

periodic abstinence: The voluntary avoidance of all genital contact during the fertile phase of the menstrual cycle, if pregnancy is not desired.

pH: A measure of acidity or alkalinity; less than 7.0 is acid, more than 7.0 is alkaline; normal vaginal pH is 3.8–4.2; normal cervical E-mucus and seminal fluid pH is 7.8–8.5.

perineal body: The skin between the back of the vagina and the anus.

Pelvic Inflammatory Disease (PID): An infection which affects the internal reproductive organs of the female.

pituitary gland: A pea-sized gland attached by a stalk to the base of the brain, directly below the hypothalamus; secretes a number of hormones, some of which control the function of the ovaries and testes; it is divided into anterior and posterior lobes.

placenta: The oval or discoid spongy structure in the uterus; the organ of metabolic interchange between fetus and mother.

polar body: The chromosomal by-product of oogenesis, containing twenty-three chromosomes, but no other cell parts.

polymenorrhea: The occurrence of menstrual cycles of greater than usual frequency.

posterior fourchette: Portion of the vagina toward the back, near the opening; anatomically the lowest part of the vagina where cervical mucus tends to collect (wiping front-to-back pushes mucus out onto perineal body, whereas wiping back-to-front tends to push mucus up into vagina, such that it will not be observed).

postlactational: State following the milk-producing phase.

postlactational involution: The return of cells and lobules to their former condition (Lobule 4 returning to Lobule 3).

post-ovulatory: After ovulation; the phase of the menstrual cycle extending from ovulation to the beginning of the following menstruation.

post-partum: After childbirth.

pre-ejaculatory fluid: A small amount of fluid that is discharged involuntarily from the penis during sexual excitement. The fluid contains a high concentration of active motile spermatozoa.

premenopause: A term commonly used to indicate that time during which a woman may notice unaccustomed irregularity of the menstrual cycles and other symptoms as a prelude to menopause.

pre-ovulatory: Before ovulation; the phase of the menstrual cycle extending from the beginning of follicular maturation to ovulation, generally considered the time following menstruation and extending to ovulation.

progesterone: Hormone produced by the granulosa cells of the corpus luteum in response to LH; also produced in corpus luteum in response to HCG in early pregnancy; later in pregnancy, produced by the placenta; causes BBT shift after ovulation; stimulates endometrium to become secretory; causes production of G-mucus in cervical glands; in pregnancy stimulates development of breast acini in the alveoli of the lobules.

prolactin: Hormone produced by the anterior lobe of the pituitary gland. It is capable of initiating and sustaining lactation. An elevated level of prolactin can cause amenorrhea.

proliferation: The multiplication of cells.

proliferative phase: *see* endometrial cycle

prostate: One of the male accessory sex glands which surrounds the lower part of the bladder and the upper urethra and whose secretions are the major component of the semen.

pseudocyesis: A condition in which a patient has nearly all of the usual signs and symptoms of pregnancy, such as enlargement of abdomen, weight gain, cessation of menses and morning sickness, but is not pregnant.

rectocele: Protrusion of rectum through vaginal wall.

releasing hormone: (Gonadotropin Releasing Factor, GTRF); a substance of hypothalamic origin capable of accelerating the rate of secretion of a given hormone by the anterior pituitary gland.

Rhythm Method: *see* Calendar Method

salpingitis: Inflammation of Fallopian tubes. May be due to the same causes as vaginitis.

scrotum: The external pouch suspended behind the base of the penis, containing the testicles.

secretion: The product (solid, liquid or gaseous) of a cellular or glandular activity that is stored up in or utilized by the organism in which it is produced.

secretory phase: *see* endometrial cycle

semen: Fluid discharged from the male reproductive tract during ejaculation; a thick, yellowish-white viscid fluid containing spermatozoa; it is a mixture of the secretions of the testes, seminal vesicles, prostate, and bulbourethral glands.

seminal vesicles: Paired sac-like structures associated with the vas deferens and located behind the prostate.

sex chromosomes: The genetic structures in nuclei of cells which determine the sex of the individual. Female cells have two X chromosomes; males have an X and Y.

sexually transmitted diseases: An array of infectious diseases (also called "venereal diseases" or, to include HIV, "sexually transmitted diseases").

Skene's glands: Located just inside urethral meatus; may contribute to arousal fluid.

sperm: The mature male sex cell (singular: spermatozoon; plural: spermatozoa).

spermatogenesis: The process of formation and development of the spermatozoon; a slow cyclic process that takes about sixty-four days; occurs in the seminiferous tubules of the testes.

spinnbarkeit: The stringy, elastic character of cervical mucus during the ovulatory period.

spotting: A quantitative term indicating small amounts of bloody vaginal discharge (red or brown) which may occur at the onset or completion of menstruation or as intermenstrual bleeding.

squamous metaplasia (cervical): The transformation zone (T-zone) formed by replacement of columnar cells of endocervix by squamous cells. The transformation occurs in response to stimuli and the process may be normal or abnormal. Cancer of cervix almost always arises from the transformation zone.

sterility: Incapability of fertilization or reproduction.

female sterility: Absolute sterility; the inability of the female to conceive due to inadequacy in structure or function of the genital organs.

male sterility: The inability of the male to fertilize the ovum; it may or may not be associated with impotence.

relative sterility: Infertility.

steroid: A large family of chemical compounds related to cholesterol that comprises many hormones, vitamins, body constituents and drugs.

Sympto-Thermal Method: Method of natural family planning in which the fertile and infertile phases of the menstrual cycle are identified by a changing cervical mucus observation, recording of daily basal body temperatures, and noting additional symptoms such as intermenstrual bleeding, pain, breast tenderness and changes in the cervix. Some Sympto-Thermal applications add Calendar Method calculations in estimating the end of the relatively infertile phase.

testis (plural: testes): One of the two male reproductive glands, located in the cavity of the scrotum; produces spermatozoa and secretes androgens.

testosterone: The main androgenic hormone formed by the Leydig cells of the testes and possibly secreted also by the ovary and adrenal gland in small amounts.

theca externa: Outer cell layer of the follicle wall and corpus luteum.

theca interna: Inner cell layer of the follicle wall, which is the site of estrogen production.

Transformation Zone: *see* squamous metaplasia

tubo-ovarian ligament: The connective tissue stretched between the Fallopian tube and the ovarian ligament.

umbilical cord: Vascular attachment between the placenta and fetus.

unusual bleeding: Any vaginal bleeding other than normal menstrual bleeding; should always be evaluated by (referred to) a physician.

urethra: A narrow canal extending from the bladder to the vulva in women and, in men, passing through the penis and opening at its extremity. The urethra in men and women conveys the urine from the bladder to the exterior of the body, and, in men, it also conveys the semen.

urethral meatus: The external opening of the urethra.

uterine cycle: Endometrial cycle.

uterus: The hollow reproductive organ of the female in which the fertilized ovum implants and develops. It has an upper rounded part called the body and a lower narrow part called the cervix which extends into the vagina. It is commonly referred to as the womb.

vagina: The hollow muscular, genital canal that extends from the uterus to the vulva.

vaginal adenosis: The presence of the aberrant growth of columnar epithelium (cells) in vagina which is normally lined by squamous epithelium. Vaginal adenosis is often found in young women whose mothers ingested estrogens, especially DES (diethylstibesterol), during pregnancy.

vaginal rugae: The circular ridges of mucus membrane in the walls of the vagina.

vaginitis: Inflammation of the vagina may be caused by infectious organisms, trauma or a foreign body.

vas deferens: Ductus deferens; commonly called the sperm duct; a long fibromuscular tube that transports sperm from the epididymis to the prostatic portion of the urethra.

vasectomy: Surgical sterilization of male by severing the vas deferens bilaterally.

viscid: Having an adhesive quality, sticky.

vulva: The external reproductive organs of the female, which include the mons pubis, the labia majora and minora, the clitoris, the vestibule of the vagina and its glands, and the opening of the urethra and of the vagina.

zona pellucida: The clear gelatinous material which forms a kind of shell for the ovum; after fertilization, it alters in such a way as to prevent the entry of another sperm cell. The zona pellucida persists until the embryo begins to implant in the uterus, five to eight days after conception.

zygote: Human being (one to four cells) at early stage of development.

APPENDIX ONE

World Population Growth Charts

Low-Income Economies

Total fertility rate[1]	1965	1990	2000[2]
Mozambique	6.8	6.4	6.7
Tanzania	6.6	6.6	6.6
Ethiopia	5.8	7.5	7.3
Somalia	6.7	6.8	6.6
Nepal	6.0	5.7	4.6
Chad	6.0	6.0	6.1
Bhutan	5.9	5.5	5.4
Lao PDR	6.1	6.7	6.0
Malawi	7.8	7.6	7.4
Bangladesh	6.8	4.6	3.3
Burundi	6.4	6.8	6.6
Zaire	6.0	6.2	5.6
Uganda	7.0	7.3	6.6
Madagascar	6.6	6.3	5.2
Sierra Leone	6.4	6.5	6.5
Mali	6.5	7.1	7.0
Nigeria	6.9	6.0	5.0
Niger	7.1	7.2	7.3

[1] Figures in italics are for years other than those specified. Total fertility rate means the number of children per couple.

[2] For assumptions used in the projections, see the technical notes to Table 26 in *World Development Report 1992*, pp. 270–71.

Total fertility rate	1965	1990	2000
Rwanda	7.5	8.3	7.6
Burkina Faso	6.4	6.5	6.3
India	6.2	4.0	3.0
Benin	6.8	6.3	5.2
China	6.4	2.5	2.1
Haiti	6.1	4.8	4.2
Kenya	8.0	6.5	5.5
Pakistan	7.0	5.8	4.6
Ghana	6.8	6.2	4.6
Central African Rep.	4.5	5.8	5.3
Togo	6.5	6.6	5.5
Zambia	6.6	6.7	6.1
Guinea	5.9	6.5	6.5
Sri Lanka	4.9	2.4	2.1
Mauritania	6.5	6.8	6.8
Lesotho	5.8	5.6	4.5
Indonesia	5.5	3.1	2.4
Honduras	7.4	5.2	4.1
Egypt, Arab Rep.	6.8	4.0	3.1
Cambodia	6.2	4.5	3.5
Liberia	6.4	6.3	5.2
Myanmar	5.8	3.8	2.9
Sudan	6.7	6.3	5.4
Viet Nam	6.0	3.8	2.9

Middle-Income Economies
Lower Middle-Income

Total fertility rate[3]	1965	1990	2000[4]
Bolivia	6.6	4.8	3.7
Zimbabwe	8.0	4.9	3.4
Senegal	6.4	6.5	6.3
Philippines	6.8	3.7	2.7
Cote d'Ivoire	7.4	6.7	5.8
Dominican Rep.	7.2	3.2	2.4
Papua New Guinea	6.2	5.1	4.0
Guatemala	6.7	5.4	4.3
Morocco	7.1	4.5	3.4
Cameroon	5.2	5.8	5.3
Ecuador	6.8	3.7	2.8
Syrian Arab Rep.	7.7	6.5	5.4
Congo	5.7	6.6	6.3
El Salvador	6.7	4.2	3.2
Paraguay	6.6	4.6	4.0
Peru	6.7	3.8	2.8
Jordan[5]	8.0	6.3	5.6

[3] Figures in italics are for years other than those specified. Total fertility rate means the number of children per couple.

[4] For assumptions used in the projections, see the technical notes to Table 26 in *World Development Report 1992*, pp. 270–71.

[5] Data for Jordan covers the East Bank only.

Total fertility rate	1965	1990	2000
Colombia	6.5	2.7	2.2
Thailand	6.3	2.5	2.1
Tunisia	7.0	3.6	2.7
Jamaica	5.7	2.8	2.1
Turkey	5.7	3.5	2.7
Romania	1.9	2.2	2.1
Poland	2.5	2.1	2.1
Panama	5.7	2.9	2.2
Costa Rica	6.3	3.1	2.3
Chile	4.8	2.5	2.1
Botswana	6.9	4.7	3.1
Algeria	7.4	5.1	3.7
Bulgaria	2.1	1.9	1.9
Mauritius	4.8	1.9	1.8
Malaysia	6.3	3.8	3.0
Argentina	3.1	2.8	2.3
Iran, Islamic Rep.	7.1	6.2	5.6
Albania	*5.4*	*3.1*	*2.3*
Angola	*6.4*	*6.5*	*6.6*
Mongolia	*5.9*	*4.7*	*3.7*
Namibia	*6.1*	*5.9*	*4.8*
Nicaragua	*7.2*	*5.3*	*4.2*
Yemen, Rep.	*7.0*	*7.7*	*7.5*

Upper-Middle-Income Economies

Total fertility rate[6]	1965	1990	2000[7]
Mexico	6.7	3.3	2.4
South Africa	6.1	4.3	3.4
Venezuela	6.1	3.6	2.7
Uruguay	2.8	2.3	2.1
Brazil	5.6	3.2	2.4
Hungary	1.8	1.8	1.8
Yugoslavia	2.7	2.0	2.0
Czechoslovakia	2.4	2.0	2.0
Gabon	4.1	5.7	6.1
Trinidad and Tobago	4.3	2.8	2.3
Portugal	3.1	1.6	1.6
Korea, Rep.	4.9	1.8	1.8
Greece	2.3	1.5	1.6
Saudi Arabia	7.3	7.0	5.9
Iraq	7.2	6.2	5.1
Libya	7.4	6.7	5.8
Oman	7.2	7.0	5.9

[6] Figures in italics are for years other than those specified. Total fertility rate means the number of children per couple.

[7] For assumptions used in the projections, see the technical notes to Table 26 in *World Development Report 1992*, pp. 270–71.

High-Income Economies

Total fertility rate[8]	1965	1990	2000[9]
Ireland	4.0	2.2	2.1
Israel	3.8	2.8	2.3
Spain	2.9	1.5	1.5
Singapore	4.7	1.9	1.9
Hong Kong	4.5	1.5	1.5
New Zealand	3.6	2.0	2.0
Belgium	2.6	1.6	1.6
United Kingdom	2.9	1.8	1.9
Italy	2.7	1.3	1.4
Australia	3.0	1.9	1.9
Netherlands	3.0	1.6	1.6
Austria	2.7	1.5	1.6
France	2.8	1.8	1.8
United Arab Emirates	6.8	4.6	3.6
Canada	3.1	1.7	1.7
United States	2.9	1.9	1.9
Denmark	2.6	1.7	1.6
Germany	2.5	1.5	1.6

[8] Figures in italics are for years other than those specified. Total fertility rate means the number of children per couple.

[9] For assumptions used in the projections, see the technical notes to Table 26 in *World Development Report 1992*, pp. 270–71.

Total fertility rate	1965	1990	2000
Norway	2.9	1.8	1.8
Sweden	2.4	1.9	1.9
Japan	2.0	1.6	1.6
Finland	2.4	1.8	1.8
Switzerland	2.6	1.7	1.7
Kuwait	7.4	3.4	2.6

APPENDIX TWO

World Sterilization Rates among Currently Married Women

World Sterilization Rates among Currently Married Women[10]

Region and Country	Year	% Using Any Method	% of Contraceptors Using Female Sterilization
Africa			
Botswana	1988	33	13
Burundi	1987	9	1
Ghana	1988	13	8
Kenya	1989	27	17
Liberia	1986	6	17
Mali	1987	5	2
Mauritius	1985	75	6
Nigeria	1990	6	0
Senegal	1986	11	2
Swaziland	1988	21	22
Uganda	1988–89	5	16
Zimbabwe	1988	43	5
Asia & Pacific			
Bangladesh	1985	25	31
China	1985	74	36

---

[10] Study done by The Johns Hopkins University Population Information Program, *Population Reports*, November 1990.

Region and Country	Year	% Using Any Method	% of Contraceptors Using Female Sterilization
Indonesia	1987	48	6
Korea, Rep. of	1989	77	48
Nepal	1986	14	45
Philippines	1986	45	24
Sri Lanka	1987	62	40
Taiwan	1985	78	33
Thailand	1987	68	33
Latin America & Carribbean			
Brazil	1986	66	41
Colombia	1986	65	28
Costa Rica	1986	70	20
Dominican Republic	1986	50	66
Ecuador	1989	53	34
El Salvador	1988	47	63
Guatemala	1987	23	45
Jamaica	1989	55	25
Haiti	1989	10	25
Mexico	1987	53	35
Paraguay	1990	48	15
Peru	1986	46	14
Trinidad & Tobago	1987	53	16

Region and Country	Year	% Using Any Method	% of Contraceptors Using Female Sterilization
Near East & North Africa			
Egypt	1988	38	5
Jordan	1985	27	18
Morocco	1987	36	6
Tunisia	1988	50	23
Turkey	1988	77	2
Developed Countries			
Germany, Fed. Rep. of	1985	78	13
Japan	1988	56	10
Netherlands	1985	72	7
Spain	1985	59	7
United States	1988	74	31

Index

For additional educational materials which complement this book:

Family of the Americas

P.O. Box 1170
Dunkirk, MD 20754-1170

Telephone (301) 627-3346
(800) 443-3395
Fax (301) 627-0847

e-mail: FAF@idsonline.com